AN ADAMS BUSINESS ADVISOR

Winning the Entrepreneur's Game

Other titles in
THE ADAMS BUSINESS ADVISORS

AN ADAMS BUSINESS ADVISOR

Winning the Entrepreneur's Game

HOW TO START, OPERATE,
AND BE SUCCESSFUL IN A
NEW OR GROWING BUSINESS

DAVID E. RYE

BOB ADAMS, INC.
Holbrook, Massachusetts

Published by Bob Adams, Inc.
260 Center Street, Holbrook, MA 02343

ISBN: 1-55850-346-3 (hardcover)
ISBN: 1-55850-345-5 (paperback)

Printed in the United States of America.

J   I   H   G   F   E   D   C   B   A (hardcover)
J   I   H   G   F   E   D   C   B   A (paperback)

Library of Congress Cataloging-in-Publication Data
Rye, David E.
    Winning the entrepreneur's game: how to start, operate, and be successful in a new or growing
business / David E. Rye.
      p.   cm. — (An Adams business advisor)
    Includes bibliographical references and index.
    ISBN 1-55850-346-3 : $29.95 — ISBN 1-55850-345-5 (pbk.) : $10.95
    1. New business enterprises. 2. Small business—Management. I. Title. II. Series.
    HD62.5.R93   1994
    658.02'2—dc20   94-8712
                                                                        CIP

This book is available at quantity discounts for bulk purchases.
For information, call 1-800-872-5627.

Table of Contents

Preface

Starting a personal business and making money at it is now a reality for millions of Americans. With the advent of sophisticated and cheap office machines like personal computers, faxes, and copiers, just about anybody can afford to set up a business. Predictions on how many of us will soon be engaged in personal businesses boggle the mind. According to the U.S. Department of Health and Human Services, half of all Americans could be working at home for corporations or in their own businesses by the year 2000. Today, many personal businesses are operated on a part-time basis, but the ranks of the full-timers are rapidly increasing.

Winning the Entrepreneur's Game was written for the countless numbers of men and women who want to set up a profitable and exciting business. We'll show you how to get started even if you currently work for a company. Important guidelines and the steps used to set up any type of personal business are covered in every chapter. The steps are progressive. You will literally build your business incrementally as you proceed through the chapters. We'll talk about the important issues you should address to determine if your business idea is viable. Should you proceed to the next step? The decision will be up to you. You should feel comfortable when you answer the probing questions asked in each chapter.

According to the Small Business Administration, 75 percent of personal businesses fail in their first year of operation. Only one out of twenty will still be in business five years from now. If it sounds like we're pessimistic, we're not. We're realists. The odds of your making it in a personal business are marginal, at best. If you accept our advice in this book, you will dramatically increase the odds of your business's surviving. *Winning the Entrepreneur's Game* is filled with real-world, jargon-free examples and explanations. They are easy to follow and can be instantly applied to any personal business.

In the initial chapters, you'll learn about the basics of establishing a personal business. Regardless of the type of business you choose to operate, there is a right way and a wrong way to set one up. You can make lots of money by either copying the success or avoiding the failure of others. In the later chapters, we'll introduce you to time-tested techniques you can use to run a winning business.

You'll get a smorgasbord of business opportunities to choose from in the appendix section of the book. Many of these can be started with little or no capital. We even include the names of important sources to contact if you need more information. Good luck at winning the entrepreneurial game.

Introduction

Starting Your Own Business

Winning the Entrepreneur's Game capitalizes on the current surge of interest in personal businesses by packaging in one book everything you need to know to build and run a personal business. The book takes you through a sequence of progressive steps to start up and run your own business. It's tailor made for people who have a desire to master the fundamentals of running a personal business without wasting time chasing fly-by-night schemes. The book is filled with practical examples and sources of information that can be instantly applied to starting any business.

You start by reading Chapter 1, "Profile of an Entrepreneur." Do you have what it takes to be an entrepreneur? Take the entrepreneurial test that's included in the chapter to see if there are any entrepreneurial areas you need to work on. What are the business basics you need to know to establish a business? You'll find the answers you are looking for in Chapter 2, "Personal Business Basics." Where can you find ideas for personal businesses? It's all there in the appendix section of the book. In fact, there are over 500 business and franchise ideas listed in the appendixes for you to consider.

You'll appreciate the progression of steps that *Winning the Entrepreneur's Game* takes you through. Each chapter builds upon what you learned in the previous chapter. Before you commit any financial resources, the book shows you how to conduct a marketing, pricing, sales, and promotional analysis in easy-to-understand chapters. The remaining chapters show you how to set up an accounting system, take advantage of the tax laws, arrange for financing, develop a strategic business plan, run your business, and a lot more.

Chapter Summaries

Chapter 1: Profile of an Entrepreneur

Do you have what it takes to be a successful entrepreneur? There are essential and basic ingredients that you must have if you are to succeed in a personal business. If you think you want to be your own boss and run your own business, but you're not sure you have the right qualifications, read this chapter. We'll show you how to compare your profile against the profiles of successful entrepreneurs.

Chapter 2: Personal Business Basics

In this chapter, we talk about the basic principles behind the building of a successful personal business. What are the issues that you need to consider before you conduct a search for the perfect business? Suppose you become interested in pursuing more than one venture at the same time? We hope you do. How do you evaluate the alternatives and select the one that is best for you? You start by building a business charter.

Chapter 3: Analyzing the Market

This chapter shows you how to analyze the market and develop a market plan. The objective of market analysis is to determine if there is a market for your products and services. What is the size of your potential customer base? Is it large enough to support your business? We'll help you answer these and other important marketing questions to determine if your business idea is viable. When you're done with the market analysis, you'll pull all the information together into a marketing plan.

Chapter 4: Pricing Strategies

If you do not have an accounting background or an appreciation for the principles of accounting, you will when you complete this chapter. For those of you who understand accounting, this is still a "must read" chapter. It contains essential information about how to analyze product and service pricing options to assure that your business makes a profit. All accounting concepts used are explained in language that anybody can understand.

Chapter 5: A Winning Sales Program

This chapter covers all of the selling steps that any business must effectively implement if it is to survive. Sales is where the rubber meets the road. You may own a business that offers a competitively priced product, but if you can't sell it, you're out of business. We'll concentrate on a set of sales techniques you can apply to make sure that doesn't happen.

Chapter 6: The Art of Promoting

The purpose of promoting is to ensure that your customers know about your business and the benefits you are offering. We'll show you how to apply advertising techniques to promote your products and services. A variety of media options will be covered, along with advertising examples that you can apply to your business. We also show you how to make your promotional campaign pay for itself and return a profit.

Chapter 7: Accounting for the Business

We have elaborated on many reasons why personal businesses fail. The inability to control costs ranks high on the list. This chapter explains in simple terms how to interpret accounting statements and use them to run your business. Examples and illustrations of accounting reports are used to reinforce the explanations. We'll also show you how to set up a tax strategy to take maximum advantage of every legal tax deduction.

Chapter 8: Creative Financing

Every business should have a carefully thought out financial plan that reflects the company's current financial position and provides the blueprint for future growth. If you are not one of the few who can draw from an unlimited bank account, you will need capital to start your business. Before you can determine where you are going to get the money, you must first assess how much you will need and when you'll need it. We'll show you how to determine your financial requirements and find sources of capital.

Chapter 9: Organizing Your Business

One of your first legal considerations will be to determine what business structure is best for you. Three primary structures are covered: proprietorships, partnerships, and corporations. Do you need the counsel of a good lawyer to help you set up a business structure? In some cases, you do. However, you can reduce your business start-up cost if you follow the do-it-yourself organizational steps covered in this chapter.

Chapter 10: Getting Into Top Form

Every time you send out a business form, such as an invoice, you have an opportunity to reinforce the professional image of your business. Do your forms have the crisp, well-designed appearance one would expect from a professional organization? Are your forms set up to make them easy to file? We'll take you through a forms design course in this chapter. We also show you how the copyright protection systems works, and how you can use it to protect and increase the value of your business.

Chapter 11: The Perfect Office

In this chapter, we'll create the perfect office, with all the equipment, hardware, and software you need to maximize the efficiency of your company. Although some of our recommendations may not apply to your particular business, treat our perfect office as a shopping list and pick the pieces that you need.

Chapter 12: The Strategic Business Plan

Many businesses fail because of poor management and the lack of a strategic business plan. The failure rate of businesses operating without a business plan is ten times that of businesses that have one. Once in place, a good business plan will provide you with systematic guidelines for running your business. The chapter includes several examples to show you how to create your own business plan.

Chapter 13: Running Your Business Right

After your business has been launched, you will encounter problems. All start-up businesses do. The growth of your business will either flatten out or begin to decline. We'll show you how to recognize the common problems and what action to take to minimize their impact on your business.

Appendix A: New-Business Ideas

Appendix A has been designed to look like a catalog so that we could present you with hundreds of examples of business opportunities. The objective of this appendix is to offer you a smorgasbord of opportunities to help you generate ideas about the type of business you want to start.

Appendix B: The Best of the New Franchises

Over the years, franchising has expanded rapidly, and accounts for $500 billion in annual U.S. sales. Franchising offers you an opportunity to own a business even if you lack the initial experience required to run a business. In this appendix, we show you how to find everything you need to know about franchises, and who to contact for more information.

Appendix C: The Small Business Administration Directory

The directory lists the addresses and telephone numbers of the Small Business Administration (SBA) offices in each state and U.S. territory. A summary of the services offered by the SBA is also included.

Appendix D: Trade Associations

The appendix covers important information that you should know about trade associations, what they do, and the benefits they can offer to small businesses. We include an alphabetical listing of trade association membership areas and show you where you can obtain more information about specific associations.

Appendix E: A Complete Business Plan

This appendix includes a complete business plan for Computech, the hypothetical personal business that we referred to throughout the book. All of the essential sections of the business plan are covered, along with important financial reports that supplement the plan.

Chapter 1

Profile of an Entrepreneur

Do You Have What It Takes?

If you think you want to be your own boss and run your own business, but are not sure you have the right qualifications to be an entrepreneur, read on. That is what this chapter is all about. What are the characteristics of an entrepreneur? How does an entrepreneur think? Is your personal profile similar to that of a successful entrepreneur? After you have read the chapter, take the entrepreneurial test to rate your own entrepreneurial potential.

Until recently, entrepreneurs were not widely studied. There was a general lack of knowledge and information about what made them tick. The recent interest in revitalizing America's dormant productivity has changed all that. Most business universities now offer courses in entrepreneurship. As a result, business professionals have learned a lot about what it takes to become a successful entrepreneur. Although no one has found the perfect entrepreneurial profile, there are many characteristics that show up repeatedly. In the sections that follow, we'll cover several important characteristics of entrepreneurs for you to consider and dispel the entrepreneurial myths.

Entrepreneurial Characteristics

A series of interviews were conducted with distinguished entrepreneurs. They were asked what characteristics they felt were essential to success as an entrepreneur. Good health was a characteristic mentioned by every entrepreneur interviewed. Entrepreneurs are physically resilient and in good health. They can work for extended periods of time, and while they are in the process of building their business, they refuse to get sick.

In small businesses, where there is no depth of management, the leader must be there. You may not be able to afford a support staff to cover all business functions, and therefore you will need to work long hours. We all know people who use part of their sick leave each year when they are not sick. Entrepreneurs are not found in this group. At the end of the eight-hour day, when everyone else leaves for home, the entrepreneur will often continue to work into the evening, developing new business ideas.

Self-Control

Entrepreneurs do not function well in structured organizations and do not like someone having authority over them. Most believe they can do the job better

---

than anyone else and will strive for maximum responsibility and accountability. They enjoy creating business strategies and thrive on the process of achieving their goals. Once they achieve a goal, they quickly replace it with a greater goal. They strive to exert whatever influence they can over future events.

In large, structured organizations, entrepreneurs are easy to recognize by the statements they make: "If they wanted that job done right, they should have given it to me." A dominant characteristic of entrepreneurs is their belief that they are smarter than their peers and superiors. They have a compelling need to do their own thing in their own way. They need the freedom to choose and to act according to their own perception of what actions will result in success.

Self-Confidence

Entrepreneurs are self-confident when they are in control of what they're doing and working alone. They tackle problems immediately with confidence and are persistent in their pursuit of their objectives. Most are at their best in the face of adversity, since they thrive on their own self-confidence.

Sense of Urgency

Entrepreneurs have a never-ending sense of urgency to develop their ideas. Inactivity makes them impatient, tense, and uneasy. They thrive on activity and are not likely to be found sitting on a bank fishing unless the fish are biting. When they are in the entrepreneurial mode, they are more likely to be found getting things done instead of fishing.

Entrepreneurs prefer individual sports, such as golf, skiing, or tennis, over team sports. They prefer games in which their own brawn and brain directly influence the outcome and pace of the game. They have drive and high energy levels, they are achievement-oriented, and they are tireless in the pursuit of their goals.

Comprehensive Awareness

Successful entrepreneurs can comprehend complex situations that may include planning, making strategic decisions, and working on multiple business ideas simultaneously. They are farsighted and aware of important details, and they will continuously review all possibilities to achieve their business objectives. At the same time, they devote their energy to completing the tasks immediately before them.

Accounting reports illustrate this characteristic. Accountants spend hours balancing the accounts and closing them out. For them, the achievement is to have balanced books. The entrepreneur only wants to know the magnitude of the numbers and their significance for the operation of the business.

Realism

Entrepreneurs accept things as they are and deal with them accordingly. They may or may not be idealistic, but they are seldom unrealistic. They will change their direction when they see that change will improve their prospects for achieving their goals. They want to know the status of a given situation at all times. News interests them if it is timely, and factual, and provides them with information they need. They will verify any information they receive before they use it in making a decision. Entrepreneurs say what they mean and assume that everyone else does too. They tend to be too trusting and may not be sufficiently suspicious in their business dealings with other people.

Conceptual Ability

Entrepreneurs possess the ability to identify relationships quickly in the midst of complex situations. They identify problems and begin working on their solution faster than other people. They are not troubled by ambiguity and uncertainty because they are used to solving problems. Entrepreneurs are natural leaders and are usually the first to identify a problem to be overcome. If it is pointed out to them that their solution to a problem will not work for some valid reason, they will quickly identify an alternative problem-solving approach.

Status Requirements

Entrepreneurs find satisfaction in symbols of success that are external to themselves. They like the business they have built to be praised, but they are often embarrassed by praise directed at them personally. Their egos do not prevent them from seeking facts, data, and guidance. When they need help, they will not hesitate to admit it especially in areas that are outside of their expertise. During tough business periods, entrepreneurs will concentrate their resources and energies on essential business operations. They want to be where the action is and will not stay in the office for extended periods of time.

Symbols of achievement such as position have little relevance to them. Successful entrepreneurs find their satisfaction of status needs in the performance of their business, not in the appearance they present to their peers and to the public. They will postpone acquiring status items like a luxury car until they are certain that their business is stable.

Interpersonal Relationships

Entrepreneurs are more concerned with people's accomplishments than with their feelings. They generally avoid becoming personally involved and will not hesitate to sever relationships that could hinder the progress of their business. During the business-building period, when resources are scarce, they seldom devote time to dealing with satisfying people's feelings beyond what is essential to achieving their goals.

Their lack of sensitivity to people's feelings can cause turmoil and turnover in their organization. Entrepreneurs are impatient and drive themselves and everyone around them. They don't have the tolerance or empathy necessary for team building unless it's their team, and they will delegate very few key decisions.

As the business grows and assumes an organizational structure, entrepreneurs go through a classic management crisis. For many of them, their need for control makes it difficult for them to delegate authority in the way that a structured organization demands. Their strong direct approach induces them to seek information directly from its source, bypassing the structured chains of authority and responsibility. Their moderate interpersonal skills, which were adequate during the start-up phases, will cause them problems as they try to adjust to the structured or corporate organization. Entrepreneurs with good interpersonal skills will be able to adjust and survive as their organization grows and becomes more structured. The rest won't make it.

Emotional Stability

Entrepreneurs have a considerable amount of self-control and can handle business pressures. They are comfortable in stress situations and are challenged rather than discouraged by setbacks or failures. Entrepreneurs are uncomfortable when things are going well. They'll frequently find some new activity on which to vent their pent-up energy. They are not content to leave well enough alone. Entrepreneurs tend to handle people problems with action plans without empathy. Their moderate interpersonal skills are often inadequate to provide for stable relationships. However, the divorce rate among entrepreneurs is about average.

MYTHS ABOUT ENTREPRENEURS

Challenges and Risks

Entrepreneurs are often thought of in terms of the risk they assume. Even the dictionary describes an entrepreneur as one who assumes business risks. However, like all prudent businesspeople, entrepreneurs know that taking high risks is a gamble. Entrepreneurs are neither high nor low risk takers. They prefer situations in which they can influence the outcome, and they like challenges if they believe the odds are in their favor.

They seldom act until they have assessed all the risks associated with an endeavor, and they have an innate ability to make sense out of complexity. These are traits that carry them on to success where others fail.

Entrepreneurs Are Born

Many people believe that entrepreneurs possess innate, genetic talents. However, experts generally agree that most entrepreneurs were not born; they learned to become entrepreneurs. The recent proliferation of college and university courses on the subject supports this point. Entrepreneurship is currently being successfully taught.

Money Motivation

Any successful entrepreneur will tell you that starting a business is not a get-rich-quick alternative. New businesses usually take from one to three years to turn a profit. In the meantime, you will do well to break even. During the business start-up stage, entrepreneurs do not buy anything they do not need, such as fancy cars. Most drive junk cars and use their surplus money to pay off debt or reinvest it in the business. Their focus is on creating a company with a strong financial base for future expansion.

Personal Life

All successful entrepreneurs work long hours, which cuts into their personal life. However, long working hours are not unique to entrepreneurs. Many corporate managers and executives work well beyond the average forty-hour work week. The primary difference between the entrepreneur and his or her corporate counterpart is schedule control. In the corporate world, you may not have control over your schedule. If some higher-level manager calls a Saturday meeting, you've got no choice but to be there.

Entrepreneurs don't mind working sixty- to seventy-hour weeks, but they will do everything they can to preserve their private time. They schedule important meetings, during the week so that they can have weekends off for their personal life, which is very important to them.

High-Tech Wizards

We are all aware of a few "high-tech" entrepreneur wizards, such as Microsoft's Bill Gates, who have made it. Media attention overplays the success of these few high-tech entrepreneurs. Only a small percentage of today's personal businesses are considered high tech, and what was considered high tech just a few years ago is not considered high tech by today's standards.

It takes high profit margins, not high tech, to make it as an entrepreneur. One has only to look at the recent problems that have plagued the computer industry to understand this basic principle. High-tech personal computers did very well when they made high profit margins. The industry went into a nose dive when profits fell.

Loners and Introverts

Initially, entrepreneurs might work alone on a business idea by tinkering in the solitude of their garage or den. However, the astute entrepreneur knows that he or she must draw on the experience and ideas of others in order to succeed. Entrepreneurs will actively seek the advice of others and will make many business contacts to validate their business ideas. The entrepreneur who is a loner and will not talk to anybody will never start a successful business.

Job Hoppers

A recent study of successful entrepreneurs showed that most of them worked for a large corporation for a number of years before they started their own business. In every instance, they used the corporate structure to learn everything they could about the business they intended to establish, before they started. Entrepreneurs are not job hoppers.

Venture Capital Users

Entrepreneurs know that venture capital money is one of the most expensive forms of funding they can get. Consequently, they will avoid venture capitalists, using them only as a last resort. Most entrepreneurs fund their business from personal savings or by borrowing from friends or lending institutions.

Deceptive Individuals

Some believe that to make it as an entrepreneur, you have to be deceptive and step on anybody who gets in your way. On the contrary, this mode of operation doesn't work for the entrepreneur. The truly deceptive entrepreneur will not be able to seek help from others or retain suppliers or customers. He or she will ultimately fail.

Limited Dedication

That entrepreneurs are not dedicated to any one thing is a myth. Dedication is an attribute that all successful entrepreneurs exhibit. They are dedicated to becoming their own boss. To this end, they'll conduct extensive research campaigns into the advantages and disadvantages of their business ideas in their dedicated drive to start a business.

SELF-ANALYSIS

If you work for a company, you probably have a steady job and income. You probably enjoy the usual fringe benefits, such as paid vacations and life and medical insurance. If work runs out, it is up to somebody else to find something for you to do. When work piles up, somebody else can be brought in to help. If you get sick, it's up to your boss to cover you. You may have some flexibility in deciding where you want to live if you work for a company with many locations.

You may even have a career path established with your company. If you follow this career path, you can probably enjoy a comfortable retirement through the company pension plan. Are you sure you want to abandon the corporate life to start your own business? Before you answer this question, let's explore the reasons people become self-employed.

Controlling Their Destiny

Many people find regular employment unsatisfying because it forces them to accept and respond to decisions others make on their behalf. They may not like the people they work for, their work location, their working hours, or their possibilities for advancement. The company may be poorly managed or in poor financial condition, or there may be frequent layoffs. Whatever the trigger, the ability to control one's destiny can be a major motivation for opening a personal business.

The Creative Urge

If you have truly developed a better mousetrap or discovered a better way of doing something, starting your own business may be the simplest and most direct way to get your idea into the market. If you succeed, there is a great deal of personal gratification in being able to say, "I did it with my idea, my way."

The creative urge can be a powerful driver that gives people the incentive to start their own business. It can also prove to be one of your worst enemies if you lose your objectivity along the way. If your unique idea proves to be not so unique after all, will you recognize the facts when you see them, and adjust your strategies accordingly?

Financial Rewards

Most people who start their own business expect financial rewards for their endeavor. They have every right to this expectation. In the business world, financial rewards increase in direct proportion to the level of risk a company is willing to take.

The banking industry provides a classic illustration of this simple concept. If you ask for an unsecured loan, what happens? The bank charges you a higher interest rate to compensate it for the higher risk of loans that are not secured by collateral.

The same principles apply if you open a business. The failure rates for personal businesses are very high. As a business owner, you have a right to expect a high rate of return to compensate you for the risk you are taking on, just as the bank does. Entrepreneurs are driven to achieve high financial rewards. They know that if they do not achieve acceptable profit levels, their business venture will not survive. Since they are in it for the long term, they reject one of the most common start-up scenarios: "I'll try it for a while to see if it works. If it doesn't work, I can always go back to my old job."

If this is your scenario, you'll probably end up back at your old job. Entrepreneurs know exactly how much money they need to make to stay in business. They are committed to the achievement of specific financial goals and do not consider their old job as a viable option.

Chrysler's Lee Iacocca was once asked, "After you joined Chrysler and discovered how much trouble the company was in, did you ever consider throwing in the towel and going back to Ford?" Iacocca responded by saying, "Never! Once I made the commitment, I never lost my determination to do everything I could to make sure the company achieved reasonable financial rewards."

THE ENTREPRENEURIAL TEST

We have discussed a few of the characteristics of entrepreneurs and myths about them. A direct mail survey of successful entrepreneurs was recently conducted to gain further insights into entrepreneurs' thought processes. We encourage you to answer the questions in the survey questionnaire and compare your responses with the responses we obtained from our survey.

Each correct answer is worth 5 points. Any score above 60 points implies that you have the right entrepreneurial instincts to run your own business. If you score between 40 and 55 points, you have the potential to do your own thing. If you're below 40 points, you may want to stay where you are. The answers most commonly given by entrepreneurs are summarized at the end of the questionnaire, along with a brief explanation of each answer.

1. You want to open a business because

    A. You want to be a millionaire.

    B. You hate your present job.

    C. You're obsessed with trying out a business idea.

2. The best work atmosphere for you is

   A. A flexible structure.

   B. A hierarchical organization.

   C. One in which you mostly operate solo.

   D. Strictly team-oriented.

3. Which example best describes your work style?

   A. You delegate tasks to subordinates.

   B. You tackle problems sequentially.

   C. You juggle three or four tasks at once.

4. Your colleagues at your current job

   A. View you as a team player.

   B. Think you are outspoken and share your ideas.

   C. See you as a "yes" person.

5. If you lost your job tomorrow, you'd find the experience

   A. Depressing.

   B. Liberating.

   C. Mildly embarrassing.

   D. Instructive.

6. If you're caught in a traffic jam, you're likely to

   A. Search for radio traffic reports.

   B. Pull off the road and wait it out.

   C. Take papers out of your briefcase and work.

   D. Try alternative routes.

7. When should you launch a business?

   A. Only when the economy is growing

   B. In a slow economy, when labor and office space are cheap

   C. Toward the end of a recession

   D. Any time in the business cycle

8. You're planning to start a business. You should first

   A. Mail your business plan to venture capitalists.

   B. Hold a press conference to generate publicity.

   C. Consult experts in the market you want to crack.

   D. Keep quiet so that nobody steals your idea.

9. You should be willing to wait as long as it takes for your business to make a profit

   A. True

   B. False

10. The economy has strained your company's resources. Several key employees are complaining about low wages. You should

    A. Tell them you can't afford raises now, but will make it up to them later.

    B. Look for employees who will work for less.

    C. Create an incentive plan that offers them a share of profits if productivity or sales rise.

11. A client who accounts for 35 percent of your sales cancels his order. You should

    A. Find out why you lost the account, and solicit new customers.

    B. Cut prices to get him back.

    C. Raise prices to make up for the loss.

    D. Cut expenses.

12. Your company has just survived its first year and you need a vacation. You should

    A. Keep working.

    B. Take a trip to recharge your batteries.

    C. Go to an industry conference.

    D. Do either A or C.

13. After just three years, your company suddenly becomes very profitable. You should

    A. Treat yourself to a new car.

    B. Invest in a friend's new business.

    C. Reinvest the profits in your business.

    D. Open a retirement account.

14. After ten grueling years, your business is consistently beating the competition. Now is the time to

    A. Sell stock to raise capital.

    B. Introduce a new line of products or service.

    C. Franchise the business.

    D. Do any of the above.

Answers:

1. *C* Most entrepreneurs are obsessed initially with trying out their new idea. They believe that the rewards will follow if they succeed.

2. *A* Entrepreneurs avoid rigid work styles.

3. *C* Entrepreneurs know that they have to be capable of handling a number of tasks simultaneously.

4. *B* Most entrepreneurs want to share their ideas so that they can seek creative solutions.

5. *D* Entrepreneurs look for lessons learned from every setback they encounter.

6. *C* Entrepreneurs hate to waste time and therefore always have something they can work on, regardless of the situation.

7. *D* If the idea is good, it can be successfully launched in any economic environment.

8. *C* Entrepreneurs know that impartial advice from experts can help them avoid costly mistakes.

9. *B* Entrepreneurs set a deadline for financial success. If they don't make it, they are not afraid to close their business and start something new.

10. *C* Key employees are your greatest resource. Give them an incentive to help you solve the problems.

11. *A* Relying on a single customer can cause the demise of your business. Call your lost customer to find out why you lost the business.

12. *D* The first years of a new business are too critical to take a vacation.

13. *C* Don't get complacent. Plow the profits back into the company.

14. *D* Look for innovative ways to expand your business, and make it even stronger.

THE SUCCESS FORMULA

Every year, hundreds of thousands of businesses are started. Most will fail, some will muddle along, and a few will thrive. Which ones thrive, and why? The reason some businesses experience spectacular sales and profit growth from the start isn't because they had a lot of money at the beginning. Their fast growth can be attributed to the fact that they were put together the right way.

In every instance, the founders either had or acquired the experience and knowledge they needed to startup and run the business. They recognized what their weak points were, subsequently nurtured alliances, and acquired the skills they needed to start their company off right. They also understood how the various parts of the business fit together to form a total structure and knew that if one part was missing, the total structure would break. For example, they knew that a successful sales plan is directly dependent upon support from the marketing and promotional plans, and that the strategic business plan acts as the glue that holds all the subplans together so that they work in concert.

The chapters in this book have been carefully arranged to build the various subplans in a logical order. We'll help you along the way by showing you how to acquire the information you'll need to properly construct each plan. Toward the end of the book, you'll pull it all together into a strategic business plan to make sure your business grows and prospers.

DEVELOPING IDEAS

Clever product and service ideas are a dime a dozen. Everybody has one, and most of them never get implemented. The successful entrepreneur starts with a basic idea. This idea is first tested to staying power. Can it be used to grow a customer base, and will it be profitable? The pseudo-entrepreneurial itch often ends before the basic idea gets tested. Studies show that a high percentage of people who open new businesses do so because they are frustrated with their current job. They'll jump into any business venture that comes along without first checking it out. Ninety percent of this group will go out of business in their first year.

Those that make it are smart enough to recognize the symptoms of their emotional state. They are acutely aware that they may be in a vulnerable position. As a result, they may hang on to the security of their current job and start a business on the side. They'll make the move to become a full-time entrepreneur when the time is right for them and after they have thoroughly checked out their business venture ideas. There are three basic concepts to keep in mind as you develop and refine your business start-up ideas.

Be Creative

The opposite of creativity is rigidity. Entrepreneurs are not rigid in their thinking. If you cling to the old ways of doing things because "that's the way we have always done it," you'll never come up with the new solutions that are demanded by today's small businesses. To test your creative ability, practice finding ways to tie together seemingly unrelated ideas.

Understand Every Problem

You must have a clear understanding of what it is you are trying to achieve and be able to identify the obstacles that stand in your way. Break each problem down so that you understand it and know what you need to do to eliminate it. For example, the problem may be that you need more space. Why do you need more space, and what are the alternatives? An alternative may pose a new set of problems, but if they reduce the magnitude of the original problem, the alternative may be a more viable option.

Brainstorming

When you come up with a solution to a problem, brainstorm the solution with as many qualified people as you can find to avoid judging your own answer. Accept modifications that make sense, and be prepared to replace the solution with a totally new and better alternative. The key to the brainstorming process is to be objective. Brainstorming is an excellent way to come up with a new set of ideas for new products, services, or improvements that could accelerate the growth of your business.

SUMMARY AND CONCLUSIONS

Do you have what it takes to be a successful entrepreneur? That was the opening question of this chapter. We established a baseline for the characteristics of entrepreneurs and dispelled the common entrepreneurial myths. In the process, we covered several reasons why people are driven to become entrepreneurs and start their own business.

Once we had set a baseline, you were invited to take the entrepreneurial test. The test allowed you to compare your answers with the answers given by successful entrepreneurs. Do you have the qualifications to become an entrepreneur? We talked about business success factors and outlined an approach you can use to develop your new business ideas. If you are interested in learning more about entrepreneurs, you may want to consider joining the American Entrepreneurs Association. For further information, write or call

American Entrepreneurs Association
2392 Morse Avenue
Irvine, CA 92714
714-261-2325

Chapter 2

Personal Business Basics

Is the Fit Right for You?

Today's personal business owners are a new breed of entrepreneur and must be capable of dealing with a variety of obstacles to achieve success. Many will start their own business as a way of getting out of the corporate world. Others will start their own business in the belief that if their ideas are properly exploited, they will be catapulted to instant success. Whatever your personal reasons, in this chapter we'll identify the obstacles that could get in your way and show you how to develop a business charter that will help you avoid these obstacles. The business charter is your first step toward creating your own business.

What if you become interested in pursuing more than one venture at the same time? We hope you do, since there are thousands of personal business ideas to consider. Several hundred ideas and opportunities are listed in Appendixes A and B. However, before you evaluate all the alternatives and select the business that's right for you, it's important that you understand what you may be giving up in your present job and the problems that you will need to overcome to be successful.

Corporate Security

Corporate security includes all the things that the company provides, such as a paycheck, health benefits, and backup support when subordinates don't make it to work. In the corporate world, if you are sick, you can stay home. The corporation goes on pretty much as before, and your sick-day benefits cover your absence. When you work for yourself, you may have to close your business if you can't afford to pay someone to run it for you. That's why good health and a high energy level are prerequisites for entrepreneurs. When you work for yourself, you are the business.

Company Feedback

The feedback loop is an addictive feature of corporate life. Some people need someone to tell them if they're doing a good job or if their performance is not up to expectations. If you work for yourself, the feedback loop is no longer a part of your working environment. It's up to you to determine if you are doing a good job.

Sociability

Sociability is something you tend to take for granted in the corporate world. The friendly chat at the water cooler, the daily choice of lunch companions, and griping about management with your peers are examples of the social aspects of corporate life. Many business owners miss the sociability of the corporate environment and find new ways to satisfy their social needs. They join groups like the chamber of commerce or become actively involved in local events to reestablish their social connections.

Support

Support services are something we take for granted when we work for someone else. Photocopies are made for us, typing is done, the mail is processed, and the wastebaskets are emptied. In your own business, who will do your typing, make photocopies, or provide you with the other basic business services? You will have to wear many different hats, and you must be careful not to let support service functions overwhelm your principal obligation, developing your business.

Identity

Corporate identity is an often-overlooked fringe benefit. We are partly defined by whom we work for. The person who says, "I'm with IBM" answers a lot of questions about what people perceive he or she does for a living. In your own business, the identity issue begins with you. Small-business owners do not have the umbrella of corporate prestige. You are the organization, and you must work hard to create your own image and identity.

Lifestyle

Most people who work for someone else can balance the demands of their job with the values they've established for their private life. For example, adjustments can be made in the office to accommodate the needs of a family. When you work for yourself, this may not be practical. The success of the business is dependent upon you, and your commitment to work may initially have to supersede all other values in your life.

People who successfully run personal businesses often have a real love for what they are doing, and work becomes their first priority. This personal commitment can lead to success, but there is a price to be paid in their lifestyle and personal life.

FINANCIAL CONSIDERATIONS

Can you afford your own business? This is a major question that all new entrepreneurs must ask themselves. Before you make a final commitment to start a business, do some basic calculations to see if you can afford to quit your current job. Do you have enough saved up to launch your business venture? Treat your life as a profit and loss statement. Set up a spreadsheet similar to the one we have prepared in Figure 2-1.

At the top of the left column, list your net income after taxes for the past twelve months. Next, list your essential annual expenses, such as utility bills, fol-

Figure 2-1
Personal Financial Analysis

Current Business Status		Projected Business Status	
Current Income	$	**Projected Income**	$
Essential Expenses		**Essential Expenses**	
Phone & utilities	$	Phone & utilities	$
Car	$	Car	$
Insurance	$	Insurance	$
Discretionary Expenses		**Discretionary Expenses**	
Subscriptions	$	Subscriptions	$
Entertainment	$	Entertainment	$
Total Expenses	$	**Total Expenses**	$
Total Income	$	**Total Income**	$
Net Income	$	**Net Income**	$

lowed by expenses that you consider to be discretionary. Subtract total expenses from current income and record the number at the bottom of the column. The number should be either zero or a positive number. If it is zero, you broke even, or spent exactly what you made. If it is positive, you had money left over, which you either added to your savings or used to pay off past debts. If the number was negative, you spent more than you made and probably had to borrow money to make up the difference.

Column 2 on the spreadsheet is a projection of what you must make from your personal business to maintain a standard of living that's acceptable to you and your family. Prepare column 2 by analyzing the income and expense categories in column 1. How would they change if you owned a business? Prepare a lean scenario by eliminating discretionary expenditures like vacations and dining out. Reduce other expenses where it makes sense, and add expenses that you didn't have before, such as office supplies and rental expenses.

When you are all done, total all the expenses in column 2. That number represents the minimum amount of money your new business must make in its first year of operation if it is to cover for your living expenses. Are the numbers realistic, and is it feasible for your business to achieve your income and expense projections? If not, can your income be supplemented from other sources, such as savings? These are important questions that we will help you analyze in this and the subsequent chapters. For now, treat your minimum income and expense needs as target goals for your business.

WHY BUSINESSES FAIL

We have all seen companies go out of business. Think about some of the businesses you used to patronize that no longer exist. Why did they go out of business? Write down the reasons as you know or perceive them and any other common causes of business failure that come to mind. Most new businesses fail within the first year of operation—50 to 80 percent, according to studies done by the Small Business Administration.

Despite tough economic conditions and high business failure rates, more people are pursuing opportunities in self-employment today than ever before. Among the most common reasons given are self-satisfaction, desire for independence, limited job opportunities, downsizing of corporations, reduction in work forces, and threats of layoffs. Unfortunately, many people start their own business for the wrong reasons. Some believe that they will get rich instantly and gain great esteem. This is not realistic, and is not a sound basis for starting a business.

Lack of a Market

Many businesses fail because there isn't an adequate market for their products or services. You must be careful not to enter a market that is contracting or changing so quickly that your business cannot achieve a sufficient volume or a sufficient share of the market. A thorough market examination and market analysis are prerequisites for anybody starting a business.

Poor Management

Lack of management skills is a cause of many small-business failures. Many people who pursue the self-employment option are not qualified for the task. Some people try to beat the odds by buying an established business or a franchise. Although these strategies can help, if the buyer lacks sound business techniques, the probability of long-term success for a purchased business isn't much better than for a start-up business.

Lack of Momentum

Start-up businesses have momentum problems that must be overcome. They start with zero momentum, and they must establish new markets. Adequate financing must be found, supplier relationships must be established, and employees must be trained. The owner must coordinate all these elements at the same time, and it is a difficult job.

Lack of Capital

The failure to recognize how much capital a new business needs and to not obtain that capital is another common mistake. Businesses that lack sufficient cash to carry them through at least the first six months of operation or until the business starts making money generally don't make it. Undercapitalizing a company is much like sending someone across a thousand miles of the Sahara Desert on foot with a cup of water, a blessing, and the hope that he or she will make it. The best management capabilities in the world cannot compensate for inadequate capital.

Mismanagement of funds or poor budgeting of expenditures can compound the undercapitalization problem. Unfortunately, a shortage of capital can become a vicious circle. If you attempt to solve the problem by borrowing, lenders will shy away from your poorly capitalized business or charge exorbitant interest rates, which further compounds the problem.

Competition

Many people fail to properly appraise the competitive and market environment of their new business. You need to know that there is a market for your product or service. Who are your competitors, and how will you successfully compete against them? What are their strengths and weaknesses? It is not uncommon for an entrepreneur to enter a new market that looks moderately competitive, only to find that his or her entry causes a pricing or promotional war. A comprehensive examination is necessary to determine whether the existing consumer demand can support all competitors currently serving the market and your new business.

Uncontrolled Growth

New businesses can encounter too much success. If they expand too quickly, they can strain their financial resources. Even large corporations can go bankrupt if they expand more quickly than their resources can support. When the profitability of a fast-growing business begins to decline, creditors will be the first to back away. Growth should be controlled throughout the business planning process. The astute entrepreneur realizes that all growth opportunities should be pursued with the same planning discipline that was used to start the business.

Location

For some businesses, location is a vitally important factor. The location of a retail business can be more important than what the business sells. Finding the right location can be a difficult task even for an experienced analyst. An in-depth investigation of potential sites could make the difference between success and failure. For example, if you are considering an existing retail location, how many businesses have moved out of that location in the past ten years? What kind of businesses were they, and why did they leave? Is the area or neighborhood changing? If so, why is it changing, and is the change good or bad for your business? Are parking facilities an important factor? These are just a few of the things you need to consider before you select a location.

SUCCESS FACTORS

How can you assure that your business will be a success? One way to succeed is to work hard at not failing by always anticipating problems before they occur. You have a better chance of success if you take a proactive posture toward running your business. You probably know of several small businesses that have succeeded, such as a favorite restaurant or supplier. Think of all the reasons why they are successful that you can name. These insights will help you think of success factors that you can apply to your business.

THE BUSINESS CHARTER

A business charter will help you clarify why you want to start a business. It will also help you explain the purpose of your business to others from whom you may be soliciting advice and provide a foundation for attracting financial support, associates, and partners.

The business charter is the foundation upon which your business will be built. You will use it to evaluate the viability of your business ideas. When you have completed the draft of your charter, step back and examine the premises of your business ideas from the perspective of an independent observer. By doing this, you can avoid making the common mistake of failing to be objective. Does your idea make sense? What additional information do you need to evaluate your ideas?

You can use your business charter to systematically and objectively deal with the critical questions about your business that will constantly arise. What business are you in? What goods or services do you sell? Where is your market, and who are your customers? How much money do you need to operate your company over time? Who are your competitors, and what is their market share? What is your sales strategy, and how will you implement it?

To answer these and other important questions, begin your business charter by defining, in writing, the type of business you want to start. Next, analyze the market that you are going after and develop marketing, sales, and promotional subplans. The financial and organizational subplans will follow.

Setting goals is an integral part of your planning process. It is important that you know where you want to be in one to three years in order to focus your attention on key objectives. The better you are able to plan now for both short- and long-term objectives, the more likely you are to reach those objectives.

Know every aspect of your business. That knowledge will be vital for dealing with problems as the business grows and changes. To be successful, you should know how to manage all of the essential business disciplines, including accounting, finance, economics, sales, marketing, and operations.

Selecting a Business

How do you determine what business is right for you? The process of selecting a business starts with the first part of your business charter. At first glance, writing a business charter may look like an exercise in futility. However, there are valuable benefits to be gained from carefully defining the type of business that you want to start.

There are two basic types of businesses to choose from: product businesses and service businesses. Product businesses include both companies that make products and companies that buy products from another source and resell them. Service businesses fall into three broad categories: the service may be performed at your business location, outside of your business location, or both. The business you select could be a combined product and service business. The basics of running a business apply equally to a product and a service business. There are some differences between the two business types that come out during the analytical process, and we will point these out to you throughout the book.

Catching and avoiding mistakes in the charter stage will translate into big savings in time and money later. The three business examples in the following sections show how entrepreneurs improved their businesses by examining their original business charters.

The boat dock

Mike and Anne owned a boat sales and service business on a lake in Colorado. According to their original business charter, they were in the marina business. However, their business had grown into a mini-conglomerate. In addition to the boat business, they operated a dockside cafe, which put them in the restaurant business. They were also in the real estate business because they were selling building lots from the property they owned around the lake.

They were involved in so many businesses that when they had an opportunity to expand, they didn't know how to allocate their resources. Mike knew that if they expanded the boat sales business, they would increase the demand for their service businesses. However, they did not have the financial resources to expand all their spin-off businesses. Mike and Anne had to decide what business they really wanted to be in.

Ultimately, they choose to concentrate on the sale and rental of boats, which was their original business. They leased the restaurant, turned their real estate venture over to a broker, and rented the boat repair facility to a service company. It's not uncommon for entrepreneurs to lose sight of why they started a business in the first place. A periodic review of your business charter will help you focus your attention on the business issues that are important to you.

The barbershop

The barbershop business has gone through some remarkable changes over the past twenty years. The typical shop of the past just cut hair. Today, most also offer hairstyling services. Frank had been a barber for fifteen years and owned his own shop in a small Midwestern shopping mall. Although his business was steady, it had not grown over the years. He decided to conduct a market analysis. He quickly discovered that hairstyling was the "in thing," and so he determined to upgrade his shop for hairstyling. He went back to school to learn hairstyling techniques and had his shop redesigned. His new shop served both men and women, at higher prices than he had been charging before.

Most of his price-sensitive clientele found another barber. However, thanks to a good advertising program, his new hairstyle business more than made up for the loss. Because of the new nature of his business, he added a profitable sideline of hair-care products. There was nothing wrong with Frank's original business charter. However, over time, it became obsolete. Fortunately, Frank recognized the symptoms and made the appropriate adjustments.

The appliance shop

Susan owned a small appliance store in an area that was quickly making the transition from a rural to a suburban community. Her business charter was focused on retail sales. To attract customers, Susan serviced all kinds of appliances, and her business was growing rapidly. Then a discount appliance chain store moved into the area. Susan could not compete with the chain's prices, and her retail sales declined significantly. However, because of the quality of her service work, her service business remained strong.

One day, as she was removing the dust from the appliances on her showroom floor, Susan had an idea. She called the manager of the discount store and offered him a service contract. Susan got the contract and quickly converted her store to a 100 percent service operation. She modified her original business charter to reflect the reality of the times. She could no longer compete in the retail market, but her service business remained competitive and continued to grow as a result of the increase in the discount store's sales.

Creating a Business Charter

Your business charter must clearly define the business you plan to start. It must be very specific, not only for your own benefit, but for the benefit of people you plan to rely on for advice and financial support. It is the first business planning step that you take and, at a minimum, should answer the following questions:

1. What products or services will you offer, and who will be your customers?
2. What are the strengths and weaknesses of your business ideas, and what action can you take to eliminate or reduce the weak points?
3. What is the market demand for your products and services?
4. Where will you locate your business, and why is it a good business location?
5. What kinds of facilities and inventories will you need?
6. Who are your competitors, and how do you plan to compete against them?
7. What makes your business unique, and how do you plan to expand your business?

You may not have all the answers to these questions, but keep them in mind as you read the balance of this book. We'll help you derive the answers along the way. This is not to say that we want to let you off the hook before you complete this chapter. At a minimum, you should create an outline for your business charter and answer the questions based upon what you now know. Add to and change your charter as you proceed through the remaining chapters. Here are some ideas you can use to help you get started on your charter:

1. Use your imagination if you don't know what type of business you want to start. What are your hobbies and the kinds of things you like to do? For example, if you like fly fishing, are there any related businesses that would be of interest to you (e.g., a fly-fishing school)?

2. Talk to business owners. Here are some key questions you may want to ask:
   - How did they get started?
   - Where did they get their financing?
   - How many people did they start with?
   - How long did it take them to go from a business idea to their first day of business?
   - Who are their competitors?
   - Are there seasonal variations in their business?
   - How do fluctuations in the economy affect their business?
   - Who are their customers, and what is their biggest market?

3. Read any applicable materials that you can find that cover personal businesses and self-employment. Sources include periodicals, journals, and the business sections of newspapers. Your public library will have all kinds of material for you to review.

4. Contact the Small Business Administration (SBA) and ask for a directory of the services it offers. The SBA also offers a variety of published information that is available for a minimum charge. We have included a directory of the SBA offices in Appendix C.

Business Charter Example

To help you get started, we have created, as example, a start-up business called Computech. Computech assembles, services, and sells personal computers and hence is a product and service business. In the interest of continuity, we'll show you how the entrepreneurs at Computech built the business as we proceed through the remaining chapters. To begin, here is Computech's business charter.

Computech's Business Charter

Products Offered
Computech produces and sells personal computers through its two retail stores, which are located in the Denver metropolitan area. The company purchases component parts from suppliers and assembles the computers in the back of one of its retail stores.

Services Offered
The company offers maintenance and repair service on all of the computers it sells. In addition, Computech conducts weekly seminars to educate people on how to use the latest and most popular personal computer software.

Location
Location is not critical to this type of business. The products (computers) are assembled in 400 square feet of office space that is directly behind one of Computech's retail stores. Computech's retail store locations offer easy customer access (i.e., parking), but they are not located in high customer traffic areas to control costs. Company seminars are conducted at the two retail locations in the evenings (i.e., after retail hours).

Equipment Costs
The equipment that is used to assemble Computech's personal computers is for the most part not sophisticated (i.e., hand tools, voltmeters, etc.). The total cost of tools and diagnostic equipment does not exceed $10,000.

Product and Service Characteristics
Computech's personal computers enjoy a reputation for being maintenance-free. Less than 1 percent of its computers are returned for repair. Computech is the only company in the area that offers a three-year unconditional warranty on its computers. Customers have responded favorably to the timely seminars offered by Computech.

Targeted Customers
Computech's target market is the professional workers who reside in the five counties that make up the Denver metropolitan area. There are over 50,000 personal computers installed in this area.

Market Strategy
Computech wants to establish itself as the premier full-service personal computer company in Colorado. It intends to mount an extensive advertising and promotional campaign to publicize the benefits and features of its products and services. Computech's management team believes that if the company is successful, it will be in a favorable buyout position in two to three years.

Growth Opportunities
Computech plans to capitalize on the expanding personal computer market by opening four new retail stores in Colorado and introducing an advanced multimedia personal computer.

SUMMARY AND CONCLUSIONS

The theme of this chapter was "choosing a business that's right for you." Do you want to open a product or a service business? Where do you start? We talked about several personal issues you need to consider before you start a business. The primary issues that cause personal businesses to fail were covered, which led us into several approaches that you can use to avoid failure. Next, we introduced you to the concept of business charters and provided you with examples showing how charters were used to guide the operations of three personal businesses.

We then walked you through the basic questions you need to address to create your business charter. In the process, we introduced you to a start-up company called Computech. A business charter was created for Computech to illustrate the process.

Chapter 3

Analyzing the Market

IS THERE A MARKET FOR YOUR BUSINESS?

Let's review where you should be in the business development process. You've got a great idea for a business, and you've drafted a business charter. The next step is to conduct an analysis of the potential market for your business. Failure to conduct an adequate marketing analysis is a major reason why many businesses fail. As you proceed through this chapter, you will learn how to perform a market analysis to determine if your business idea is viable. To help illustrate the process, we'll conduct a market analysis and create a marketing plan for Computech.

You'll need marketing information to start the analysis process. Marketing information is readily available, but where do you look? When you find what you are looking for, how do you know if it's the right information? How can you tell if the information is accurate? We'll answer these and other important marketing questions in this chapter. When you have finished the chapter, you will know how to create your own marketing plan.

WHAT IS MARKETING?

Marketing includes all the activities a business performs to assure that its products and services are accepted by customers. The customer is therefore the focal point of marketing. The components of marketing that you must understand before you can develop a viable marketing plan are outlined as follows:

> *Product mix* refers to whatever combination of products and services you offer for sale.

> *Price* is what buyers are willing to pay for your products and services. Because price is a critical factor, we have devoted a separate chapter to the subject.

> *Location* includes the location of your business and the distribution channels you use to move products and services to the consumer. In a product-driven business, distribution also includes inventory, warehousing, and transportation.

> *Promotion* covers advertising, personal selling, sales techniques, and public relations. Promotion is used to create consumer awareness of and preferences for your products and services.

MARKET ANALYSIS

Many new businesses fail because the owners neglected to obtain sufficient information to accurately analyze the market. Having good hunches about what will sell is a valuable entrepreneurial quality. Before you risk your resources on a new venture, however, it is important to get an objective picture of your prospective market.

A market analysis is the orderly, objective process of gathering and evaluating information about potential customers. Who are your customers? Where do they come from? How many are there, and how do you appeal to them? Market analysis also includes an evaluation of the factors that will influence the size and profitability of your market to help you forecast the total sales for your business. The results of your market analysis serve as the foundation of your sales and financial plans.

Most investors require solid market information before they will consider backing a new venture, and so should you before you start your venture. Whether you need outside investors or not, the market analysis will help you understand the needs and wants of your customers. Once your business is underway, market analysis becomes an ongoing process that you can use to adjust to changes in the marketplace.

MARKET RESEARCH

Market research is the process used to gather the information needed to complete the market analysis. The research effort focuses on understanding the customer. It may involve asking prospective customers questions, studying existing customer data, and collecting and interpreting the information. The research findings should identify your potential customers and answer important marketing questions: What do your customers like and dislike? How can your business best satisfy their needs? There are four steps that you go through to complete a market research project:

1. *Target market identification* is the research process in which you define the target market for your business. Who are the primary customers for your products and services?

2. *Market information* involves the research processes employed to find the information that is already available to answer target market questions.

3. *Research programs* are used to obtain additional information that is not readily available to complete the market analysis.

4. *Data analysis* is the process in which you analyze the information collected from all sources and formulate your conclusions in a market strategy and plan.

The first and last steps in the research process are the most critical. They focus on the information you must have to make critical marketing decisions. Is there a viable target market for the products and services of your business?

Target Market Identification

The target market is the market you must penetrate to build a customer base. Your market may be limited to a defined geographical area or may spread cross regional, and even national boundaries. Market research must be designed to provide you with important information about your target market.

1. What types of people make up your target market (i.e., sex, age, etc.)?

2. What factors affect their decisions to buy products and services similar to the ones you propose to offer (i.e., price, quality, etc.)?

3. Are their buying patterns influenced by changes in the seasons?

4. What specific geographical areas do they come from (i.e., neighborhood, city, state, etc.)?

5. Who are the competitors in your target market, and what are their market shares?

These are examples of target market questions that you may need to address. Other questions that pertain to your particular business should be added to the list.

Marketing Information

Marketing information that already exists is called *secondary information*. In most instances, it's available in printed form for little or no cost. Gather as much secondary information as you can to build a market intelligence system for your business. There are many sources of secondary marketing information. The following is a partial list of common sources.

- You can obtain information about customer characteristics such as lifestyles and attitudes from periodicals, newspapers, and other media sources.

- Demographic characteristics of your prospective customers, such as the number of people in your area and their age, sex, and income level, are available in the Federal Census Report. You will find a copy of this document at your local library.

- You can investigate the industry using standard industry data sources such as Moody's and Standard & Poor's publications. The public library or the business library of a college near you will contain these resources. Newspapers such as the *Wall Street Journal* and the *New York Times* can help.

- Franchisers of businesses similar to yours may have prepared a customer profile for your area. You can obtain this information by calling the franchiser and expressing interest in the franchise. We have listed the names and addresses of a number of franchise companies in Appendix B, which also tells you how to obtain more information about other franchises.

- You can gather valuable information by talking to people who may see your business from a perspective different from yours. Talk to vendors who serve similar businesses in your area or talk to owners, employees, and customers of businesses similar to yours to obtain firsthand information.

- Check for existing surveys that have already been conducted to obtain information about customer characteristics for a specific market. Graduate schools of business at nearby universities may have the survey results that you need.

- Observe businesses comparable to the one you are planning to start. What are they doing to attract customers? For example, if you are planning to open a retail store, one of your best research strategies is to find a comparable store that you can use as a source for research data. You might arrange to talk with the owner to discuss your personal observations or even volunteer to serve as an unpaid helper.

- Check the Yellow Pages to see how many businesses similar to yours already exist. Call them to find out how long they have been in business.

- Call the competition and tell them about your plans to open a business. If they are willing to share their experiences, you may interpret this as a sign that they are doing well and have ample business. A new entry may not be a threat to them.

- Talk with potential customers and ask them what they like and don't like about your competitors. Look for opportunities to offer something customers want but can't get from the competition.

- The chamber of commerce may have data about your market, including consumer demographics and the number of competitors in a geographical area.

- Contact local, state, and federal government agencies to find out if they have data about your market. Most of the data they collect is on public record and is available free or for a minimal charge. Check the telephone directory under the local, state, and federal government headings to find appropriate agencies to contact.

- Test-advertise by placing a small advertisement in the local newspaper to solicit interest in your business idea. Evaluate the positive and negative response you get.

- Trade associations are excellent places to locate valuable marketing information. Trade associations operate like clubs. They're made up of members who share a common business interest (e.g., retail, wholesale, services, etc.). It most cases, members pay dues for the privilege of belonging to the association. There are thousands of associations in the United States. Any good public library has copies of the national and international association directories (see Appendix D for more information about associations).

- Small business periodicals feature marketing articles about personal businesses every month. Personal business magazines include *Money*, *Home Office Computing, Inc.*, *Profit*, *Entrepreneur*, and *Income Opportunity*. Visit a store that specializes in magazine sales to purchase appropriate magazines. The local library is another source of current and back issues of relevant magazines. Here are some market specialty periodicals:

  Advertising Age
  Crain Communications
  70 Rush Street
  Chicago, IL 60611
  (800) 678-9595

  Adweek
  BPI Communications
  1515 Broadway
  New York, NY 10036
  (212) 536-5336

  Direct
  Cowles Business Media Inc.
  911 Hope Street
  Stamford, CT 06908
  (203) 358-9900

  Direct Marketing Magazine
  Hoke Communications
  224 Seventh Street
  Garden City, NY 11530
  (800) 229-6700

  InfoText
  The Interactive Telephone Magazine
  InfoText Publishing
  34700 Coast Highway, Suite 309
  Capistrano Beach, CA 92624
  (714) 493-2434

  Interactive World
  VPI Inc.
  4141 N. Scottsdale Road, Suite 316
  Scottsdale, AZ 95251
  (602) 990-1101

  Target Marketing
  North American Publishing
  401 North Broad Street
  Philadelphia, PA 19108
  (215) 238-5300

- Competitors' advertisements can give you some hint about how your competitors are doing. For example, if one of your major competitors is always running help-wanted ads in the Sunday paper, you may arrive at one of two conclusions. Its business is growing or it has a high employee turnover rate.

- Annual reports are issued by public corporations. They are free and available to anybody for the asking (i.e., by letter or telephone call). If you are aware of a national corporation that offers products and services similar to those you want to offer, order its annual report. It could tell you where that company thinks the market is going based on its market research programs.

- Trade shows are an excellent way to find out in one short visit what others in your business area are doing. Competitive products and services, research and development information, and management philosophies are often disclosed in displays, brochures, and presentations. Trade show participants will overwhelm you with helpful brochures and handout materials. (This assumes that there is a trade show that covers your business or industry. Your local library can provide you with a directory of trade shows that indicates where and when they will occur.)

- The library research desk has been referred to indirectly throughout this section. When we said, "See your local library," we were indirectly referring to the research librarians stationed at the library research desk. These people have been trained in the art of finding anything. Ask them any question, and they will tell you where to find the answer within the confines of their library. They can even show you how to use the library's computer systems to search for the information you need.

- Marketing organizations offer many sources of marketing information. The names and addresses of the major marketing organizations are as follows:

  American Marketing Association (AMA)
  310 Madison Avenue
  New York, NY 10017
  (212) 596-8100

  American Telemarketing Association (ATA)
  5000 Van Nuys Boulevard
  Sherman Oaks, CA 91403
  (800) 441-3335

  Direct Marketing Association (DMA)
  11 West 42nd Street
  New York, NY 10036-9096
  (212) 768-7277

  Promotion Marketing Association of America (PMAA)
  322 Eighth Avenue, Suite 1201

New York, NY 10001
(212) 206-1100

Public Relations Society of America (PRSA)
33 Irving Place
New York, NY 10003
(212) 995-2230

As you can see, there are many sources of marketing information. When you begin your information search, be creative and objective. Use your creativity to devise innovative methods for learning more about the marketing characteristics of your business. As a rule, try to balance the subjective information you collect with quantitative information so that you can objectively evaluate the accuracy of the information collected.

Research Programs

Personal interviews

The personal interview is a technique many marketing professionals favor for gathering primary information. *Primary information* is marketing information that is not available through published sources. The interview process allows face-to-face interaction between the interviewer and the respondent. The interviewer can explain complex questions using audiovisual aids, pictures, and diagrams to further clarify questions directed at the respondent.

On the negative side, personal interviews require more time than other survey techniques. They can be expensive, and the presence of the interviewer can bias the survey. Some respondents may alter their responses in an attempt to please the interviewer. The way in which the interviewer presents a question, such as his or her tone of voice, may unwittingly influence the answer received. Interviewing is an art, and training is required to minimize these problems.

In the past, interviews used to be conducted in the home. With the increase in working couples, home interviews are no longer popular. They have been replaced by shopping mall intercept interviews. Interviewers approach people in a mall and solicit their responses to questions.

Focus groups are another popular interview technique. Groups of eight to twelve people are brought together to offer their views on a set of marketing issues. The sessions are informal, and a moderator controls the discussion by asking questions.

Telephone surveys

Telephone interviews are the most frequently used survey method. They are fast and easy to conduct. The response rate tends to be high. People are more willing to respond to a stranger on the phone than they are in a face-to-face situation. Telephone interviews are cost effective even for national surveys when WATS lines are used. Interviewing by telephone allows the interviewer to probe for a response. On the other hand, telephone interviews do not allow for observation or the use of visual aids, such as product pictures, to supplement the interview.

Direct mail surveys

Direct mail questionnaires are the least flexible of the market survey techniques. The foundation of the survey is a standardized questionnaire. Questionnaires must be short and easy to complete (five minutes or less) if you are to get a good response rate.

Direct mail surveys eliminate interviewer bias. Questionnaires can be returned anonymously, which can result in more honest responses. Direct mail surveys generally cost less than personal and telephone interviews. The major disadvantages of mail surveys are their low response rates, which are often below 10 percent, and that they allow little room for probing. Techniques for increasing direct mail response rates include

1. Personalizing the questionnaire package, such as printing the respondent's name on the questionnaire

2. Offering a monetary or gift incentive to those who complete and return the questionnaire

3. Including a self-addressed return stamped envelope with the questionnaire

4. Sending a follow-up postcard one week after the questionnaire is mailed to remind people to respond

5. Using follow-up phone calls to remind people to respond

Designing questionnaires

Designing a successful questionnaire is an art. Fortunately, there are some established principles and procedures that you can apply. We will cover the basics in this section and finish with an example of a questionnaire that was used by Computech.

Each question should be directed at obtaining information you need to define your market. All solicited responses must provide you with the information you need to solve your marketing problems. Questions should be easy to answer. Whenever possible, use checklists to solicit answers.

Questions should be phrased in simple and unambiguous words and phrases. Avoid using any words or phrases that could irritate the respondents. Each question asked should stand on its own and not conflict with other questions. For example, if you asked the question, "Do you like our product idea?" and in the next question you asked, "What is it that you don't like about our product idea?" you could confuse those respondents who indicated that they liked your product idea in the first place. Perhaps a better way to phrase the follow-on question would be to ask, "Are there any improvements you would you like to see in our product idea?"

After you have designed your questionnaire, pretest it. Show it to your friends and ask them if they understand the questions you're asking. How would they respond? If you are using checklist responses, find out if you have all the possible response options covered. The questionnaire that Computech used to analyze the market for its personal computer is shown in Figure 3-1.

Figure 3-1

Computech's Direct Mail Survey Questionnaire (Check One Block for Each Answer to a Question)

1. On average, how many hours do you use your personal computer each day?	1	2	3	4	5	6
2. Please rate your level of personal computer expertise.	Novice		Average		Good	Expert
3. What is your favorite personal computer application?	Word processing		Database		Spreadsheet	Other
4. Where do you purchase most of your personal computer software and hardware?	Computer store		Department store		Mail order	Other
5. What sources do you use to find out how to use your personal computer hardware and software?	Manufacturing manuals		Magazines		Books	Other
6. Please answer the following personal status questions.	Sex		Age		Marital status	Number of children

When you are satisfied with the format of your questionnaire, cross-check the answers you're looking for against the marketing problems you are trying to solve. Will the answers provide you with the information you need to answer the questions in the market analysis? Will you know more about your target market when you have completed the survey?

Let's take a few moments and analyze how Computech developed the questions in its personal computer questionnaire. The questionnaire was sent to Computech's target market, people who owned a personal computer that was three or more years old. The computer that Computech wanted to promote was designed for the casual user. The first two questions in Computech's questionnaire address this market.

One of the planned features of the computer is free software, which is addressed in questions 3 and 4. Questions 5 and 6 have been designed to obtain valuable customer profile information that Computech can use in its advertising campaign. Note that the questionnaire can be completed in less than a minute by checking off preprinted responses. A stamped return envelope and a free newsletter offer were included with the questionnaire to encourage consumer responses.

Research services

Up to this point, we have assumed that you will be conducting your own market research program. However, there are firms that specialize in providing market research for a fee. There are three types of research firms. *Syndicated firms* sell specialized marketing information. For example, you can buy demographic profiles for just about any geographical location you want from syndicated companies. *Custom firms* design customized market studies tailored to your exact specifications. *Specialty line companies,* the final category, perform specialized functions such as field interviewing, telephone interviews, and direct mail surveys.

Research fees vary depending upon the type of work you want. Some firms will quote a fixed price for a defined project, whereas others may charge an hourly rate that varies depending on the level of effort required. If you are interested in learning more about research firms, you will find them listed in major metropolitan area Yellow Pages. Look for them under the heading "Market Research."

Sampling procedures

The selection of survey participants is an important part of the survey process. In most cases, you do not need to include every possible respondent in the survey. A sample of the people in a target market population is usually sufficient to derive conclusions about the total target market.

The obvious benefit of surveying a sample of the population, as opposed to the entire population, is the saving in money and time. Sampling can also produce more accurate results. Imagine how long it would take if you attempted to interview every fisherman in Colorado. By the time you finished the interview process, the business environment might have changed. The results you obtained during the early stages of the interview process might no longer be valid.

Random sampling

How do you select a sample population for your survey? There are two basic sampling procedures you can use: random sampling and selective sampling. in random sampling, all members of the target population have an equal chance of being included in the survey. Sampling is done according to statistical rules that leave no room for the researcher's judgment. For random sampling, a complete list of the target market members is obtained. Names are randomly selected from the list until you have a sample of the desired size.

For example, suppose you had a list with a thousand names that represented your target population. You could number the names from 1 through 1,000, sequentially put each number on an individual card, and mix the cards in a barrel. You could then choose the sample by randomly selecting cards from the barrel until you had a random sample of, let's say, 100 names.

Selective sampling

Selective sampling uses the researcher's judgement in the selection of respondents. The target market is divided into subgroups. Each subgroup is treated as an independent market, a sample is selected from each according to the rules of random sampling. This approach is used when the researcher knows or suspects that certain subgroups in the target population might have special characteristics that could skew the overall results of the survey.

For example, suppose that the research objective was to determine the average amount of time people spend using personal computers for home use. People who are retired probably have more time for home use than working people. Thus, to ensure that the sample does not reflect the bias of either retired people or working people, the researchers might divide computer users into two groups, working people and retired people; and survey the two groups independently.

Sample Size

How many people do you need to survey to obtain accurate results? The answers to sample size questions are covered in detail in any good statistics book. If you intend to conduct extensive surveys, you owe it to yourself to learn more about how statistics is used to determine sample sizes. For those of you who have no interest in learning any more than you have to about statistics, this section offers you a crash course on the subject.

First, let's establish what it is that we are trying to accomplish when we survey a sample of a target market. We hope that the answers obtained from the sample represent the answers we would have gotten had we surveyed 100 percent of the target market. This basic principle is the foundation of market research, and it's supported by the statistical laws of probability.

Two aspects of the sampling procedure ensure that the answers obtained from the sample reflect the answers of the total target market. The random selection process covered in the previous section is the first aspect.

The second aspect is the sample size. Suppose the target market was a population of 1 million people. If we chose to ask one person out of the million about our product, would we be able to formulate conclusions about what the remaining 999,999 people thought? The answer is obviously no.

Would we be able to form significant conclusions if we randomly surveyed 1 percent of the population? The statistical answer is yes. Statistics tells us that there is an inverse relationship between the percent of the total surveyed, and the size of the target population. The percent surveyed decreases as the target population increases. Again, this is covered in any good book on basic statistics.

Figure 3-2
Survey Sample Size Estimates

Market Size	Minimum Sample Size
Over 1 million	1.0%
500,000 to 999,999	2.5%
300,000 to 499,999	3.0%
100,000 to 299,999	3.5%
50,000 to 99,999	5.0%
25,000 to 49,999	6.0%
Below 25,000	7.7%

As a rule of thumb, we have identified the sample sizes you should use for a survey, given different target market population sizes, in Figure 3-2. The sample sizes assume that all respondents were selected randomly.

Tabulating Survey Results

Marketing people use a variety of techniques to turn raw marketing data into useful information. First, they tabulate all the data they collected from interviews, surveys, and secondary sources. The support data they collected is carefully organized into marketing categories. The next step in the analysis process is to determine whether the support data reinforces the primary marketing information.

Three numbers are typically derived in the market analysis process: the mode, median, and mean. The mode is the number that occurs most often. The median is the number in the middle; it divides the list in half. Half of the responses are above the median, and half are below the median. The mean is the average, or the sum of all scores divided by the number of respondents. Figure 3-3 illustrates how these numbers would be calculated from a market survey.

Figure 3-3
Mode, Median, and Mean Calculation (200 People Surveyed)

Question: On average, how many hours do you use your personal computer per day?	1	2	3	4	5	6+
Results from the survey	55	45	50	35	10	5
Mode	1 hour					
Median	Between 2 and 3 hours, since 50 percent use their computer 2 or fewer hours per day and 50 percent use their computer 3 or more hours per day.					
Mean	The sum of the total number of usage hours divided by the number of respondents; 515 hours/200 people = 2.575 hours.					

In Figure 3-4, we have provided you with an example in which the marketing information from Computech's direct mail survey and from secondary information sources are correlated. In the sophisticated world of market research, cross-reference techniques can be complicated, and may require computer support.

Figure 3-4
Correlating Computech's Primary and Secondary Marketing Information

Primary Marketing Information from Direct Mail Survey	Secondary Marketing Information and Sources	Computech's Conclusions Based on the Information Collected
50 % use their computer less than 2 hours a day.	*Datamation* magazine survey confirms primary findings.	Personal computers should be targeted to the casual user.
55% rated themselves as novice computer users.	No secondary information available.	Information corroborates casual user assumption.
85% ranked word processing as the most popular application.	Information confirmed by WordPerfect survey.	Emphasize word processing software.
75% indicated that they use outside sources for education.	Microsoft survey confirms findings.	Feature seminars and pamphlets for self-teaching.
65% rely on the business sections of major newspapers for important product announcements.	Information confirmed by *Denver Post*.	Consider placing display ads in business sections of newspapers.

THE MARKETING PLAN

At this point, let's assume that we have analyzed all the marketing information that we collected. We now understand our market, and we feel confident that we can use the information to develop a good marketing plan. Our marketing plan will identify where we want to go and the marketing objectives we want to accomplish. If properly designed, the plan projects the events that are likely to occur in the future. It is used to implement changes and to minimize the effect on our business of any adverse conditions. The plan can also be used to take advantage of positive conditions when they occur (e.g., a major competitor goes out of business).

There are two critical parts to a marketing plan. The sales forecast comes first and shows anticipated sales in dollars and units. The second part is the market strategy that, when deployed, will produce the figures in the sales forecast. Like all good plans, the marketing plan is dynamic. You are constantly adjusting and tuning it as changes occur in the business environment. A good plan anticipates changing conditions and includes "what if" strategies. If a change occurs, you are not taken by surprise and forced into a reaction mode. You simply implement the subset of your plan that was designed to accommodate that change.

Sales Forecast

Sales are the lifeblood of any business. A business must have a certain volume of sales in order to survive. In this section, we show you how to apply market research data to derive a sales forecast. Because of the importance of sales, the subject is covered in more detail in Chapter 5.

Let's walk through a simple example to see how a sales forecast could be prepared. In our example, we plan to open a retail store. The store will sell widgets, which we will assume everybody needs. There are three competitive stores selling widgets in the geographical area we plan to serve. All widgets are the same. There is no product differentiation, and the retail price of a widget is fixed at one dollar.

Our market analysis shows that 75,000 widgets were sold last year. That's an increase of 10 percent over the previous year. Our analysis concludes that since we will be the fourth store to enter the widget retail business, we should be able to capture 25 percent of the total market. Our sales forecast calculations are shown in Figure 3-5.

Figure 3-5
Sales Forecast for Widgets

Forecast Item	Actual Widget Sales from Three Competitors	Forecast for Your New Widget Store	Your Forecast Rationale
Annual widget unit sales last year	75,000 widgets	18,750 widgets	18,750 widgets sold per store (75,000/4 stores = 18,750)
Percent widget sales increase over last year	10 percent	20,625 widgets	18,750 widgets x 110% = 20,625 widgets
Average price per widget	$1.00	$1.00	No change in price, since all widgets are the same
Projected sales forecast dollars	$82,500	$20,625	75,000 widgets x 110% x $1.00 each/4 stores

In our simple widget sales forecast example, we made several marketing assumptions that were not realistic and used a minimum of marketing information. Let's use the market research data we collected for Computech to develop a more realistic sales forecast for personal computers. The marketing research data that we collected is summarized as follows:

1. Each year, 5,000 personal computers are sold in the Denver metropolitan market area.

2. The average consumer spends about $475 on computer supplies, software, and related services each year.

3. There are four personal computers on the market that compete with Computech's personal computer. The average retail price of the competitive computers is $1,195. Competitors' average annual unit sales are 1,675 personal computers.

4. The state's population has an annual growth rate of 3 percent.

The sales forecast for Computech's personal computer is shown in Figure 3-6. Here is how we derived the numbers for Computech's sales forecast. We know from our market research data that there are four competitive personal computers on the market. Last year, our competitor sold 1,675 units at an average price of $1,195. We believe our personal computer is considerably better than the competitive products. However, the competitive products have been on the market for many years and have developed name recognition.

Figure 3-6
Computech's Sales Forecast for Personal Computers

Forecast Item	Forecast	Computech's Forecast Rationale
1,675 computers were sold last year at an average price of $1,195 each	$2,001,625	1,675 computers x $1,195 each = $2,001,625 annual sales
Computech's first-year unit sales forecast	335 computers	20 percent of 1,675 computers = 335
Average price for Computech's computer	$955	20 percent markdown from competitors' computers
Computech's projected dollar sales forecast	$319,925	335 computers x $955 = $319,925

Our market survey showed that consumers will shop for the best price when they buy personal computers. We believe we can capture a conservative 20 percent of our competitors' market share by lowering the price of our computer to $955 or 20 percent below the competitors' average price. Unit sales are projected to increase by a conservative 5 percent in years two through five. The increase will result from population growth in Colorado and improved name recognition of Computech's products and services.

The Market Strategy

The second half of the marketing plan is the market strategy. There is a tendency for businesses to rely totally on sales volumes and profit margins to measure the marketing progress of the business. This approach overlooks the fact that profit levels for different products and services vary. You may be tempted to concentrate on the higher-margin items and ignore lower-margin items. A "margin only" market strategy could have adverse effects on your business.

The classic bakery story illustrates this point. Once upon a time, there was a bright young man who had just received his MBA from the University of Colorado. He decided to open a bakery and apply all of his MBA knowledge to make it highly profitable. He set up an elaborate cost accounting system that would show him the exact profit he made on each item sold (cookies, bread, etc.). His market strategy was very simple: make 20 percent profit on every item sold. He opened his bakery, and after the first month, he was delighted with the financial results.

He was making 20 percent profit on every item sold except cookies, which were making only 10 percent profit. He immediately solved the profit problem by eliminating cookies from his product line. When he closed out his second month, he discovered that he was no longer making 20 percent profit on bread. He stopped making bread. You know the rest of the story.

Customers who came to the bakery to buy low-margin cookies also bought high margin bread. When the bakery stopped making cookies, it lost those customers. Our bakery entrepreneur continued to eliminate marginal products. Over a short period of time, he lost all of his customers and went out of business.

The profit margins of separate products and services must be looked at from a marketing standpoint if your business is to prosper. At a minimum, your market strategy should address the following questions:

1. What is the key focal point of your marketing strategy?
2. Who are your competitors, and what advantages do they offer over your business? What are their weaknesses?
3. How will you use your strategy to compete against your competitors?
4. What product and service mix will you offer? What are the marketing advantages of your offerings?
5. What pricing strategy will you use and why?
6. Where will you locate your business, and why is it a good location?
7. What are your advertising and promotional strategies? How will you know if they are working?
8. What product and service warranties do you plan to offer?
9. What special or unique services do you plan to offer?
10. What type of ongoing market research program do you plan to have once you are in business?
11. In your first year of operation, what would be your worst-case scenario? What would you do to recover?
12. In your first year of operation, what would be your best-case scenario? What would you do to take advantage of the opportunity?

Let's apply the market research data we collected and develop Computech's market strategy (see Figure 3-7). Our example will not be as elaborate as most market strategies, since our intention is to provide you with ideas on how to approach your own market strategy questions.

When you combine the sales forecast in Figure 3-6 with the marketing strategy from Figure 3-7, you can derive the marketing plan summarized in Figure 3-8. Your marketing plan should be in tune with the pricing, sales, and promotional strategies that you will develop in the succeeding chapters.

Figure 3-7
Computech's Market Strategy for Personal Computers

Demographic Characteristics	Findings	Primary Data Source	Secondary Data Source
Total population	50,000 computer users	None available	Denver Chamber of Commerce
Geographic location	Five-county region surrounding Denver	Telephone survey	*Datamation* magazine
Target market	85 percent are college graduates	Direct mail survey	*Denver Post* business section
Personal status	41 is the average age, and 72 percent are married with an average of 2.1 children	Direct mail survey	None available

Figure 3-8
Computech's Marketing Plan for Personal Computers

Year	Sales	Cost of Goods Sold	Operating Expenses	Net Profits
1	$319,925	$277,500	$40,900	$79,600
2	$418,225	$292,750	$41,630	$83,845
3	$425,045	$297,555	$42,480	$85,010
4	$460,250	$322,175	$55,230	$82,845
5	$508,875	$330,770	$71,240	$106,865

SUMMARY AND CONCLUSIONS

Much of what you have learned in this chapter will be carried over into the remaining chapters. We started the chapter by defining what marketing is all about. We showed you how to fit the elements of marketing into an overall marketing strategy. A strong case was made for understanding your target market by applying a process that we called market research and analysis. Market research was used to collect the information needed to complete the analytical process. We showed you how to apply primary and secondary marketing information to develop and refine your marketing strategy. It all came together in the marketing plan, which was made up of a sales forecast and a market strategy.

Chapter 4

Pricing Strategies

How Much Should You Charge?

The pricing strategy of your business must be compatible with your overall marketing goals and objectives. Pricing strategies are used to achieve market and growth objectives. Your business may enjoy a variety of pricing advantages based upon its competitive position, product uniqueness, and distribution channels.

Economic survival is the primary consideration underlying all pricing decisions. At a minimum, the survival of your business requires that product and service prices cover all costs so that your business does not incur a loss. Beyond that, it must earn some profit to offer an incentive to investors. Cost recovery is the first basic component of a pricing strategy. You must analyze the relationships of costs and sales volumes to ensure that your business recovers all costs.

Unfortunately, cost and pricing analysis is one of the least understood business concepts. Most new business owners don't know how to apply the principles of cost accounting to determine costs and calculate a price that will generate a profit. The success of your business will depend upon your understanding of the cost and pricing principles that we present in this chapter. To help simplify the explanations, we'll develop and analyze the cost and price structures for Computech's product and service lines of business.

Cost Comparisons

A telling sign of a company's financial health is its competitive cost and price position. Cost comparisons are particularly important in businesses where there is intense price competition. The low-cost producers usually control the industry. Even in businesses where product or service differentiation exists, competing businesses have to keep their costs in line with rivals' or risk losing their competitive advantage. The cost of producing comparable products or services will vary among competitors. Some reasons for cost disparities are as follows:

- There are differences in the prices paid to suppliers for such items as raw materials, parts, utilities, and capital leases.
- There are differences in cost resulting form the levels of technology different businesses use to produce their products and services. Technology issues affect the efficiency of the business.

- Economies of scale may contribute to lower cost. Different operating costs are associated with different production volumes, overhead expenses, and development costs.

- There are differences in marketing, sales, and advertising costs since these services and their related costs are tailored to the unique requirements of a business.

- Distribution cost and retail markup policies differ among competitors. Distribution costs include the cost of transporting the product or service to retail distribution points. Retail markup policies cover price breaks offered by different businesses.

Given the numerous opportunities for cost variances among businesses, you must be on the "cost alert" to survive. To be competitive, you need to know what the cost categories are and how to control all costs. Every function must pay for itself by adding value to the product or service sold. If a function does not add value, then that function and its associated costs should be eliminated. Examples of functions that add value are processes that lower manufacturing cost or improve service quality.

There are two types of costs that are an integral part of the total cost and pricing formula: fixed costs and variable costs. Fixed costs are relatively stable over time and do not change with the level of sales output. Variable costs do change with the level of sales output.

Fixed Costs

Fixed costs are sometimes called *period costs* because they are related to the passage of time. Examples are rent, lease payments, insurance, and property taxes. The fixed costs to produce Computech's personal computers are illustrated graphically in Figure 4-1. Note that fixed costs are unchanged regardless of how many computers Computech sells. That makes sense if you consider a fixed-cost example. Assume that Computech pays $5,000 a month for office space, which is considered a fixed cost. What is Computech's fixed cost if it sells one computer a month? The answer, of course, is $5,000, since fixed cost does not change when sales volumes change.

Figure 4-1
Computech's Fixed Costs to Produce Personal Computers

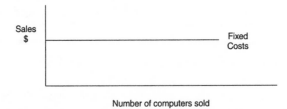

Unit fixed cost is an important extension of fixed cost. If we divide Computech's total fixed cost by different numbers of computers sold, we get very different cost levels. The unit fixed costs for different sales volumes are given in Figure 4-2.

Figure 4-2
Computech's Unit Fixed Costs per Computer at Different Sales Volumes

Fixed Costs	Total Sales Units (Computers)	Unit Fixed Cost per Computer
$100,000	100	$1,000
$100,000	300	$333
$100,000	500	$200
$100,000	750	$133
$100,000	1,000	$100

Unit fixed costs decrease in proportion to increases in the quantity of units sold. This relationship can result in significant cost savings. It also forms the basis for what economists call *economies of scale*. The larger the scale of an operation, the lower its unit fixed costs, which can give a high-volume business a decisive advantage over a low-volume competitor. The relationship of unit fixed costs to sales volumes is graphically illustrated in Figure 4-3.

Figure 4-3
Unit Fixed Costs at Different Computer Sales Volumes

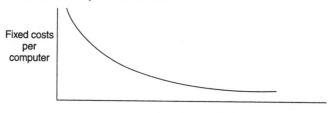

The unit fixed cost curve for Computech's computers slopes downward and to the right. As the volume of computer sales increases, the fixed cost per computer decreases dramatically. The company is experiencing the advantages of economies of scale. If we return to our original $5,000 a month office rent example, unit fixed costs are $5,000 for the first computer sold but drop to $2,500 per computer when Computech sells two computers, and to $50 when 100 are sold.

Variable Costs

Variable costs are directly related to the number of units produced and change when this number changes. Examples of variable costs are product- and service-related materials, direct labor, and distribution and selling costs. The total variable costs for Computech's computers are illustrated graphically in Figure 4-4. Note that variable costs change in direct proportion to the number of computers Computech sells. That makes sense if you consider the fact that it costs Computech a certain amount to produce each computer. For example, assume that Computech pays $750 for parts (variable costs) for each computer that it produces. What are Computech's variable costs if it sells one or a hundred computers in a given month? The answer, of course, is $750 and $75,000, respectively, since variable costs change when production output volumes change.

Figure 4-4
Computech's Variable Costs for Personal Computers

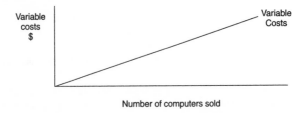

The variable cost curve for Computech slopes upward and to the right. As sales output increases, variable costs increase.

Total Costs

Total costs are all of the costs that are associated with producing and selling a given number of product or service units calculated by adding total fixed costs to total variable costs. Computech's total costs for different computer sales volumes are given in Figure 4-5.

Figure 4-5
Computech's Total Costs for Personal Computers at Different Sales Volumes

Total Sales Units (Computers)	Fixed Costs	Variable Cost ($750/computer)	Total Costs
100	$100,000	$75,000	$175,000
300	$100,000	$225,000	$325,000
500	$100,000	$500,000	$600,000
750	$100,000	$562,500	$662,500
1,000	$100,000	$750,000	$850,000

Total costs at different computer sales volumes are graphically illustrated in Figure 4-6. If total sales dollars exceed total costs, then the business is making a profit. Or conversely, if total sales dollars fall below total cost, the business is in a loss position. The price at which total sales dollars equal total costs is called the *price floor,* or the lowest price that you can accept and still stay in business. You cannot make less than your total costs without taking a loss. To arrive at a selling price, you add the profit you wish to make to the price floor.

Figure 4-6
Computech's Total Costs for Personal Computers

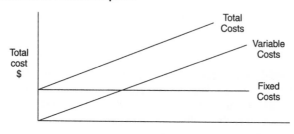

Number of computers sold

Break-even Point

Entrepreneurs are constantly faced with decisions about what to sell based upon competitors' prices and variable and fixed costs. They must decide how to acquire and use resources economically to meet their profit objectives. Inadequate cost and sales forecasts can have undesirable or even disastrous effects on the company's profits. Costs can change at any moment in time. Therefore, sales decisions are often made, and changed over short time periods, based upon what is called the *break-even point.*

All businesses want to make money. To do so, they must exceed the break-even point, or the point where total sales equal total costs. It is the point at which zero profits or losses are incurred. Total sales are dependent upon consumer demand and the prices consumers are willing to pay for a product or service. Total costs vary with the number of units produced. Thus, the break-even point varies with the number, cost, and price of units sold. We show this relationship in Figure 4-7.

You make profits when you move above the break-even point. You incur losses when you move below the break-even point. The objective of performing a *break-even analysis* is to find the optimum profit point. This is the point at which profits will be the highest. To determine the location of this point, you must consider all costs associated with various levels of demand and prices.

Figure 4-7
Computech's Break-even Point for Personal Computers

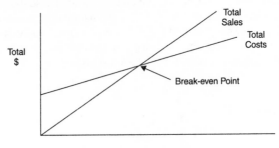

To illustrate the break-even point, suppose you plan to sell personal computers for $955 each. Your variable cost per computer is $750. You have decided to rent retail space and equipment at a total fixed cost of $5,000. How many computers must you sell each month to break even? The solution to the problem is calculated as follows:

Let X be the number of computers to be sold to break even.

$$X = \frac{\text{fixed cost}}{\text{price} - \text{variable cost}}$$

$$= \frac{\$5,000}{\$955 - \$750}$$

$$= \frac{\$5,000}{\$205}$$

$$= 24 \text{ computers/month}$$

Profit Margins

Profit margin is the excess of sales over total costs. To determine a reasonable profit, you must know what your competitors charge for comparable products and services. If you don't know what their costs are, assume that they are the same as yours. For example, if a competitive auto repair shop charges $210 for the same job that costs you $175, subtract your cost from the price charged ($210 – $175) to estimate the competitor's profit ($35 or 20 percent—20 percent is a good profit margin in any industry).

There are many ways to compute your profit margin. The way that was just described is a common-sense approach that assures that you are in the ball park. To use this method, you need to know what your competitors charge and know or be able to estimate what their costs are. Another method is to determine what you believe is a reasonable profit margin for your business. It should be highly competitive with the prevailing rates of return from alternative investments.

For example, if certificates of deposits are offering 8 percent interest, you may want to set your profit margin above that level. Certificates of deposit are a relatively safe investment, whereas your business is more of a risk for investors. You may therefore determine that your business needs to make a 20 percent profit to attract investors. Then, to determine your price, add your profit margin to your total cost for the job. In the example, you would add 20 percent, or $35 to the total cost of $175 to arrive at a price of $210 ($175 × 120% = $210). After you decide on a price, check it against your competitors' prices. A third way to arrive at a price is to add a surcharge to each cost category. Assume that you want to match your competitor's price and realize a profit of $35. Here is one formula that you might use:

Direct material cost	$50.00 × 10% = $5
Direct labor cost	$40.00 × 25% = $10
Overhead	$80.00 × 25% = $20
Total price	$175.00 + $35 = $210

The control of costs can have a significant effect on business profits. As we have seen, costs are affected by many factors. Product or service pricing, the mix of products and services produced, and the efficient use of resources such as labor and materials are examples of factors that influence cost. Profit assumptions involve estimated levels of sales, costs, and volume. A change in any estimated cost will alter total profits. If the profit is known, the change in profits resulting from a change in sales volume is easy to calculate.

We have seen what happens to profits when sales volume changes. We could have changed any or all of the variables affecting profit and calculated the subsequent impact on profits. This profit concept is useful for analyzing problems or developing business strategies. For example, if your business is operating at a loss, you can determine how much the loss will either increase or decrease with each dollar change in one or more of the variables. A high profit percent will provide greater profits than a smaller percent as sales dollars increase above the break-even point. The opposite holds when sales volume falls below the break-even point, where the higher the profit percent, the greater the losses as sales volume decreases.

Changes in Costs

Both the profit and the break-even point are altered by changes in variable costs. In the earlier example, if the cost of producing Computech's computers increased by $25 per unit, the gross profit would fall from $205 to $180 per computer. The break-even point would increase from 24 to 28 computers, as we have shown in the following calculation:

Let X be the number of computers to be sold to break even after a variable cost increase.

$$= \frac{\text{fixed cost}}{\text{price} - \text{variable cost}}$$

$$= \frac{\$5,000}{\$955 - \$775}$$

$$= \frac{\$5,000}{\$180}$$

$$= 28 \text{ computers/month}$$

Variable costs are subject to various degrees of control at different production and sales levels. When business is booming, all you think about is producing all the computers you can at any cost. You know that each computer produced will generate a profit. When business is slack, you may want to ride herd on all costs.

As with variable costs, changes in fixed costs will also alter the break-even point. Unlike variable costs, fixed costs are not subject to control when sales volumes change. For example, let's assume that you decide to lease a manufacturing facility that costs $10,000 per month. The new facility has sufficient capacity to produce 100 computers per month. When business is booming and you are running at maximum capacity, you have nothing to worry about. You can sell every computer you produce, and therefore, you are selling computers at the lowest possible unit fixed cost ($100 each, or $10,000/100).

Suppose the economy takes a sudden turn for the worse. There is high unemployment, which causes consumers to cut back on their demand for new personal computers. Computech can now sell only fifty computers per month. As we have seen from our previous discussion, you can take immediate steps to reduce your variables cost. But what happens to your fixed costs? They remain unchanged at $10,000 per month. The lease payment on your factory space is still due each month. You cannot change your plant to a smaller and less expensive facility to accommodate the lower sales volumes. This scenario is illustrated in Figure 4-8, which shows what happens to the break-even point when the fixed cost per computer doubles.

Figure 4-8
Computech's Break-even Point when Fixed Costs Increase

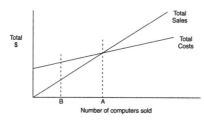

Computer sales decreased from point A to point B in the figure when fixed costs moved to a higher-cost point on the curve. Two important fixed cost characteristics are illustrated. First, total fixed costs do not change when sales volume changes. However, as we showed in our earlier discussions, fixed costs per computer change dramatically when sales volume changes.

PRICING STRATEGIES

Deciding how much to charge can be a challenge to even the best cost accountant. Many new business owners tend to underprice their products. As a rule, it's better to overprice in the beginning than to underprice. It is much easier to lower your prices if you discover that they are too high than to raise them later.

There is also a tendency to adopt a cost-plus pricing policy. This means that you determine what your total costs are and add a reasonable profit. Although this approach ensures that you cover all costs, it is not a good way to determine price. The customer will pay whatever the product is worth. Your costs do not enter into the customer's buying decision. If your product is worth three times what it cost you, why should you charge less than this? This point is so important that we will reiterate the rule: Your product's price should be whatever the customer is willing to pay for it. This concludes our discussion of pricing and the basic approaches you can use to make sure you cover your costs.

SUMMARY AND CONCLUSIONS

Small businesses find that there are many factors affecting the prices of their goods and services. We emphasized the important role that cost plays in determining prices. Controlling total costs led us into a discussion of fixed and variable costs. Each cost category exhibits a different behavior when sales quantities change. We showed how to derive total costs by adding fixed and variable costs together. Next, we plotted total cost and total revenue to create a break-even chart. Techniques for tracking all profits on the break-even chart were illustrated. Several charts and computations were used to provide a framework for our analysis of changes in costs and sales volume and as a technique for evaluating sales performance. In the final analysis, we showed you how to pull all of the sales and cost control concepts together to maximize profits.

Chapter 5

A Winning Sales Program

SALES IS THE HEART OF ANY BUSINESS

Sales is one of the most important functions in any business organization. Sales pay for expenses and ultimately produce the profits of the business. Somebody has to sell. It is amazing how many companies go out of business because of the owner's failure to understand this simple fact. Many new business owners assume that they can easily sell their "perfect" product or service. Their concept of a sales plan is to run an ad in the local paper and wait for the phone to ring off the hook. It will not happen. The problem is particularly acute if the owner does not have a sales or marketing background.

Regardless of how good your product or service is, it will not sell itself. A "full charge" sales process has to be in the forefront of all of your new business planning efforts if your company is to succeed. In this chapter, we'll talk about the various components of the sales process and show you how they work. Several examples will be used to illustrate the process and to help you develop a viable sales plan for your business. We'll also show you how to refine the sales forecast that you developed in Chapter 3.

SALES AND MARKETING

There has always been some confusion over the difference between the sales and marketing functions. The sales function interacts with the customer directly and includes the following activities:

- Initial sales calls
- Follow-up sales calls
- Price quotations
- Proposal preparation and presentations
- Order taking and processing
- Customer relations and service

Marketing functions support the sales organization. They include many behind-the-scenes business activities, such as the following:

- Market research and information analysis
- Competitive analysis

- Profitability analysis
- Pricing strategy
- Advertising and promotional programs
- Distribution analysis
- Technical service

Nothing happens until somebody in the business sells something. Your sales plan must clearly show how you will generate sales and distribute your products and services. Your plan must be supplemented and supported by your marketing plan and your pricing strategy. These three components (marketing, pricing, and sales) should fit together like a finely balanced race car engine.

SALES TACTICS

Selling requires the use of basic survival skills and must be an integral part of every aspect of your business. All successful entrepreneurs develop basic core selling skills. The Dartnell Corporation recently conducted a sales skills survey of more than 1,700 sales professionals. They were asked to rank fourteen sales skills in order of importance. The results of the survey are summarized in Figure 5-1. Sales skills are used to motivate people to buy something or to initiate a desired action. In addition to selling to customers, you'll be constantly selling your employees and partners on what you are trying to accomplish.

Figure 5-1
Sales Skills Ranked in Order of Importance

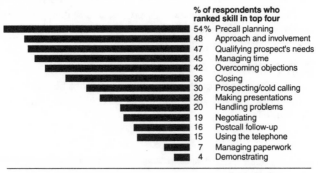

% of respondents who ranked skill in top four	
54%	Precall planning
48	Approach and involvement
47	Qualifying prospect's needs
45	Managing time
42	Overcoming objections
36	Closing
30	Prospecting/cold calling
26	Making presentations
20	Handling problems
19	Negotiating
16	Postcall follow-up
15	Using the telephone
7	Managing paperwork
4	Demonstrating

Source: Survey of 1,233 sales managers and 437 sales reps at companies with sales of $5 to $35 million, the Dartnell Corp., Chicago, 1992.

Prospective customers must be sold, and that takes time. Time is something that you are going to be short of in the early start-up stages. Developing a reliable base of customers will be one of your most difficult tasks. Entrepreneurs recognize this fact and are actively involved in the sales process from the start. If you do not like sales or elect to turn the entire sales operation over to someone else, that person will probably own your business at some point in time.

This issue is so important that it demands elaboration. A lady who was attending one of my entrepreneur seminars made the following statement: "Dave, I hate sales and I refuse to participate in any sales activities. What are my chances of becoming a successful entrepreneur?" When I told her, "Zero," she promptly left the seminar room. As an entrepreneur, you are the chief sales officer of your business. It will be up to you to make crucial management decisions to balance the various segments of your business. The impact of your management decisions on sales will significantly influence these decisions. Therefore, you must become actively involved in every aspect of your sales program.

For example, suppose Production wants to reduce costs by reducing the number of products offered. Sales wants more products in order to increase sales. The accountants want to reduce product inventory levels. Sales wants more inventory so that they can instantly satisfy customer demands. Your research department wants to develop a new product, and Marketing wants to improve upon the old product's design.

What do you do? You must be prepared to make a decision on each of the issues raised. And in every instance, you will have to base your decision upon its impact on total sales. In order to make informed decisions, you need to understand how your sales process works. There is no substitute for getting out in the field and making sales calls to further your understanding of the process.

PRODUCT MIX

Businesses have a tendency to overrely on sales revenues as the primary measure of their success. This overlooks the fact that different products may have different levels of profitability. Business owners are often tempted to expand in the product and service areas that are the easiest to sell, which are also often the lower-margin items. They may succeed in increasing sales and reducing profits at the same time.

If your business involves just one product, delivered in one grade or type, you have no product mix concerns. Those who perform a variety of services or handle a variety of products should know the marginal or incremental profitability of each in order to control total profits. This doesn't mean that you always eliminate low-margin products. They may help by carrying part of the fixed costs or bringing in customers.

In determining your product mix, you have to focus on more than just total sales revenue. It has to specify the volume of each product or service, so that profits can be computed. The profit margins of different products or services must also reflect differences in hidden benefits. For example, a product may have a low margin, but may at the same time draw customers to your business.

THE SALES PROCESS

Selling is not for everyone, but every business owner should learn the rudiments of selling. It doesn't require an innate capability that only a few chosen individuals have. Selling involves a rational set of procedures. This may be different from what you've heard at sales seminars, where they try to convince you that selling is the art of psychological manipulation.

Most of us realize and appreciate the real value of selling. Selling is the exchange of information that one can use to make a purchase decision. A customer tells you what he or she needs, and you tell the customer what you have that will satisfy these needs. If you offer the right product or service, a sale is made.

There are four stages in a successful sale. First, you must find a customer who is interested in buying what you are offering. Second, you must provide the customer with the information he or she needs to make a buy decision. Next, you close the sale, and finally, you follow up with the customer to make sure he or she is satisfied.

Finding Customers

Where do your customer prospects come from, and what are their characteristics? It's marketing's function to help the sales organization identify the type of customer that would be interested in buying the company's products and services. Marketers pass this information to their counterparts in Sales to help them increase their chances of making a sale. Advertising is used to help draw customer prospects into your business, but in the final analysis, it's up to salespeople to contact the prospects and convert them into customers.

There is an important distinction that needs to be made between prospects and customers, although it may seem subtle and many salespeople forget it. A prospect is someone who is thinking about buying your product. A customer is somebody who has already bought your product.

Prospects are a dime a dozen. You need to sort out the ones who are legitimately interested in buying. The challenge is to qualify viable prospects who have a high probability of becoming customers early in the preselling stage. At one end of the spectrum is the "hot" prospect who says, "I need a personal computer to track my stock investments." At the other end is the prospect who says, "I might be interested in buying a personal computer. What can they be used for?" The object of sales is to learn how to qualify sales leads so that you can use your sales time wisely.

Sales Objections

Customer prospects may come up with all kinds of objections to explain why they shouldn't buy your product. How do you convert negative objections to positive statements? You start by listening to objections carefully before you offer a response. Prospects rarely come up with objections that are easy to handle. "I like it, but I don't know" is an example of an objection that tells you nothing about what your prospect is really thinking. All good salespeople have an incredible amount of patience. Don't try to rush your prospect into making a decision. Ask probing questions that will help you understand the prospect's concerns. "What is it that you don't know about?"

In most instances, prospects want you to overcome their objections so that they can feel comfortable about making the purchase. Over a period of time, you will learn to recognize the most common objections about your product or service line and learn how to respond to the common objections in the most appropriate manner during the course of the sale discussion. In the interest of helping you get started, we have covered common objections and responses in the sections that follow.

Wants and needs

"It isn't what I need" is a common objection. The prospect is saying "need" instead of "want." It is important that you recognize the major differences between these two words. "Need" is a finite word. "I need this brand of paint in this color to match what I already have." You either have it or you don't have it.

A "want" statement implies that while the customer is looking for something that you do not have, he or she might be satisfied with a reasonable alternative. If we continue with the paint scenario, the customer's objection may state, "I want paint, but you don't carry brand X." Assuming that you are familiar with brand X, you could enter into a dialog that will convince the prospect to buy your brand instead of brand X. "Our brand is better than brand X because. . . ." If you don't know anything about brand X, you'll lose the sale. Go out and learn all you can about competitive products.

Price objections

Price is often a primary objection. A good answer to the price objection is what separates good salespeople from the amateurs. The mediocre salesperson is always pressing for lower prices because that is the only way he or she knows how to sell. If you give everything away, you don't need salespeople.

The price objection takes two standard forms: quality and value. Let's talk about the quality issue first. The sales scenario follows: "It's not worth the price." Obviously, your prospect believes that there is another, more competitive product that has higher quality than yours. In this instance, the sales conversation should shift to a quality comparison of the two products rather than price.

On the other hand, the objection may be, "I love your product, but I can't afford it." In this case, don't try to tell your prospect about the added benefits of your product, since she has already indicated that she likes it. Instead, talk about financing options, volume discounts, the real price after tax deductions, and the value-added features of your product.

Best value objections

"It's not the best value" is another common objection. The implication is that one of your competitors offers a product with a perceived better value. If you start off with an immediate counterattack on your competition, your customer may become reluctant to discuss the issues. Not only will you lose the sale, you will not have gained access to valuable competitive information.

Ask the customer to tell you why he prefers the competitive product, and listen. Even if you think he is wrong, listen, and ask probing questions that will help you understand the reasons for his perceptions.

Responses to value objections fit into two categories. The first one assumes that the customer's objections are based upon wrong facts. You could simply tell the customer that he or she is wrong and proceed with your attempt to recover the sale. However, the professional salesperson will bend over backwards to be more tactful. This conversation could follow: "You mentioned that we do not include clip art with our graphics software. You would be pleased to know that we now include clip art with every package we sell. You would prefer the 3.5-inch disk over the 5.25-inch disks because they are easier to handle. While I agree with you on the handling issue, are you aware that you get more reliable data transfer off 5.25-inch disks?"

In both sales scenarios, the salesperson did not attack the customer's objections. The customer was wrong about the clip art, but the issue was eliminated by saying, "We now have it." The disk size handling objection was offset by a more important benefit—the data reliability of the larger disk.

Customer trust objections

The customer may bluntly state the trust objection as follows: "I don't trust your company." Trust objections are seldom expressed in such a straightforward way, but they can be among the most difficult objections to handle. Once trust has been lost, it's hard to recover. There are four trust issues that you should avoid or, if applicable, resolve as quickly as possible:

False statements. A salesperson may exaggerate the features of a product to make a sale. Other techniques include understating prices, not mentioning hidden costs, or telling customers that you have the product in stock when you know you don't.

Reputation. If your company has a bad reputation, you must do something to fix the problem. If your industry has a bad reputation, you may have to take action to differentiate yourself from the industry.

Sucker deals. These are offerings that the customers perceive too be to good to be true. Some will ask, "What's the catch?" The rest will just back away with an "I don't trust you" attitude that may not be apparent to you. If you are truly offering an exceptional deal, make sure that it is fully disclosed in any advertising or sales contacts.

Hard sells. These encounters are not easily forgotten by pressured customers. Good selling is a courtship in which both parties provide give and take during the exchange process. In the end, the customer purchases the product in a conducive environment. The opposite occurs in a hard-sell confrontation. If the consumer is forced into buying the product, you can rest assured that he or she will tell the hard-sell story to anybody who will listen, which will cripple your business.

Honest selling is extremely important, particularly if you are selling in highly competitive markets. A simple rule that you can use to build consumer goodwill is to always be honest when dealing with customers. Offer them an out if they choose not to buy your product. The sales dividends that you will gain in the long run will be worth it.

Sales Presentations

Sales presentations are used to introduce your product or service to a customer in an organized manner. A good sales presentation is made up of modules that can be broken apart or combined to meet specific customer needs. Rambling verbal presentations don't cut it. There are six basic steps in preparing a presentation:

1. List the benefits or your product of service in order of importance.

2. Write a short sales pitch for each benefit listed.

3. Identify the features of the product that support each benefit and describe why these features are important to customers.

4. Whenever possible, back up your benefits and features claims with brief proof statements that you can document.

5. Use graphics and images to replace words when it makes sense to do so. People can grasp the meaning of a good picture much faster than they can grasp the meaning of words in a paragraph.

6. Rehearse the presentation in front of as many friends as you can get to listen. Do the features and benefits jump out at the listener? Does everything in the presentation flow? If you use pictures and illustrations, do they convey the right message?

A good sales presentation will have gone through countless revisions and modifications. Add relevant material to your presentation as you discover it. If a local newspaper just published a flattering article about your business, include a copy of the article in the proof section of your presentation. Be prepared to modify your presentation based upon what you learn when you make your pitch to each customer. Expand the parts that they like and eliminate the sections that they don't like.

Closing Sales

After you have answered all customer questions and neutralized any objections, you are ready to close the sale. Closing is the process in which you encourage the prospect to make a commitment to buy. The formalities of closing may be accomplished when the customer issues you a purchase order, signs a contract, or hands you a check. Amateur salespeople often think that closing is automatic—if you answer all of the questions, the prospect will buy. However, a professional salesperson will tell you that if you don't ask for the sale at some point in the conversation, the sale will not occur.

There are different types of closing techniques that you can use in different situations. Every salesperson has a favorite closing technique. Try to master as many techniques as you can, rather than relying on a single approach. The most common closing techniques are covered in the sections that follow.

Request close

The most basic of all closes is the request close, where you simply ask the customer for the sale. This straightforward approach saves time and can be used to qualify a hesitant prospect. Even if the prospect doesn't respond with a yes, you may get an objection that you can counter before you again ask for the sale. The disadvantage of a request close is that it generally demands a yes or no response. It can be difficult to convert no responses to yes responses. Prospects are put in a position where they would have to reverse themselves and admit that they made a mistake.

Request closes are popular for subsidiary sales closes. Subsidiary sales are sales that are made after the main sale. This technique is particularly popular after a big-ticket item has been sold. The customer is generally in a good frame of mind and assumes a go-for-broke attitude. He or she will often agree to buy add-ons or other items that have no relation to the primary purchase if you ask the right question: "Would you also like to buy . . . ?"

Pressure close

Like all closes, the pressure close is designed to force a commitment from the prospect or to get the prospect to divulge objections. As its name implies, this closing technique applies pressure on the prospect. Examples include, "This is the last day at this price." or "This is the last one in stock. When it goes, we won't reorder. How would you like to pay for it—cash or charge?" The pressure close is used as an inducement to motivate the prospect to make a buying decision.

Negotiation close

The negotiation close relies on negotiations between the salesperson and the prospect. This close is based on the assumption that prospects will buy when the offering is right. The art of the negotiation close is to identify the prospect's primary objection. When you are certain that you understand the objection and you have formulated a response that will neutralize it, move in for the close.

Repeat the objection and ask the prospect to verify that this is, in fact, the main objection. Then answer and neutralize the objection. The sudden annihilation of the objection will leave your customer with little alternative but to buy your product. An example of a negotiated close would be, "You indicated that the only colors you will accept in this product are white or pink. If I can get you a white one, will you buy it?"

Conditional close

The conditional close uses the prospect's primary objection to close the sale. Like the negotiated close, it assumes that you know what the objection is and how to eliminate it. During the sales dialog, the prospect is asked to make a conditional commitment. "Would you buy this product if I could find one in the white color that you want?" You then tell the prospect that you've got one in white, and the sale is made. The whole point of the conditional close is to get the prospect to take the initiative—"I'll buy a white one if you have it." Once the demand has been made, if you meet the demand, the sale is made.

All closing techniques have several common elements. The salesperson must listen carefully to what the customer is saying. Questions should be carefully phrased to clarify the issue raised by the prospect. Objections must be clearly understood before you counter them and start the closing process.

Follow-up Sales

One of the most neglected parts of many sales programs is follow-up sales. After you close a sale, your prospect becomes a cherished customer. Customers should be considered one of the most important assets of your company. You can learn lots of things about your customers after they have made a purchase. How do they like the product or service? How did they like dealing with your salespeople? Take the bad with the good and use it to improve your operation. Follow-up techniques can include

- Recurring customer telephone calls to check on how customers are doing
- A thank-you letter sent immediately after the sale is made
- Special fliers announcing sale items to preferred customers
- Birthday cards
- Newsletters containing helpful information

Existing customers are your best source of new sales. Positive word-of-mouth advertising is impossible to buy. Getting repeat business from existing customers takes a fraction of the time and cost it takes to get a new customer.

COMPETITIVE ANALYSIS

Knowing your competition is essential to the success of any sales program. You must analyze your direct competitors, those with whom you will be actively competing. Your indirect competition can have as big an influence on your business as your direct competitors. For example, if you are in the trucking business, other truckers in the area are your direct competitors, and you must know as much as possible about how they operate. But you will also be competing indirectly with other means of transportation, such as railroads and air freight companies. Know who your indirect competitors as well as your direct competitors are and how to compete against them. Competitive issues to consider are summarized as follows:

- How much of the market does each competitor control?
- How do your competitors appeal to their customers?
- How do your competitors price their goods and services?
- How do your competitors manage their operation?

If you are opening a unique business that does not have any immediate competitors, you will probably be competing against some other form of business. For example, if you are planning to open the only nonalcoholic nightclub for teenagers, you may be competing with other entertainment that appeals to teenagers. Competing businesses could include movie theaters, restaurants, amusement parks, and bowling alleys.

SALES FORECASTING

Sales forecasting is a process in which you estimate your sales volume, expenses, and projected net profits for the first three to five years of your business. It represents the goal you expect to reach through the combination of your marketing, pricing, and sales strategies. The completed sales forecast becomes an important part of your business plan and will help you accomplish the following:

- Determine markets for your products and services.
- Plan and implement business strategies.
- Develop sales quotas.
- Determine whether salespeople are needed.
- Decide on distribution channels and alternatives.
- Develop pricing strategies for products or services.
- Analyze new product or service offerings.
- Determine total profit and sales potential.
- Determine advertising alternatives and promotion budgets.

The sales forecast should show the dollar volume for each product or service for each month over a three-year minimum time period. If possible, it should also show to whom the products or services will be sold (major customers or account categories). Businesses with industrial customers should identify the prospective buyers and sales volumes by product type. Retail businesses should break their sales forecast down into product and service categories.

Although there is no scientific way to come up with a perfect forecast, the use of a systematic approach will improve the forecast's accuracy. Before you estimate your sales volume, analyze the marketing and pricing information that you have collected. Estimate your sales for the first year as accurately as you can. Be conservative in your projections for the next four years. This process forces you to take a hard look at what you can reasonably expect, rather than focusing on false business hopes.

Market Share Forecasts

One way to estimate sales volume is to calculate the total sales potential for your market, then, estimate the percentage of that market that you believe you can capture. The total sales potential for a market is the total amount the products or services currently being sold by all of the businesses (i.e., competitors) in that market. You could calculate the total market potential for your business for the first year by multiplying the number of customers for this product or service by their average per capita expenditures for it.

Secondary research may be required to develop an estimate of per capita expenditures. One way is to determine the total sales for your type of product in the geographical region you plan to serve and divide the sales number by the region's population. For example, the per capita expenditures for Computech's personal computers can be calculated from secondary research data. Computech has determined that there are 500,000 people in the Denver metropolitan market area who own personal computers. According to a survey that was conducted by the Department of Commerce, these people spend $23,750 million annually on personal computers and related products and services. From this data, you know that the average computer user will spend $47.50 on personal computer products and services ($23,750,000 ÷ 500,000 = $47.50).

Per capita expenditures for a variety of items can also be obtained from government and private publications. The *Editor and Publisher Market Guide* (New York) and *Survey of Buying Power* (Sales Management Inc., New York) are two publications containing expenditure data. Other information, such as the income level of customers in your target market, can be used to refine your estimate.

When estimating your share of the total potential market, take into account the total number of competitors you will face, their size, and the similarity of their products or services to those you plan to offer. Factor these considerations directly into your calculations. If there are only a few competitors with products similar to yours, estimate your market share in proportion to the number of competitors. For example, if Computech knows that there are four competing personal computers in its market area, then its product entry will be the fifth product. Computech may conclude that it will gain a 20 percent share of the total market.

Square footage is another method commonly used to estimate market share in retail businesses. Competitive space is determined by preparing an inventory of the total square footage of retail selling space in a target market area devoted to the sale of merchandise similar to that you intend to offer. Estimate the size of your proposed store and calculate market share using the following formula:

$$\text{Percent market share} = \frac{\text{square feet of proposed store}}{\text{total square feet of all competitive stores}}$$

Adjust this percentage to reflect other competitive advantages, such as location, attractiveness of retail space, price, merchandise quality, marketing techniques, and size of advertising budget. Be conservative in making these adjustments. Adjust the forecast for each sales year for factors such as population growth, name recognition, and changes in per capita income. Finally, calculate sales volume as follows:

$$\text{Sales forecast} = \text{percent market share} \times \text{total market \$}$$

Another approach for estimating sales volume in small businesses that have cash operations uses primary research data. Find a business similar to the one you plan to start and observe it long enough to estimate the volume of traffic it is handling. On that basis, project its sales and determine how your operation would do by comparison. The validity of your conclusions will depend upon the rigor of your observation methods and the accuracy of your assumptions.

Regardless of the approach you use to forecast sales, you will need to make more than you spend. After calculating fixed and variable expenses for your business, determine what is a realistic sales plan. Your worst-case scenario should reflect good information, based on research, about market realities. As long as your worst-case sales projection suggests that your business is viable, you can feel safe in proceeding with your venture.

SUMMARY AND CONCLUSIONS

In this chapter, we covered a number of important issues that you need to take into account when you develop and implement your sales program. We defined the sales process and showed you several ways to close a sale. Next, we showed you how to employ several methods to develop an accurate sales forecast, which becomes a critical part of your financial and business plans. We thought we would close this important chapter by listing twenty ways to increase your sales.

1. Contact the right person and don't waste time on non-decision makers.
2. Be creative in everything you do in sales.
3. Focus on what your customer cares about.
4. Let people know why your company is the best there is.
5. Make your offer a good one.
6. Always be in the right place at the right time.
7. Create a distinctive name for your product or service.
8. Be relentless in your pursuit of a better sales program.
9. Tell your customers everything you know.
10. Always look for new customer prospects.
11. Work at creating a business identity.
12. Always focus on why people should do business with you.
13. Develop a sense of excitement in your sales program.
14. Make your marketing program support everything you do in sales.
15. Personalize everything you do in sales.
16. Take advantage of customer testimonials.
17. Listen to everything your customer says.
18. Never sell a customer something he or she doesn't want.
19. Perform after-sale follow-up to check on customer satisfaction.
20. Advertise benefits and features.

Expand upon and refine our list as you find and develop new ideas that enhance your sales program. The success of your sales program is the single most important factor in the overall success of your business.

Chapter 6

The Art of Promoting

MAKE ADVERTISING PAY FOR ITSELF

Advertising is like weight lifting: If you don't do enough of it, you're wasting your time. The amount and type of advertising you do depends on many factors, which will be discussed in this chapter. When you write or create an advertisement, you don't want your customers to tell you that they find it creative. You want them to find it so interesting that they buy your product or service.

Poor advertising can be financially catastrophic for any business. New businesses don't have the luxury of advertising merely for the sake of advertising. Advertising has to pay for itself in new sales and profits. Monitor your advertising carefully to see if your dollars are being well spent. Plan and stretch your advertising budget by making sure you can answer the following questions:

- Who should see or hear your advertisement?
- What are your competitors doing with their advertising programs, and are they successful?
- How much can you afford to spend, and what are your expected returns?
- Is there any way to save dollars and have a powerful advertising program at the same time?
- Where and when should you place your advertising?
- What do you want to emphasize in relation to consumer needs and wants?
- How effective is your advertising? Is it getting the job done?

A serious attempt to answer these questions will greatly improve your chances of developing a successful ad campaign. Conversely, if you don't analyze your market and you set advertising strategies haphazardly, your advertising dollars will be wasted. Advertising dollars should be considered an investment, not an expense. Avoid using the "whatever is left over for advertising" scenario. Your sales can go downhill fast if you do not maintain an adequate advertising program.

HOW MUCH SHOULD YOU SPEND?

There's no magic answer to how much you should spend on advertising. As a start, get data on your industry or look at popular financial guidebooks such as

Dun & Bradstreet's or Robert Morris Associates' annual industry studies, which give ballpark figures on advertising expenditures for comparable industries. The overall yardstick for advertising is between 1 and 5 percent of gross sales, but this amount varies depending upon the type of business you are in. At a minimum, your advertising program should accomplish three objectives:

1. It must offer consumers features and benefits that they need.

2. Your offerings should be tied directly to the promised benefit or solution offered by your product.

3. The features of your product or service must be clearly communicated throughout the ad.

If you keep these guidelines in mind when you create your advertising program, your advertising dollars will return new sales and profits to your business. You don't want your limited dollars scattered among too many types of media. One rough guide is that you should spend 80 percent of your advertising budget for media and 20 percent for producing the ad copy, including layout costs. Before placing an ad, make sure you can answer the following questions to your satisfaction:

- To whom do you want to advertise, and where are your customers?
- What types of media are they most likely to respond to?
- How can you economically reach them, and when is the best time to appeal to them?
- What kind of message do you want to deliver, and can you test it before you place the ad?
- What is your total cost of placing the ad, and what is your cost per contact or per thousand viewers or readers?
- Does the market and geographic exposure of the medium under consideration cover or exceed the geographical region covered by your business?
- How do the visual or sound quality features of media under consideration compare?
- What are the lead times for placing the ad?
- How much assistance can you expect to receive from the different media?
- How much advertising clutter is there in the various media under consideration?
- If you have used a medium before, what was its performance in reaching your advertising goals?

Each medium has strengths and weaknesses. When you want speedy action, look to radio or newspapers, where turnaround time may be less than twenty-four hours. Magazines may take months before an ad is actually printed. After you make your media decisions, you must develop strong copy and that clearly communicates your advertising message to the targeted audience.

MEDIA ALTERNATIVES

Successful businesspeople realize that they must achieve top results from their advertising dollars. Advertising is a necessary investment, but you must squeeze every penny out of your program. "I know that half of my advertising is wasted, but I don't know which half" is a systematic problem statement. Leverage your advertising dollars by adopting creative techniques. Here are some suggestions for you to consider:

- Radio stations, newspapers, magazines, and other media outlets will frequently give valuable free help on advertising strategies.
- Ads placed during off-hours or in unusual print locations generally cost less to run.
- Avoid expensive ads that rapidly deplete your funds. Most of the time, your customers will need more than one exposure if they are to remember your business.
- Always repeat successful ads.
- Shop for last-minute discounts on unused time or space.
- Provide a toll-free number in your ads to get immediate responses and feedback.
- Try cheaper classified advertisements to see if their drawing power is comparable to that of more expensive display ads.
- Use piggyback advertising material in mailings, such as combining invoices with ad fliers.
- Take advantage of any media discounts you're offered, such as for paying cash in advance.
- Consider advertising in regional geographic editions of national publications, where the costs are lower.
- Share your advertising with neighboring businesses that have common interests, such as retailers in a mall or shopping center.
- Try reducing the physical size of your ad or the time of a broadcasting spot. A full-page ad or sixty-second commercial may not be twice as effective as a half-page or thirty-second ad. Sometimes frequency is more important than the size of the ad.
- Develop tight production controls to minimize the need to change ad copy. Copy changes can result in additional charges.
- Aim your ads at the prospects or consumers who give you the greatest returns.
- See if your suppliers offer free point-of-purchase promotional material. Some offer excellent promotional in-store display racks and sales literature.
- Sponsor a community or civic event that will be publicized through community service ads, which are usually free.

- Match advertising media, such as radio and newspapers, with the target markets you want to penetrate. Poor target marketing wastes advertising dollars. Challenge the media representatives to clearly identify the profile of their viewers, listeners, or readers.

- Fully exploit the advantages of the various types of media. For example, television ads give you the opportunity to demonstrate your offerings and allow visual impact.

- Saturation advertising is costly. Carefully coordinate all forms of advertising to develop a consistent, systematic approach. With the proper integration of public relations, personal selling, telemarketing, and advertising, you'll develop a powerful synergistic impact on the marketplace.

- Test advertising alternatives to find the one that works best for you. For example, Computech found that its sales orders increased from eight orders per hundred calls to forty orders per hundred calls when brochures were sent to customers prior to the sales call.

- Writing a paper in editorial style that provides informative suggestions can position you as an expert in the readers' mind. People prefer to buy from experts.

- Develop ad copy that appeals to your market and that differentiates you from your competitors. Experiment with unusual approaches, such as color, music, slogans, humor, or media selection, to attract customer attention and interest.

- Consider alternative advertising media, such as advertising on parking meters, electronic billboards, balloons, blimps, and bus stop benches.

- Keep close tabs on how well certain ads and different media types are doing. You cannot afford to spend money on advertising that is not generating sales.

- Use cooperative advertising by combining the promotional efforts of several retailers to reduce costs. All parties are identified in the ad and share the advertising costs. Co-op advertising is one way to stretch your ad budget. If carefully managed, this arrangement can develop into a positive partnership.

These suggestions should give you some practical and economical ideas for advertising. Although they may not all be relevant to your situation, they illustrate the importance of planning and controlling your advertising budget. When working on your ad budget, set some money aside for special situations. You can never accurately forecast your competitors' actions, economic downturns, or business opportunities that may suddenly surface. For example, if one of your competitors suddenly goes out of business, you may want to run an accelerated advertising campaign.

Classified Advertising

Classified advertising refers to ads placed in newspapers, magazines, or weekly shoppers that are arranged by product or service category. Typeface, layout freedom, and size are usually limited. Because of the low cost of classified ads, they are a popular advertising medium. Classified ads offer an inexpensive and effective way to start a modest advertising campaign. Here are some techniques you can use to increase classified ad response:

- If an address is required in the ad, use a street address instead of a post office box.
- Use words or phrases that are power-packed, such as "free," "new," "amazing," "how-to," "easy," and "now."
- When requesting money, offer money-back guarantees.
- Advertise consistently, since many people respond only after seeing classified ads repeatedly and becoming familiar with your name.
- Avoid charging for sales literature.
- State the offer in twenty-five words or less. The average classified ad is twenty to twenty-five words.
- Code ads to see which ones are getting the best response rates. For example, use an ad-unique department number for ads that require mail-in responses.

Your message should spur customer prospects to take action and encourage purchases. Consider using the following tactics if they are applicable and true:

- Statement that quantities or time periods are limited.
- Statement that this a one-time-only offer.
- Free estimates and demonstrations.
- Bill me later statements or zero-interest financing.
- Discounts for the first 100 customers.
- Special prices with cutoff dates.
- Guarantees and free trial periods.

Display Advertising

Display ads appear on selected pages of newspapers and magazines. They differ from classified ads in that each is custom designed by the advertiser. They may include artwork, color, illustrations, and photographs to supplement the text copy. If properly presented, they can make a message come alive, gain attention, and create excitement. Often your audience will remember the visual elements of a display ad more than the words. Here are some design considerations to take into account when you create a display ad:

- Are the names of your products and your business noticeable at a glance?

- Does your ad contain information on where, when, and how to locate your business or buy your products?
- Do photos and graphics clearly convey and illustrate the intended message of your ad?
- One dominant picture or illustration is usually more effective than many pictures or illustrations.

These suggestions are illustrative points, not absolute rules. Develop the copy by identifying benefits. Consider offering a reward for anyone who patronizes your business. Coupons placed in the lower right-hand corner of display ads are an excellent way to draw customers. Be sure the coupon looks like a coupon to avoid confusion. Use key words to help draw people to your ad:

New—People like novelty.

Saved—Everyone wants to save time, money, or energy.

Safety—This shows long-lasting quality.

Proved—People like documentation.

Love—It gives inner satisfaction.

Discover—People like excitement.

Guarantee—Consumers want some assurances.

Healthy—The health consciousness of the 1990s is applicable to many products.

Results—Every consumer wants some reward for the purchase.

You—This could be the most persuasive copy word of all.

Brochures

You see brochures all the time, but how many do you actually read? The brochures that get the most attention are the ones that talk directly to the customer and are loaded with tantalizing graphics and interesting copy. After reading an effective brochure, you feel as if you've learned something important in only a few minutes.

Brochures are an excellent promotional tool if they are carefully planned and designed (see Figure 6-1). They are not a tool for bragging about your company, but rather a means of making readers feel that they have benefited in some way by reading your brochure. Here are a few points to consider when you design a brochure:

- What is the purpose of your brochure? Do you want to introduce a new product or service line? Will it emphasize benefits and features?
- Who is your audience? Are they present customers or prospective customers? Prioritize the benefits you want to convey in the brochure and don't try to include everything you do.
- Choose a style of type for the brochure that reflects your company's personality and the image you want to project.

Figure 6-1
Layout Design Template for Sales Brochure using Aldus PageMaker

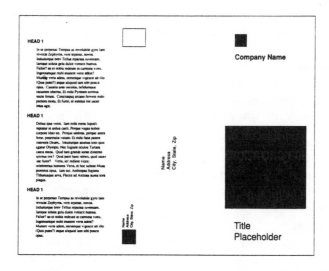

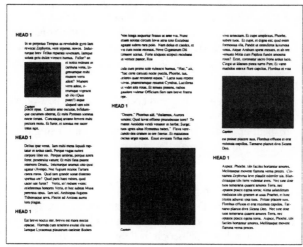

- Use a writing style that suits your readers. Don't use technical industry jargon if your audience does not normally use it. Avoid using jargon whenever possible.

- Illustrations and photos should clearly communicate the message in the brochure.
- Give your company's address and phone number in a convenient and highly visible place for reader response.
- If you plan to mail your brochure, make sure your mailing list is up to date to avoid wasted postage. Don't overlook leaving brochures at locations like supermarkets.

Joint Advertising

All small businesses have the same problem, how to advertise as inexpensively as possible. Joint advertising with other businesses can save money and generate income. In some cases, the appropriate partner for joint advertising is obvious; for example, a photographer doesn't need much imagination to hook up with a bridal shop or a caterer. Your business may require a bit more thought. For instance, if you are a computer consultant, would your customers also purchase computer supplies? If you don't sell supplies, you could hook up with a computer supply store and offer to give your customers its business cards if it will give its customers yours.

Free Consultants

Students need projects. Why not offer your business to your local college's business program as a case study? To fire up the professor, provide an interesting advertising problem for the students to solve—for instance, "I'd like to try to market my service to Hispanics, but I don't know where to start."

One of the most exciting programs is an offshoot of the Small Business Administration called the Small Business Development Center (SBDC). The 250 centers offer all kinds of business counseling, including marketing help.

Customer List

It's generally easier to keep old customers than to attract new ones. Your customer mailing list may be the most important asset your business owns. You can track every prospect or customer on a personal computer using database software. Anyone whom you meet on a sales call or who phones should be asked for his or her name and address. To get this information, offer to send the caller a free brochure, newsletter, or other item.

Ask current customers for referrals. If appropriate, offer them a reward or discount in exchange for names. Don't ignore the membership rosters of organizations you belong to. To avoid wasted postage, make it a practice to call anyone you'd like to add to your list. Ask people if they would like to receive the latest news about your particular industry.

Fliers

Like brochures, fliers quickly tell readers how they can benefit from a special offer. However, fliers are typically one-page handouts that are less expensive to produce. Fliers are often used to announce special opportunities to consumers,

Figure 6-2
Layout Design Template for Sales Flier using Aldus PageMaker

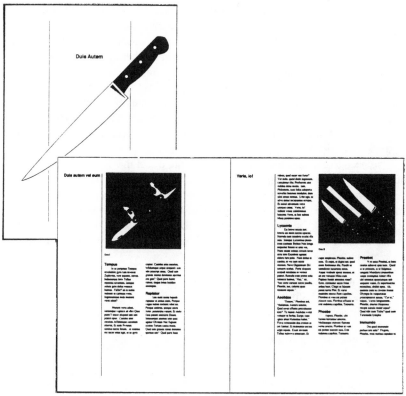

such as limited offers, sales, or coupons. The message should be short and to the point (see Figure 6-2).

Your flier should look different from everybody else's if it is to stand out from the clutter of junk mail. Having a different look may simply mean using a different color ink or a different size flier. Everybody uses black ink. If you have to pay a small additional charge for a multicolored flier, do it. The extra cost is trivial if it encourages people to read your flier rather than toss it into the trash.

To reduce printing costs, design your flier to get three cuts out of a standard sheet of paper. Check with the printers in your area to find the best way to go. There are many small, independent printers competing for business, so it should be relatively easy to find reasonable prices. Many printers are willing to negotiate a price.

Direct Marketing

Direct Marketing magazine, a leading publication in the field, defines direct marketing as "an interactive system of marketing which uses one or more advertising media to effect a measurable response." Direct marketing involves the use of such techniques as telephone sales, mail order, promotional postcards, television home shopping, billing inserts, party plans, or door-to-door selling to get your advertising message across. The best direct marketing approach for your business depends on your product and service offerings.

Direct marketing has several unique requirements and characteristics. It requires a database system to record and retrieve the names of customers and prospects. A mechanism must be in place to measure the actual purchases that occur as a result of the direct marketing program. Ongoing direct communication with prospects or customers is also a part of the program.

You need to evaluate the impact of a specific direct marketing effort. One of the benefits of direct marketing is that you can track your selling efforts to see if they are working. For example, you could count the number of returned coupons from a magazine display ad, the number of orders from a coded address of a classified magazine ad, the number of calls received from a mail order or radio advertisement. If you want to learn more about direct marketing, there are two associations to contact:

Direct Marketing Association
6 East 43rd Street
New York, NY 10017

Direct Selling Association
1776 K Street, N.W.
Suite 600
Washington, D.C. 20006

Business Cards

Every business owner needs business cards. Handing out business cards is a normal business activity and is an acceptable, low-cost form of advertising. In fact, your contacts, prospects, and associates expect to receive your business card. Business cards are easily filed away and can be used at the recipient's convenience. Since they are small, plentiful, inexpensive, and used frequently, it is easy to become complacent about developing an effective card. Here are some ideas to consider:

- Make your cards 1/4 inch larger than normal size to make them stand out.
- Distribute your cards to both prospects and their secretaries, since executives will frequently rely on their secretaries to file cards.
- Avoid giving your cards a cluttered look.
- Don't use more than one symbol or logo per card.

- Prominently display your logo, if you have one.
- Be consistent. All members of your firm should use the same card design.
- Place a printed calendar for the year on the back of your card. This will encourage prospects to keep your card and use it for future reference.

If you use your cards as a selling device, consider printing sales incentives, such as sales discounts or coupons, on the back of the card. In the presence of the prospect, add your home address and phone number. You'll create a special feeling in the customer's mind that you care about him or her personally.

MEDIA ADVANTAGES AND DISADVANTAGES

Up to this point, we have covered a number of advertising and promotional alternatives. Some of the general advantages and disadvantages of the various media alternatives were also mentioned. The purpose of this section is to provide you with a detailed comparison of the advantages and disadvantages of each of the media types that we have covered.

Newspapers

Advantages

- Your ad can be as large as necessary to communicate as much of a story as you care to tell.
- The distribution of your message can be limited to your geographic area.
- Free help in creating and producing ad copy is usually available.
- The ad you decide to run today can be in your customers' hands in one to two days.

Disadvantages

- Your ad has to compete for attention with large ads run by supermarkets and department stores.
- Poor photo reproduction limits creativity.
- Newspapers are a price-oriented medium; most ads are for sales.
- Newspapers have a short shelf life.
- You may be paying to send your message to a lot of people who will probably never be in the market to buy from you.
- Newspapers are a highly visible medium, so your competitors can quickly react to your prices.

Magazines

Advantages

- High reader involvement means that more attention will be paid to your advertisement.

- You can place your ads in magazines read primarily by buyers of your product or service.
- Better-quality paper permits better photo reproduction and full-color ads.
- The smaller page (generally 8 1/2 by 11 inches) permits even small ads to stand out.

Disadvantages

- Long lead times mean that you have to make plans weeks or months in advance.
- Space and ad layout costs are higher.

Yellow Pages

Advantages

- Everyone uses the Yellow Pages.
- Ads are reasonably inexpensive.
- You can easily track responses.

Disadvantages

- All of your competitors are also listed, so you run the ad as a defensive measure.
- Ads are not very creative, since they follow certain formats.

Radio

Advantages

- Radio is a universal medium enjoyed at home and at work.
- Most people listen to the radio at one time or another during the day.
- Radio permits you to target your advertising dollars to the market most likely to respond to your offer.
- Radio permits you to create a personality for your business using only sounds and voices.
- Free creative help is usually available.
- Rates can generally be negotiated.
- During the past ten years, radio rates have seen less inflation than those for other media.

Disadvantages

- Because radio listeners are spread over many stations, you may have to advertise simultaneously on several stations to reach your target audience.
- Listeners cannot refer back to your ads to go over important points.

- Ads are an interruption in the entertainment. Because of this, a radio ad must be repeated to break through the listener's "tune-out" factor.
- Radio is a background medium. Most listeners are doing something else while listening, which means that your ad has to work hard to get their attention.

Television

Advantages

- Television permits you to reach large numbers of people on a national or regional level.
- Independent stations and cable offer new opportunities to pinpoint local audiences.
- Television is very much an image-building and visual medium.

Disadvantages

- Ads on network affiliates are concentrated in local news broadcasts and station breaks.
- Creative and production costs are high.
- Preferred ad times are often sold out far in advance.
- Most ads are only thirty seconds long or less, which limits the amount of information you can communicate.

Direct Mail

Advantages

- Your advertising message is targeted to those most likely to buy your product or service.
- Your message can be as long as is necessary to fully tell your story.
- You have total control over all elements of creation and production.
- Your ad campaign is hidden from your competitors until it's too late for them to react.

Disadvantages

- Long lead times are required for creative printing and mailing.
- Direct mail requires coordinating the services of many people (artists, photographers, printers, etc.).
- On average, 20 percent of the population moves each year. You must constantly update your mailing list.
- Likewise, a certain percentage of the names on a purchased mailing list are likely to be no longer useful.

Telemarketing

Advantages

- You can easily answer questions about your product or service.
- It's easy to prospect and find the right person to talk to.
- It's cost-effective compared to direct sales.
- Results are highly measurable.
- You can get a lot of information across if your script is properly structured.

Disadvantages

- Lots of businesses use telemarketing.
- Professionals should draft the script and perform the telemarketing in order for it to be effective.
- It can be extremely expensive.
- It is most appropriate for high-ticket retail items or professional services.

Specialty Advertising (Balloons, Key Chains, Etc.)

Advantages

- They can be attention grabbers if they are done well.
- They can create instant awareness.
- They get your name in front of people.

Disadvantages

- Targeting your market is difficult.
- This can be an inappropriate medium for some businesses.
- It's difficult to find items that are appropriate for certain businesses.

ADVERTISING AGENCIES

As your business grows, your advertising may become more complicated and time-consuming. Eventually, you may decide to hire an advertising agency. Although agency services increase your cost, agencies are in business to increase your advertising effectiveness. Depending on the contractual agreement and your own needs, an agency can offer you the following:

- Analyze your business strengths and weaknesses.
- Study your industry and competition and, based upon its findings, make recommendations for your business.
- Plan your advertising strategy, select media, and purchase space and time.
- Produce ads, including copy, visuals, layout, sound, and video production work.

- Create finished ads in the physical format required by different media.
- Keep records of your advertising expenditures and schedules, and perform research studies to measure results.

The two most popular agency services are the production of the ads and the liaison work with different media. To help minimize the time you spend selecting an agency, develop selection criteria to guide your choice.

What you get when you hire an agency is personal attention to your specific advertising needs. Small agencies typically rely more on customer references for growth, and they may be more interested in your business. How do you know if an ad agency is good? You'll know whether an agency is potentially good and interested in your business after you have met with its people. Here are some basic questions to ask during the interview process:

How long has your agency been in business?

Do you specialize in serving any one industry?

Do you have experience in serving businesses with modest budgets?

Can you give me some examples of successful advertising programs that you have put together for businesses like mine?

If there are account problems or disagreements, how are they resolved?

Please explain all the costs that will be incurred in using your services.

Are there any positive or negative comments that you want to make about my account?

The chemistry you feel between you and the people you would be working with will be a big factor in choosing the right agency. Will there be any personality conflicts? Will you be able to get along with the agency's creative people as well as with the person managing your account? Ask for references and review the work that the agency has done for other companies like yours.

Ad agencies are listed in the Yellow Pages. Or you can read the annual issue of *Advertising Age*, which lists advertising agencies by rank and size. Another source is the *Standard Directory of Advertising Agencies*. Both directories should be available in your local library. The American Association of Advertising Agencies is the national association that most agencies belong to. It can provide you with a list of agencies that are in your geographic area or that specialize in unique advertising programs. Its address is

American Association of Advertising Agencies (AAAA)
666 Third Avenue
New York, NY 10017

If you decide to work with a large agency, make sure your small account is not lost in the shuffle. Challenge the agency to suggest unique ways to advertise effectively with a modest budget.

MISTAKES TO AVOID

Every business makes advertising mistakes. You will not be immune from them, but you should know how to avoid the common ones. Don't try to do too much with too few advertising dollars. You cannot afford to be something to everyone. Too often, businesses try to say too much by using many different media or expensive, one-time, flashy ads.

A clear focus with just one powerful message may be all you need to create a successful advertising program. Choosing a medium based on its low total cost rather than on its cost per thousand readers, listeners, or viewers can be an expensive mistake. You should compare audience size, audience image, and selling results for businesses that have advertised in various media. Don't just look at a medium's ad rates.

Not advertising frequently enough is another common mistake. You may need to run several ads to increase customer awareness and recall of your message. Don't make an advertisement bigger than it needs to be. Make sure your advertisement concentrates on the reader, listener, or viewer. Don't expect too much from creativity in copy and art. A flashy, innovative ad will not make up for a defective product.

Failing to fully utilize the unique advantages of the medium, especially television, is another common mistake. For example, if you use TV, don't just talk through a TV script, demonstrate the virtues of your product. If you use billboards, avoid using excess words. People will not have time to read them. Always capitalize on the inherent features of your product, service, or company. Match your market's preferences with the strengths of your offerings.

Measure the success or failure of every ad you place. Otherwise, you will never know which ads are working and which are not. Evaluate your ads to see if they're drawing customers into your business. Discover what it takes for advertising to succeed. Advertising cannot overcome a structural business weakness, nor is it an automatic solution to all of your problems. If your prices are too high or you are in an inconvenient location, you've got problems that go beyond your advertising campaign.

If advertising is a major part of your business, subscribe to magazines like *Advertising Age* or *Adweek* to help you improve your ad program. Excellent advertising articles also appear in publications such as *Business Marketing, Entrepreneur, Inc., Inside Business, Marketing News, Small Business Report, Venture,* and *Nation's Business.*

CUSTOMER RELATIONS

According to the Federal Office of Consumer Affairs, 95 percent of all dissatisfied customers never bother to complain to the seller. They make their dissatisfaction known in other ways—by taking their business elsewhere and by criticizing your business whenever they get the opportunity. Replacing lost customers is an expensive proposition. Unfortunately, many businesses pay more attention to acquiring new customers than to retaining existing customers. It makes good dollars and sense to keep your current customers. The advertising costs of attracting new customers are five times greater than those of selling to existing customers. Here are some ideas that you can use to keep your customers:

- Solicit customer criticism and suggestions by installing a customer suggestion box.
- Teach all employees the importance of respecting your customers.
- Constantly remind employees of the value of good customer relations.
- Conduct telemarketing programs with new customers to gauge their level of satisfaction.
- Use direct mail surveys to measure overall customer satisfaction.
- Conduct personal customer interviews to determine customer's level of satisfaction.
- Use hired shoppers (shoppers hired by the employer) to determine how well employees are treating customers.
- Use conveniently located comment cards to encourage customer response.
- Use toll-free numbers to solicit comments from out-of-town customers.
- Establish a special complaint department to review and objectively evaluate every customer complaint.
- Publish a newsletter featuring product and service use bulletins, helpful news briefs, and calendars of local events.
- Conduct educational seminars at which you can discuss different features of your business and offer product demonstrations.
- Offer goodwill gifts or special discounts to key customers to show your appreciation.

Testimonials

If you've been in business for more than a few weeks, you should have satisfied customers. Why not let them help you promote your business? While customers may occasionally send you complimentary letters without any prodding, you'll generally need to ask. If a customer says something positive about your product or service, ask if you can quote him or her. If the customer agrees, ask a few qualifying questions.

For example, suppose a customer tells you, "I was really impressed that you processed my order so fast!" you might ask, "Why did you need that order processed so quickly? What would have happened if you had not gotten it for another week? Would you recommend my company to your friends?" Document the answers for future reference.

Another way to solicit testimonials is by sending a thank-you letter after the sale. In addition to expressing your appreciation, you might state, "If you have any questions or comments regarding the product, please call me at 555-5555." Businesspeople may not have a storefront or window display, but they can still give prospects the opportunity to view testimonials. Enlarge a few of the best and post them on your office walls. Try to get testimonials from local celebrities. If you succeed, you might place a photograph beside the letter.

Position Yourself

You may be an expert in your field, but if no one else knows it, you're missing out on a real marketing opportunity. And if you're not an expert, it may be relatively easy to become one in the eyes of the buying public. When you own a business, people expect you to know something about it. You are, in other words, the expert. Now all you have to do is get the word out.

Offer to write a brief column for your local newspaper. Expert writing is generally not required. Try a question-and-answer format and list one or two common questions your customers ask you. Although your customers may not read trade publications, anything you have published in them can enhance your image. Reprint the article and offer it to your customers or include a copy when you send out your invoices.

Depending on your product or service, if you speak better than you write, consider giving seminars, lectures, or demonstrations. Even if you've never taught before, once you come up with an interesting topic, you may be able to offer a course through an extension of your local university or college, chamber of commerce, public library, or nonprofit organization.

Phone Manners

You don't get a second chance to make a first impression. For many people, that first impression is made by phone. The human voice can convey an astounding range of emotions. If you sound angry or brusque when you answer the phone, you start things off on a bad note. Worse yet, you may drive away a potential customer.

What should you say when you answer the phone? It's generally best to use your company's name in the greeting because it reassures callers that they have reached the correct number. Find out what kind of impression you make by taping your phone greetings. For about $10, you can purchase a device that attaches to the phone and a tape recorder. For one day, turn the recorder on each time you answer the phone. When you replay the tape, listen for flaws in diction. Can you easily recognize the name of your company? Does your voice exude enthusiasm or boredom? Finally, if the phone rings when you are under pressure, don't rush to answer.

SUMMARY AND CONCLUSIONS

We kicked this chapter off by stating that advertising is an investment and therefore must pay for itself. Several basic advertising issues and elements that go into a productive advertising program were covered. You were introduced to a number of advertising media and alternatives. The advantages and disadvantages of the various media were listed to help you select the media that are right for your business. We then introduced you to advertising agencies, which can play an important role in your ad program. The importance of maintaining good customer relations was also emphasized.

Chapter 7

Accounting for the Business

COUNT THE PENNIES AND WATCH THE DOLLARS GROW

The accounting system that you set up for your business will be a major source from which you can derive information. Besides telling you how well you are doing, accounting reports can be used in developing business strategies and investigating reasons for the success or failure of existing strategies.

All accounting systems produce financial statements that contain two primary reports: the *income statement* and the *balance sheet*. They show your business's performance over a period of time and provide a financial picture at a given moment in time.

THE BALANCE SHEET

The balance sheet is a record of the dollar value of three accounting categories: assets, liabilities, and owners' equity. A simplified example of Computech's balance sheet is shown in Figure 7-1.

Figure 7-1
Simplified Version of Computechs Balance Sheet

<table>
<tr><td colspan="2" align="center">Computech
Balance Sheet
End of February</td></tr>
<tr><td>Assets</td><td></td></tr>
<tr><td>Cash</td><td>$41,000</td></tr>
<tr><td>Accounts receivable</td><td>$10,000</td></tr>
<tr><td>Inventory</td><td>$20,000</td></tr>
<tr><td>Plant & equipment</td><td>$12,000</td></tr>
<tr><td>Less: Depreciation</td><td>($10,000)</td></tr>
<tr><td>Total assets</td><td>$73,000</td></tr>
<tr><td>Liabilities</td><td>$55,000</td></tr>
<tr><td>Owners' equity</td><td>$18,000</td></tr>
<tr><td>Liabilities & owners' equity</td><td>$73,000</td></tr>
</table>

Assets are those items owned by your business that have an identified value. The amount of money that you have on deposit in checking and savings accounts is an example of a current asset. Inventories of raw materials, inventory of finished products, and equipment owned by the business are all considered assets.

In Figure 7-1, we deducted an item called *depreciation* from the plant and equipment account. Depreciation is an accounting term used to record a decrease in the value of property as a result of wear, deterioration, or obsolescence. For example, suppose you bought a personal computer (an asset) for $1,200, and you expect this particular computer to last five years before it wears out. The depreciation period for the computer would therefore be five years, and the depreciation rate would be $240 per year ($1,200/5 years) or $20 per month ($240/12 months).

The value of the machine at the end of the first month would be $1,180 (asset value – depreciation or $1,200 – $20). This is an example of the straight-line method of calculating depreciation. It is the simplest and most common method, used by most businesses.

Liabilities are obligations or responsibilities of the business to pay for assets purchased or for services received. Liability claims or loans are generally held by banks and suppliers. Accounts payable and notes payable are two examples of liability accounts.

As a business owner, you have a claim to the assets, that remain after all your liability obligations have been met. The difference is called *owners' equity* or *retained earnings*. It is the difference between total assets and total liabilities.

How To Read A Balance Sheet

An expanded version of our original balance sheet for Computech is shown in Figure 7-2. The headlines of the report include the name of your business and the point in time that the report pictures (the end of February in our example). If you start from the top of the report, you can see that Computech has accumulated $73,000 in assets. The business has $21,000 in a checking account and $20,000 in an interest bearing savings account. Computech's customers owe the company $10,000 (accounts receivable).

Figure 7-2
Computech's Expanded Balance Sheet for February

Computech
Balance Sheet
End of February

Assets		Liabilities	
Cash in checking account	$21,000	Accounts payable	$25,000
Cash in savings account	$20,000	Notes payable	$30,000
Accounts receivable	$10,000	Total liabilities	$55,000
Computer inventory	$12,000		
Parts inventory	$8,000	Owners' equity	
Plant & equipment	$12,000	Retained earnings	$18,000
Less: Depreciation	($10,000)		
Total assets	$73,000	Liabilities & owners' equity	$73,000

The company owns $20,000 in computer and parts inventories. Plant and equipment are property owned by Computech that is not intended for sale and represent $12,000 in assets, less $10,000 for depreciation. Plant assets include land, buildings, and fixtures. Equipment assets include office computers, fax machines, and any other such equipment owned by Computech.

Two liability accounts are shown. Accounts payable are short-term obligations to suppliers and vendors ($25,000). The business owes the bank $30,000 for money that was perhaps borrowed to buy equipment (notes payable).

The difference between total assets and liabilities is retained earnings ($18,000), or the owner's equity in the company. It represents what Computech would be worth (retained earnings) if it were to go out of business and sell off all of its assets.

THE INCOME STATEMENT

The income statement identifies the profits or losses of a business over a stated period of time. A simplified version of Computech's income statement is shown in Figure 7-3. There are three primary accounting categories in the income statement: sales, costs, and profit. *Sales* are the revenues that a company derives from the sale of goods and services.

Figure 7-3
Simplified Version of Computech's Income Statement

Computech
Income Statement
February

Total computer sales	$30,000
Less: Total costs	($25,000)
Net profit	$5,000

The *costs* of doing business are deducted from sales to determine the amount of *profit* that was made. If costs are greater than sales, the profit figure will be a negative number, reflecting the dollar amount of loss to the business.

We have expanded our simplified version of Computech's income statement to show more detailed information about the performance of the business. Figure 7-4 breaks out the business's sales by type and gives shows a breakdown of the costs for February. Notice that the expanded income statement includes a year-to-date column, which accumulates the previous months' totals.

Figure 7-4
Computech's Income Statement for February

Computech
Income Statement
February

Sales	Current $	Units	YTD $	Units
Service sales	$9,500	170	$16,500	313
Product sales	$20,500	2,950	$37,975	5,323
Total sales	$30,000		$54,475	
Cost of Goods Sold				
Product materials	$5,200		$13,110	
Direct product labor	$4,000		$2,605	
Direct service labor	$2,400		$4,000	
Total cost of goods sold	$11,600		$19,715	
Operating Expenses				
Utilities	$650		$1,210	
Salaries	$7,200		$13,390	
Payroll taxes & benefits	$1,475		$2,740	
Advertising	$400		$745	
Office supplies	$325		$605	
Insurance	$490		$910	
Legal & accounting services	$125		$235	
Telephone	$165		$305	
Depreciation expense	$1,010		$1,880	
Travel & distribution	$460		$855	
Total operating expenses	$12,300		$22,875	
Other expenses	$400		$745	
Notes payable interest	$700		$1,300	
Total expenses	$25,000		$44,635	
Net Profit	$5,000		$9,840	

Here is how you would interpret the income statement in Figure 7-4. Total sales are $30,000, broken down into product and service sales. During the month of February, the company sold $20,500 in products and $9,500 in services. We cannot tell by looking at Figure 7-4 what types of products or services were sold in February. However, the people at Computech maintain a detailed sales log to track monthly sales. The sales log for February is shown in Figure 7-5. The detailed sales log can be used to track sales of individual products and services to analyze sales growth and decline patterns.

Figure 7-5
Computech's Sales Log for February

Computech
Detailed Sales Log
February

Service Sales	Current $
Seminars	$4,500
Computer maintenance	$4,000
Total service sales	$9,500
Product Sales	
Personal computers	$12,300
Computer supplies	$4,200
Other	$4,000
Total product sales	$20,500
Total sales	$30,000

Cost of goods sold follows the Total Sales line and shows the costs that are associated with producing each of the two types of sales. The product materials costs direct product labor and direct service labor costs that are associated with producing products and services are separated before they are totaled. This approach allows Computech's owner to analyze the profitability of its product business independent of its service business.

Operating expenses are expenses that cannot be directly tied to the production of products or services. They include utility costs and insurance payments. Other expenses include payments on notes and other types of loans. Total expenses are determined by adding the cost of goods sold, operating expenses, and other expenses. Net profit is obtained by subtracting total expenses from total sales.

Profit

The "bottom line" of the income statement is called net profits or net losses. If total sales are greater than total costs, then profits will be a positive dollar amount ($5,000 in Figure 7-4). If costs exceed sales, then the company incurs a loss and the bottom-line figure will be negative.

FINANCIAL STATEMENTS

Up to this point, we have discussed the components of the balance sheet and the income statement as though they were separate, unrelated reports. On the contrary, there is a direct relationship between these two financial statements that should not be ignored. There are decisions that you can make as a result of your interpretation of the income statement that can have a positive or negative effect on the balance sheet.

For example, how can you change the equity position of your business? In Figure 7-4, Computech made $5,000 in net profit. This represents a surplus of money that the company earned after the current month's expenses have been met.

Let us assume that all earned income is deposited in Computech's checking account. If Computech had earned $10,000 more, or $15,000, in February, cash on hand would have been $31,000 ($21,000 + $10,000). Computech's revised balance sheet for February with the increase in the checking account balance is shown in Figure 7-6.

Figure 7-6
Computech's Balance Sheet after a $15,000 Profit

Computech's
Balance Sheet
End of February

Assets		Liabilities	
Cash in checking account	$31,000	Accounts payable	$25,000
Cash in savings account	$20,000	Notes payable	$30,000
Accounts receivable	$10,000	Total liabilities	$55,000
Computer inventory	$12,000		
Raw materials inventory	$8,000	**Owners' equity**	
Plant & equipment	$12,000	Retained earnings	$28,000
Less: Depreciation	($10,000)		
Total assets	$83,000	**Liabilities & owners' equity**	$83,000

Now, reverse the example and assume that Computech lost $5,000 in the same period (a $10,000 change). Computech would have had to withdraw $10,000 from its checking account to pay for added expenses. If the cash on hand in the checking account is now $21,000, the cash balance after the withdrawal would have been $11,000 ($21,000 – $10,000).

The effect on the balance sheet of a $10,000 change in profit is shown in Figures 7-7. As you can see, a relatively small change can significantly affect the balance sheet. In our previous example, the increased profit assumption resulted in a favorable equity position of $28,000 while the loss assumption reduced owners' equity to $8,000 (see Figures 7-6 and 7-7).

Figure 7-7
Computech's Balance Sheet after a $5,000 Loss

Computech's
Balance Sheet
End of February

Assets		Liabilities	
Cash in checking account	$11,000	Accounts payable	$25,000
Cash in savings account	$20,000	Notes payable	$30,000
Accounts receivable	$10,000	Total liabilities	$55,000
Computer inventory	$12,000		
Raw materials inventory	$8,000	**Owners' equity**	
Plant & equipment	$12,000	Retained earnings	$8,000
Less: Depreciation	($10,000)		
Total assets	$63,000	**Liabilities & owners' equity**	$63,000

FINANCIAL RATIOS

Financial ratios are used to gauge the overall financial performance of a business and to identify potential or pending problems. What is considered an acceptable ratio will vary from industry to industry. We'll show you how to use various financial ratios and apply common business guidelines to determine how well your business is performing. To find ratio guidelines and values that apply for your industry, consult the *Almanac of Business and Industrial Financial Ratios*. It should be available at your local public library.

Profit Margin

Computech made a $5,000 profit in Figure 7-4. The formula to calculate Computech's profit margin is shown below:

$$\text{Profit margin} = \frac{\text{net profit}}{\text{net sales}}$$

$$= \frac{\$5,000}{\$30,000}$$

$$= 17\%$$

Debt-to-Equity Ratio

The debt-to-equity ratio will reveal the borrowing leverage that exists in your business. To determine Computech's debt-to-equity ratio, divide the company's total liabilities by the owners' equity on the balance sheet in Figure 7-3.

$$\text{Debt-to-equity ratio} = \frac{\text{total liabilities}}{\text{owners' equity}}$$

$$= \frac{\$55,000}{\$18,000}$$

$$= 3.1$$

In general, the higher the ratio, the greater the likelihood that the company will not be able to meet its payment obligations. Banks use this ratio to determine loan risk.

Inventory Turnover

Inventory turnover is a useful ratio for any business that maintains significant levels of inventory. It measures the average number of times a company's inventory turns over in a one-year period. A high ratio is good and indicates that a relatively low level of on-hand inventory is supporting a relatively high sales volume. The ratio is calculated by dividing the cost of goods sold from the income statement (Figure 7-4) by the value of the inventory reported on the balance sheet (Figure 7-2).

$$\text{Inventory turnover} = \frac{\text{cost of products sold}}{\text{value of product inventory}}$$

$$= \frac{\$9,200}{\$12,000}$$

$$= 0.76$$

Keeping inventory costs down is especially critical during periods of high interest rates. Any ratio for a month that is equal to or above 1.0, indicating that the company is turning its inventory at least once a month, is considered good.

Return on Investment

The return on investment (ROI) ratio represents the rate of return you are receiving on your investment in your company. The higher the ROI, the more attractive your business is to outside investors. ROIs are often calculated on individual company investments, such as the acquisition of a specific piece of capital equipment that will save the company money. To determine the rate of return for Computech, apply the following calculation by using information from the previous figures:

$$\text{Return on investment} = \frac{\text{net profit}}{\text{owners' equity}}$$

$$= \frac{\$5,000}{\$18,000}$$

$$= 0.28 \text{ or } 28 \text{ percent}$$

ROI should be compared with the prevailing interest rates and rates of return on other investments. Anything above a 10 percent ROI is usually considered acceptable.

COST REDUCTION STRATEGIES

As you can see, all of the financial ratios are driven by cost containment. Your daily operating strategy should include a continuous effort to reduce your costs. Survey the insurance marketplace at least annually. The availability of coverage can change if a new insurance company enters the local market. Increase deductibles in areas where you seldom make claims.

Investigate all of your service contracts to ensure that your service charges are acceptable. Review supplier costs to make sure you are getting the best deal you can at acceptable quality levels. If you are buying in low volume, find out what larger-volume orders would do to your overall supplier costs and other costs as well. Look into reducing your service costs by combining with other businesses in your area to contract for services.

If yours is a growing company that spends most of its time developing new products and services, it may be vulnerable to employee theft and fraud. Minimize your risks by implementing a system of safeguards. Randomly compare expense checks to avoid excessive reimbursement of expenses. Require backup documentation of all expenses. Prevent employees from setting up dummy businesses and then submitting fraudulent bills by analyzing all new or unfamiliar suppliers. Conduct random spot checks of deliveries from new suppliers to make sure that goods received match invoiced goods.

Watch for inventory theft. For example, someone in inventory control could be selling your inventory out the back door. Look for trends that don't make sense like sudden decreases in inventory in a warehouse from which no shipments were made.

ACCOUNTS RECEIVABLE

Accounts receivable are like IOU accounts. You have agreed to sell a product or service on credit. The credit gets recorded in the IOU or accounts receivable account on your company's balance sheet. Computech's balance sheet (see Figure 7-2) showed that the company had $10,000 in its accounts receivable account and intended to collect the money from its customers at some future point in time.

You cannot determine from Computech's balance sheet what specific customers owed the company money. However, the accountants at Computech maintain what is called an Aged Accounts Receivable Report (see Figure 7-8) that shows this information.

Figure 7-8
Computech's Aged Accounts Receivable Report for February

Computech's
Aged Accounts Receivable Report
End of February

Account Name	Total Due	Current	30-59	60-89	90-119	Over 120	Action Taken
John Doe	$2,200	$200	$500			$1,500	No more credit until paid
ABC Corporation	$5,400						
Ajax Inc.	$4,359					$4,359	Turned over to collection agency
Susan Jones	$750			$750			Promised to pay in two days

The left-hand column identifies the individual Computech customers that owe money. The next six columns identify the total amount due and the past due status for each account. Current means that the sale was made in the current reporting month (i.e., February). Older receivables are reported in 30-day increments. The last column in the report, the Action Taken column, is used to report and track account collection activities.

Collection Agencies

When receivables remain unpaid despite dunning letters and telephone calls, consider hiring a collection agency. Collection agencies are in business to help you collect past due accounts. As a general rule, if an agency collects nothing, you pay nothing. If it collects, the agency retains a percentage of the amount collected. The amount is based on the nature, size, and age of the account. Most agencies are small businesses and operate from a single location.

Each collector is trained to establish a rapport with a debtor and sympathize with his or her problems while setting up a payment plan. No two agencies are alike, so shop the agencies in your area. Don't accept initial quotes. Examine agency conditional terms, such as fees charged if merchandise is returned in lieu of payment.

BOOKKEEPING

It is imperative that you establish a basic record-keeping system before you start your business. Accurate books and records are essential for business planning and will help you make informed management decisions. You should analyze the record-keeping needs of your business to determine the bookkeeping system that's best for you. All systems should provide the following:

- Detailed operating statements (i.e., balance sheet and income statement)
- Comparison of current results to budgets and prior periods
- Information for tax returns and reports to regulatory agencies
- Sufficient control to protect assets and detect errors

Each business has special needs that must be considered when establishing a bookkeeping system. Factors that you should take into consideration include the legal structure of your business, your industry, the number of employees you have, and the number of products or services you sell.

CASH FLOW MANAGEMENT

The goal of cash flow management is to always have enough cash on hand to meet the cash requirements of the business. There are several fundamental cash flow principles that you can apply to manage your cash and to make sure you have the cash when you need it. It all starts with the preparation of a cash flow projection report similar to the one of Computech in Figure 7-9.

Figure 7-9
Computech's Monthly Cash Flow Budget

Account Description	Current Month Budget	Current Month Actual	Deviation
Sources of Cash			
Beginning cash balances	$12,500	$10,000	($2,500)
Accounts receivable	$7,500	$8,500	$1,000
Cash sales	$10,000	$9,500	($500)
Total available cash	$30,000	$28,000	($2,000)
Cash disbursements			
Materials	$12,500	$12,500	0
Labor	$8,500	$9,500	($1,000)
Loan payments	$2,250	$2,140	$1,100
Insurance	$1,200	$1,300	($100)
Equipment	$2,000	$500	$1,500
Supplies	$1,000	$500	$500
Taxes	$2,000	$1,000	$1,000
Total disbursements	$29,450	$27,440	$2,010
Ending cash balance	$550	$560	$10

The cash flow projection attempts to predict the cash needs of the business by showing when cash will flow in and out of the business. The source of the flow is also shown. Cash flows in from sales, collections of accounts receivable, and the sale of assets. Cash flows out of the business to meet its expenses and debt obligations.

SELECTING AN ACCOUNTANT

A good accountant is the single most important outside advisor a small business has. One of the basic rules of accounting in small businesses is never to scrimp on the use of good accounting services. During the start-up stages, you need to establish tight financial controls over your business and you need to develop an understanding of the basic tax laws that affect your business. Here's what a good accountant can do for you:

- Help you select a record-keeping system and billing software.
- Set up a bookkeeping system that will give you valuable information about your business over time.
- Tell you when to buy and when to lease new equipment.
- Set up a tax-deferred retirement plan for you and your employees.
- Figure out the best organizational structure for your business and tell you when it may make sense to change the structure.
- Help you write your business plan and produce the data needed for getting a loan.
- Tell you when to borrow and when to pay cash.
- Provide you with references for attorneys, management consultants, or marketing experts when you need them.
- Figure out which products and services you are making money on and which you aren't.

The best way to get the most out of your accountant is to select one that is right for you in the first place. Start with an accounting firm that specializes in small businesses. You probably can't afford to hire a national accounting firm like Coopers & Lybrand. Smaller accounting firms are more likely to understand the scale of your budget and have more time to spend on your account. Look for an accounting firm with knowledge of your field or industry. Tax issues for service businesses are different from those for product businesses. Ask people you know for recommendations.

COMPUTERIZING YOUR BOOKS

There are problems associated with computerizing a company's accounting systems. The larger and more complicated your accounting system is, the longer computerizing it will take and the more it will cost. If you are going to computerize, do it when you are small and things are relatively simple. As your business grows, you can expand your computer system so that it grows with you at a comfortable pace.

If you want to computerize your accounting system, there are a number of excellent personal computer software packages to choose from. Many are available for less than $100. The good accounting systems are relatively easy to use.

TAX PLANNING

The first step in tax planning is to organize your records. Set up a filing system for papers that you need regular access to. A filing cabinet with hanging folders is a good choice. An accordion folder is a good solution for documents that get filed with your tax return. Papers pertaining to different tax categories can go into the different sections of the folder. When you finish your return, you can record the tax year on the folder and file it.

Remembering where you keep everything is as important as keeping it. When you set up your filing system, you may think that everything is logical and that you'll remember where your important files are stored, but you won't. Create a master list that identifies where you keep your files.

Income taxes are the primary reason for storing most records. Tax records are used not only to justify tax deductions you've taken, but also to remind you of deductions you should take. Guidelines for how long records should be kept are provided by the Internal Revenue Service (IRS). The IRS can audit returns up to three years after you file the return, or up to seven years after a tax return is filed if auditors suspect fraud. To be safe, keep all pertinent records for seven years. The following is a list of the important documents you should save and how long you should save them:

Annual tax records. These include receipts, canceled checks, auto logs, any proof of deductible expenses, and proof of income.

Annual tax returns. These should be saved forever. They take up little space and are a concise record of your financial life. You may need them in the future to prove that you paid Social Security taxes.

Home basis data. If you own your own home, keep a running tally of the money you've put into it for such permanent features as new roofs, kitchen renovations, or permanent landscaping. This will reduce the capital gains tax on your home when you sell it. Keep all of the associated receipts and canceled checks, even if you sell your home and buy another, because the taxable capital gain will probably roll over into your new home.

Income statements. Save these reports forever. You may want to use them to analyze your business, apply for a loan, or appraise the market value of your business if you decide to sell it.

Personnel records. If you hire employees and withhold income, Social Security, and unemployment taxes, you are required to save the records for seven years.

Equipment records. Keep payment records for all equipment that you depreciate on your tax return for four to seven years after you've filed the last return on which the equipment is listed. If you write off some of this equipment in one year, keep the records for four to seven years after the return on which you take the deduction.

Pension records. If you've established a 401(k) plan or an IRA for yourself, keep those records forever. Keep the plan documents as well as the statements. Most banks, brokers, and mutual fund companies send a complete annual statement. Throw out the monthly or quarterly statements that come during the year if everything is covered on the annual statement. If you are investing money that is not tax-deferred in stocks or mutual funds, keep records of all of your transactions so that you can create a basis for those assets when you sell them.

Losses. Keep records pertaining to losses for at least four years after the last loss has occurred.

Record Not Needed

Throw out old bank statements, manuals for software that you no longer use or have been updated, insurance policies that have lapsed, payment schedules for loans you've paid, registration cards, expired warranties, and tax-related receipts that are more than seven years old. All the miscellaneous canceled checks that were used for non-business-related items can be discarded.

Tax Deductions

Retirement accounts are one of the best financial breaks for self-employed workers. Every $100 you contribute to your retirement can save you as much as $40 right now if you are in a top tax bracket. And the money will compound tax-free until you need it.

Tax Schedule C will walk you through every calculation to ensure that you maximize your legitimate business deductions. Deductible expenses include the costs of setting up your office, office utilities, applicable interest payments, and equipment depreciation.

As a general tax strategy, write off equipment as quickly as possible. The tax code allows small businesses to deduct up to $10,000 worth of equipment each year immediately, rather than depreciating it over time. This doesn't have to be high-tech computer equipment. It can include office furniture and furnishings as long as they're used for legitimate business activities. Other deductions include stationery supplies, Federal Express bills, client gifts ($25 limit per person), business trips, hired help, and subscriptions to periodicals that you use to help run your business.

Deduct the wear and tear on your car. If you haven't kept complete records of your car expenses for the year, estimate the mileage for business trips. Be careful about travel expense reimbursements. If you take a trip for a client, charge the airline tickets to your credit card. If the client reimburses you, when the client sends you and the IRS a 1099 form stating how much you were paid, the cost of the tickets will be included in the total. If this happens, make sure you deduct the tickets as a business expense. Otherwise, you'll end up paying taxes on the tickets as income.

SUMMARY AND CONCLUSIONS

Every business must have some type of accounting system in order to function efficiently. We introduced you to the two essential accounting reports: the balance sheet and the income statement. In the process, we showed you how to interpret the accounting information that's on these reports and how the two reports interact. Financial ratios were covered to provide you with a relatively easy way to monitor the financial health of your business. Important supplemental accounting functions such as aged accounts receivable analysis and cash flow management were discussed. We concluded the chapter with a crash course on tax laws and record-keeping requirements.

Chapter 8

Creative Financing

How to Get the Money You Need

If you ask any entrepreneur what he or she thinks is the greatest obstacle to starting a business, the answer will be financing. Poor financial management and undercapitalization are among the most common causes of business failures. New entrepreneurs tend to be rich in ideas and enthusiasm, but poor when it comes to start-up capital. And with the banking industry becoming more conservative, entrepreneurs are finding start-up loans more difficult to obtain.

Up to this point, we have concentrated on personal considerations, and sales, marketing, and accounting factors that are essential to starting a business. In this chapter, we'll discuss the financing of the business. If you are to succeed as a business owner, it is essential that you start off with adequate financing. Your understanding of the various financial elements will be critical for the future of your business.

Financial Guidelines

To develop your financial plan, you should work closely with your accountant long before the start-up date for your business. An accountant's guidance in the planning stages can literally make the difference between success and failure. As you develop your plan, pay particular attention to questions that your plan must address, such as

- How will you find the capital needed to launch your venture?
- What are the financial prospects for your business, including cash flow, profit, and income statement projections for a the next three to five years?
- What is your break-even point? What will be your return on investment?

The amount of capital you need will depend on the scope of your venture. If you will provide a one-person service and work from home, you will probably need little start-up capital. However, you must consider your living expenses until the business generates enough revenue to support you. If your living expenses must be covered by savings, how long will your savings last?

Start-up costs include the costs of investigating your business ideas, such as legal and accounting fees. Most business professionals charge an hourly rate for

---

their time. Fees vary with the type of work, so get an estimate of the total charges before you engage professional services. Other start-up costs include

- Purchase of space
- Lease deposits
- Equipment and fixtures
- Inventory and materials
- Deposits for public utilities
- Advertising and promotion
- Remodeling
- Office supplies
- Insurance premiums
- Travel
- Franchise fees
- Licenses and permits
- Taxes

WORKING CAPITAL REQUIREMENTS

Most professional business advisers recommend that you keep some capital in reserve for unexpected contingencies. You will also need enough money for the daily operation of the business. This is called *working capital*. Working capital is the financial fuel that stokes the furnaces of your business. It is the capital that keeps your business running.

All businesses need working capital. Employees must be paid, and suppliers may demand cash for your purchases. If you pay your suppliers on delivery, your customers are slow to reimburse you, and you need more inventory, then you need more working capital.

Financial advisers recommend that start-up businesses have working capital equal to three to nine months of anticipated sales. The procedures for estimating cash flow that were covered in the previous chapter are used to determine working capital needs.

Cash flow analysis is used to evaluate the effects of business decisions on a company's cash needs at given points in time. The goal of good cash flow management is to have enough cash on hand when you need it. This is a simple concept, yet in practice, it eludes even the biggest operations.

The expression *cash flow* indicates that cash leaves a company's beginning cash balance, does something for a while to attract customers, and returns to the company's ending cash balance. You need to anticipate the balance in your cash account at given points in the future to determine your cash requirements.

There are several fundamental cash flow rules that you can apply to your business. First, get your customers to pay you as soon as possible, and ask your vendors to allow you to pay them as late as possible. Vendors want to grow and may be willing to extend liberal payment terms to your business. Every dollar you collect in receivables this morning that isn't needed for expenses until tonight is yours to use all day.

Figure 8-1
Computech's Three-Year Cash Flow Requirements Budget

Cash Flow Item	1st Quarter	2nd Quarter	3rd Quarter	4th Quarter	Total Year 1	Year 2	Year 3
Beginning cash balances	$2,500	$12,456	$29,515	$51,598	$96,069	$78,023	$147,163
Net sales	$90,170	$96,758	$103,785	$111,296	$402,009	$425,000	$440,000
Other income	$550	$675	$900	$875	$3,000	$3,200	$52,000
Total available cash	$93,220	$109,889	$134,200	$163,769	$501,078	$506,223	$639,163
Cash disbursements							
Payroll	$12,115	$12,056	$12,390	$12,862	$49,423	$53,790	$67,238
Advertising	$2,062	$2,045	$1,765	$1,750	$7,622	$35,000	$43,750
Sales commissions	$5,038	$6,019	$8,230	$10,500	$29,763	$18,675	$23,344
Cost of goods sold	$22,180	$23,094	$24,275	$21,437	$90,986	$98,555	$123,194
Interest expense	$4,038	$4,019	$4,130	$4,287	$16,465	$14,300	$17,875
Taxes	$8,076	$8,037	$8,260	$9,970	$34,343	$35,435	$44,294
Equipment leases	$8,884	$8,841	$9,086	$9,432	$36,243	$37,430	$46,788
Building rent	$15,345	$15,271	$15,694	$15,517	$61,827	$65,875	$82,344
Total cash disbursements	$77,738	$79,378	$83,830	$85,746	$326,692	$359,060	$448,825
Cash after disbursements	$15,482	$30,511	$50,370	$78,023	$174,386	$147,193	$190,338

The challenge is to determine when payments will be due and to have the cash to meet them. You can do this by preparing a cash flow projection similar to the one in Figure 8-1. A forward-looking cash flow analysis recognizes the significant differences among debt-service arrangements that call for interest plus principal, interest only, balloon payments, revolving credit lines, and so on. Financing a $10,000 computer, for instance, may become more attractive if it's done through borrowing rather than with company cash. The problem with loans is that you have to pay them back.

DETERMINING CAPITAL NEEDS

Depending on the size and complexity of your business, you may wish to explore both personal and outside sources of financing. How do you know if you have enough resources to cover the start-up requirements? If you plan to use your own funds, calculate your net worth. Calculating your net worth allows you to

- Identify your assets and liabilities.
- Give your financial advisors the raw data they may need to advise you.

- Become aware of resources you could draw on when or if your income falls below your operating expenses.
- Identify assets that might be redeployed to get a better return on an investment or to support your new venture.

Suppose you wish to raise cash using personal resources. You could obtain a home equity loan to raise the cash you need. You could also borrow against the cash value of a life insurance policy or sell stocks. Before we move on to external sources of financing, it is important that you project your monthly personal expenses. Do you know exactly how much it costs you to live on a monthly basis and what effect inflation will have on your living costs? Project these figures over a period of several years to see the impact of certain business assumptions that you may have made.

FINDING A LENDER

The banking industry's past troubles are in large part responsible for its reluctance to lend to small businesses. The savings and loan crisis and the billions of dollars it took to bail some banks out led to increased government regulation of banks. Bankers found themselves constrained by mounds of costly paperwork that had to accompany every loan they made. Consequently, getting a loan to expand or improve a small business is difficult. Getting a loan to start one can be next to impossible.

Finding a lender isn't a scientific task, but there are several steps you should take when you look for a bank with which to do business. Talk with other business owners about loans. You don't have to come right out and ask people how much they're borrowing and at what rate. Ask, "How's your bank treating you?" You'll probably elicit more information than you were looking for. Stay abreast of who's lending and who's getting loans by watching the newspapers. Banks often run ads in the business section of local papers to announce new clients.

Look for a bank that knows your industry and has done business with companies like yours. Seek out a loan officer with eight to ten years' experience and a certain amount of authority. Knowing what your banker can authorize on his or her own will help you expedite your loan. If your banker doesn't have final authority, try to meet the next person up the chain of command.

LOAN PREPARATION

The two biggest mistakes small-business owners make when applying for a loan are not being adequately prepared and not shopping around for the right bank and banker. Before you approach a lender for a business loan, be prepared. Have in hand solid cash flow and financial statement projections covering at least the next three years. Banks focus heavily on cash flow lending rather than straight asset-based lending. Be sure your marketing strategies are outlined in detail to lend credence to your sales projections.

In addition to the numbers, be prepared to give your lender other insights into your business that may enable him or her to more easily approve your loan or to be a more effective advocate on your business's behalf. You should be able to answer these questions from your banker in detail:

> "How much money do you want?" The days of answering this with "How much will you lend me?" are gone. Be as exact as possible, and don't forget to add a little extra for contingencies.

> "What are you going to do with the money?" There are only three things you can do with a loan—you can buy new assets, pay off old debts, or pay for operating expenses. Never say you're just going to use the money for working capital.

> "Why is this loan good for your business?" You may regard all banks as heartless money machines but they want their business to be productive, just as you want yours to be. Be prepared to go into detail about what the money will do for you and why your business is a good risk.

> "Why don't you have enough of your own money to do this?" Your banker is trying to find out if an internal management problem is to blame for your financial need. Have a well-thought-out answer to this question.

> "When will you pay the loan back?" Your cash flow projections will help you formulate a repayment time frame.

> "How will you repay the loan?" This isn't the time to be vague. Use your financial projections and business plan to convince the banker of the long-term profitability of your business and your ability to repay the loan.

> "What happens if your plans don't work out?" This is why you have collateral. Banks may require abundant collateral, and you may be required to give a personal guarantee in order to get the loan. Your mission is to reassure the banker of the value of your collateral in case your business doesn't work out. While entrepreneurs are generally positive about their chances of success, bankers are inevitably skeptical.

SOURCES OF CAPITAL

Once you have calculated your net worth and expenses, you may find that you lack the necessary cash to launch your new business or you may decide to use a mix of your savings and outside funds. Most sources of external financing want owners to have some of their own cash invested in their business.

Bank Loans

Unless you are an established businessperson with a good credit rating and a sizable bank account, banks often will not lend you the money to start a business. If they do, they usually expect you to have raised at least 50 percent of the money you need. Banks are more willing to supply financing after your business is established. Lending officers look for borrowers with good credit ratings, experience in the business they propose to enter, and business plans that demonstrate an ability to repay the loans. Interest rates and repayment schedules will vary from bank to bank.

A line of credit may be extended to a business; this is a sum of money that can be used as the business owner sees fit. Lines of credit extend from thirty days to as long as several years. The interest on a credit line is computed on the amount actually used. Fees are sometimes charged for keeping credit line funds in reserve. Some banks have special loan programs aimed at helping small businesses in general and minority entrepreneurs in particular. Check with business associates to find banks with special programs.

Small Business Administration (SBA) Loans

The Small Business Administration (SBA) was started in 1953 to help small businesses start, grow, and prosper. Among other things, it provided a program to make long-term, low-interest loans available to businesses that would otherwise have a hard time finding capital. Today, the SBA has loan funds that are distributed both as direct loans and through loan guarantees administered by local banks.

In its forty years, the SBA loan program has helped over a million small-business owners get the money they need to develop products, hire employees, purchase equipment, and make building improvements. Many borrowers get SBA funding after they've been rejected by other lending institutions. The SBA focuses less on the business owner's collateral and more on repayment ability. It wants to see a detailed cash flow projection showing how the loan will be paid back.

The SBA makes several different types of loans. Understanding the different programs before you start your search puts you that much closer to getting the money you need. Most people think of SBA loans as money going straight from the government's coffers into an entrepreneur's hands. This rarely happens.

Direct loans are only a small percentage of SBA loans. They are given to applicants who are unable to secure a bank loan with or without an SBA guarantee. The SBA's most active lending arena is the Guaranteed Loan Program. Through a working partnership with local banks and other lending institutions, the program guarantees small-business loans issued by qualified lenders.

Business owners gain significant advantages from SBA-guaranteed loans, such as longer terms. At least 50 percent of traditional business loans by banks are for less than one year. The average maturity for most SBA working capital loans is between five and seven years. Because payments are amortized over a longer period of time, they are smaller and more manageable. Another advantage is that applying for SBA-guaranteed loans helps build relationships between bankers and business owners.

Your regional SBA office can tell you what SBA loan programs are available and how to apply. There is no central clearinghouse for information on SBA loans. The best way to find these programs is to ask around at business events, chambers of commerce, or business group meetings.

For businesses planning to expand their markets, the SBA offers several financing programs through its affiliation with the Office of International Trade. Although its primary purpose is to educate small-business owners on the benefits of exporting, the SBA's Export Financing Program also provides partnership financing programs and revolving lines of credit for exports.

Before you contact the SBA, be aware that certain enterprises are not eligible for SBA loans. These include magazines, newspapers, religious bookstores, most live entertainment, nonprofit ventures, and multilevel marketing businesses. You can't use an SBA loan to make speculative investments or to pay off non-business-related debt. The SBA also imposes certain limits on annual revenues and number of employees.

If you satisfy the basic requirements, you can begin the application process, which involves a considerable amount of paperwork. Both the bank and the SBA will want a detailed analysis of your business, with cash flow numbers and research data to back up your sales projections and cash flow needs. Here are some of the application elements you'll need to provide:

- A business description and strategy
- Management capability summary
- Capital requirements
- Personal financial statement
- Financial plan and cash flow
- Investment statement
- Loan application

The entire process can take as little as sixty days depending on the bank's backlog and your own preparation. If there are any complications or the information you supply is incomplete, it will take additional time. It's not easy to get financing through the SBA. If your business doesn't qualify for a loan now, keep trying. In the meantime, learn as much as you can about the many non-financial resources the SBA has to offer. Then when it's time to grow your business, you'll be ready.

In summary, the SBA exists solely to support and make loans to small businesses. Like banks, the SBA may limit the loan amount to 50 percent of the capital needed. In some cases, it will consider ventures with less capitalization if it is convinced of the favorable prospects for the business. A list of regional SBA offices is included in Appendix D, or consult the telephone directory for the office nearest you.

Personal Loans

In many ways, friends and family seem like the logical place to go for a loan. Soliciting a loan from your inner circle of friends and relatives may seem your only viable alternative. In fact, friends and family are the second most popular source of business start-up capital, after personal savings. After all, friends and family know you're trustworthy and competent, so lending money to you doesn't seem so risky.

However, taking money from people you know has its own risks. It can threaten the relationship if your business fails and you can't repay the loan. A bad loan to a family member can result in lingering hostility. Mixing money and friendship creates a potentially explosive combination. There are ways to control this delicate process without upsetting anybody. If you handle the situation in a professional manner, both you and your friends can benefit from the union.

Document everything in writing. "I'll just pay you back when I can" won't cut it when you're borrowing from friends. Many budding business owners erroneously assume that if you get a personal loan from a friend, you can take your time paying it back. This is wrong. You've got to treat a loan from a friend exactly as you would treat a loan from the bank. Set up a repayment schedule and pay the prevailing market interest rate.

Some people are willing to put up money to get your business going, but they assume that the investment gives them free license to meddle in your business affairs. If the person who's lending you money has some business experience that you can use, you may want to make that person a partner in your business. However, if you're looking for a straight investment, as opposed to a partner, make it clear from the start that the loan doesn't entitle the lender to dictate how you run your business.

Before you ask your friends for a loan, measure their interest by holding an informal meeting. Tell them about your venture and your need for capital to see if they are receptive to the idea. Whatever you do, don't pressure someone to give you money. Don't use emotional blackmail to coerce friends or relatives to invest. This tactic only puts added stress on the relationship. Give people an out and let them know that your relationship won't be affected if they don't invest. Avoid friends who are too willing to help or who may offer you a loan when they can't really afford it.

Once you've assessed a person's willingness and ability to make an investment, arrange a more formal meeting to hammer out the details of the agreement. Go in armed with a formal business plan and a brief contract outlining the terms of the loan and the payback schedule. Show the lender how you plan to make your business profitable enough to repay the loan in the prescribed time period. During your meeting, try to separate your personal relationship from the business transaction. This may be the most difficult aspect of securing a business loan from a friend or relative, but it is also one of the most important.

You don't need to go to a lawyer to have the loan contract drawn up. Writing the contract yourself will save you costly attorney's fees. If you don't feel comfortable drafting a financial document, take what you've written to a lawyer to make sure you've included all the essential points. This will still cost less than having the lawyer draft it from scratch.

Once you have the loan in hand, your association with your friends isn't over. When people have invested money in a venture, they take a marked interest in its progress. You should make an effort to keep investors informed about your business's development. Open communication should prevent them from becoming anxious about what's happening to their money.

Your accountant, lawyer, banker, friends, or relatives may know of local businesspeople who are interested in financing new businesses. Check the classified ads in local newspapers, usually under business opportunities for people with money to invest, or run your own ad.

Loan Guarantees

The words "options" and "alternatives" seem to be the key to finding financing in these tough economic times. Entrepreneurs must be flexible and creative in their efforts to fund a start-up business by investigating both traditional and non-traditional lending alternatives.

Lending cash isn't the only way friends and family can help you get your business out of the starting blocks. Loans can come in other forms as well. A parent or friend may sign a bank loan guarantee or put up assets as collateral for a loan on your behalf. Although this is not a direct cash loan, the person is still ultimately liable, so this is not something to enter into lightly. Finding someone who is willing to put up his or her house as collateral or to cosign a loan may be easier than finding someone who can write you a check for thousands of dollars. Keep this option in mind as an alternative to cash loans.

Commercial Finance Companies

Commercial finance companies typically charge exorbitant interest rates for small-business loans, but they make higher-risk loans. Consider a finance company only if you can't find another lender and can afford the high interest payments. Commercial finance companies are listed in the Yellow Pages.

Supplier Loans

Suppliers of merchandise or equipment can furnish capital in the form of credit. They do this by permitting extended payment terms that, in effect, add cash to your working capital. Suppliers will sometimes offer trade credit to attract new business.

In trade credit, you secure a loan with your merchandise, which is placed either in a public warehouse or under the control of a bonded employee. A receipt is given to the bank, and merchandise is released as the loan is repaid. A typical inventory loan will be 50 percent of the value of your merchandise.

Accounts Receivable Loans

Many banks and finance companies will lend money on the basis of your accounts receivable. Generally, you can get as much as 80 percent of the value of your receivables, depending on the payment patterns of your customers. In most cases, you continue to handle customer billings; however, some lenders may take on this task.

Although most banks will not make a loan on the basis of a contract you hold on which you have yet to perform, finance companies will. They will need assurances that you will perform satisfactorily and that the firm granting the contract is reliable. Interest rates for contract loans are very high.

Seller Loans

If you are buying an existing business, you may be able to get financial help from the seller. If the seller does not participate in the financing, you may have trouble getting money from banks and other lending institutions. They may feel that the seller lacks confidence either in you or in the future of the business.

Normally, you would be expected to pay between 20 and 40 percent of the purchase price up front and to get financing to cover the rest. If possible, try to get the seller to consider the balance as a loan bearing the lowest interest rate you can get. Don't accept the argument that interest rates will never go down again. Try to get the repayment terms extended (e.g., twenty years) with an agreement that you will have the right to prepay without penalty.

If you cannot get the seller to finance the entire balance, try to negotiate financing for a substantial amount. You can then approach conventional lenders for the rest of your financing requirements with some prospect of success. You will have the expressed confidence of the seller and the past track record of the company to support your request.

Equity Financing

Exchanging cash for ownership is called *equity financing*. It is another method of generating capital. To raise equity dollars, you can persuade friends and relatives to participate in the ownership of the new enterprise. The agreements can take the form of joint ventures, partnerships, limited partnerships, or other equity arrangements. Outside investors can also share in the ownership of the new company. Negotiated terms include the profit and loss distribution, percent ownership over time, and other considerations.

Venture Capitalists

Venture capitalists are professional investors who give advice and money in return for ownership in companies. They are looking for business ideas that may ultimately grow into multimillion-dollar companies. Venture capitalists are usually investment bankers or private capitalists and syndicates. Most have a minimum size venture that they will consider. Less than 1 percent of venture capital proposals get funded.

Small Business Investment Companies (SBIC)

SBICs are private investment companies that supply small businesses with equity capital and long-term financing. They are private and not directly connected with the SBA. Like venture capitalists, they take an ownership position and a strong hand in the management of the ventures they sponsor. There are hundreds of SBICs in the United States. Many of them are subsidiaries of banks and other financial firms. For more information, contact

National Association of Small Business Investment Companies
618 Washington Blvd.
Washington, DC 20005

Advertise for a Loan

To find prospective lenders, you need to show your proposal to a large number of interested investors. There is a way to reach thousands of potential investors cost-effectively. It's called advertising. Advertising is the way consumers learn about most products and services, so why not use it to attract investors? There are ways to advertise to attract investors and increase your odds of raising capital. The two best places to advertise for a loan are newspapers and magazines.

Newspapers reach thousands of people every day. If you place a good advertisement, you can achieve excellent results. If you're looking for a small number of investors, try the classified section of your local Sunday paper. Under the heading "Business Opportunities," you'll see many companies looking for investors or partners. For a relatively small fee, you can place an ad that could bring you thousands of dollars.

Classified ads in local newspapers work well if you want to raise $100,000 or less. If you need more money or more investors, you may need more exposure. Consider placing a display advertisement in the business or sports section of your local newspaper. This type of advertisement is more expensive, but is seen by a wider audience.

If you want to reach an even larger audience, try a classified ad in a national newspaper such as the *Wall Street Journal* or *USA Today*. These publications have specific sections for investment ads. The *Wall Street Journal* has regional editions, so you don't have to pay to advertise to the entire country.

Magazines are also a good medium for advertising for investors because they are read over an extended period of time. Try placing a classified advertisement in a trade magazine or journal that covers your business. When placing an ad in a magazine, remember that magazines have a long publication lead time. Your ad must be placed well in advance of the publication date.

Creating loan ads

There are three basic parts to a loan ad: the heading, the copy, and the close. Here's an example of a loan request ad.

Investors Needed

Sporting goods manufacturing company growing like wildfire. Retailers can't keep our products in stock. Excellent sales and profit. Desperately need investors to take company national. Exceptionally big return on your investment. Call or write. . . .

An alternative to a classified ad is a display ad, which usually costs more to run. You may require help from an advertising professional to create an effective display ad. If you decide to go this route and an advertising agency is beyond your budget, look for a freelance graphic designer who specializes in advertising to help you.

How you handle responses is just as important as how you attract prospects. Designate someone with sales expertise and the ability to communicate excitement about the investment to handle calls from prospects. Once you have mailed any requested information, follow up with a phone call to answer any questions. Whenever possible, arrange for a personal meeting to discuss your opportunity.

LOAN CONDITIONS

There comes a point when you've shown your lending institution everything you've got and told them everything you can think of to get your loan approved. Now it's simply a matter of waiting for an answer. Once a bank has turned you down, it's almost impossible to get those in authority to change their minds unless you can point to some error that cost you the loan.

Rather than trying to coax your loan officer to reconsider, a better tactic is to arrange an interview with him or her to see what your problems were and how they can be corrected. Most loan officers are reluctant, if not downright unwilling, to do this, so proceed with that in mind.

One of the most important parts of the loan process is what happens after you get the money. Maintaining a good relationship with your lender is essential to making sure things go smoothly. It's important to negotiate an agreement you can live with. When you sign the loan agreement, you are signing a covenant with the lender, and there can be serious consequences if you default. If you agree to unrealistic repayment terms and fail to meet them, the lender can call the loan. Most loan covenants mandate a certain debt-to-equity ratio for your business, so you must build the financial ratios that we covered in Chapter 7 into your cash flow and financial projections.

STRETCHING A LOAN'S LIFE

When small-business owners talk to lenders about financing, they usually try to bargain over things like interest rates and collateral. One thing that few try to negotiate is how long they'll have the use of the funds and the schedule for paying them back. Usually, a borrower starts paying off the principal right away. However, the longer you can use the full amount, the more flexibility you'll have.

Most loans are written for a period of about a year, so the potential for extending the average life of capital is limited. Slowing down the principal payments can reduce the pressure of thinking about the next round of financing. Lenders want to get their money back sooner rather than later, so don't expect them to offer suggestions. Here are some points to consider.

Longer Maturity

If you need money to buy equipment or assets you'll be using over a long time, negotiate for the longest loan term possible.

Less Frequent Principal Payments

Once the maturity has been set, negotiate for as few regular principal payments as possible, such as quarterly or semiannual payments.

Moratorium on Principal Payments

An attractive alternative is to press for interest payments only for some portion of the life of the loan.

Balloon Payments

If possible, negotiate to make a single payment of the principal, or at least as much of the principal as possible, when the loan matures.

LEASING OPTIONS

In times when capital is tight, many companies choose to lease equipment rather than borrow the money needed to purchase it. According to the Equipment Leasing Association, equipment leasing has tripled since 1980 and exceeds $125 billion a year. Even if banks are willing to make loans, they require a large down payment for capital purchases. Leasing companies can usually find money because they can use the equipment as collateral for their loans.

There are many advantages of leasing, in spite of the fact that it is more expensive than buying. Companies that lease can bypass down payment requirements and finance 100 percent of the purchase over several years. If the equipment becomes outdated during the term of the lease, they can upgrade the asset with little or no penalty.

Before you consider leasing, you need to understand the different types of leases. Capital leases generally require a company to purchase the equipment at the end of the lease term at a percentage of the original price. Operating or open-ended leases allow you three options after the term expires: (1) purchase the equipment at its fair market value, (2) extend the lease, or (3) simply terminate the agreement. For tax purposes, payments on operating leases are treated as operating expenses and can be deducted from revenues to reduce tax liabilities. If you elect to buy the equipment at the end of the lease, the purchase becomes a capital expense.

If your business uses assets that have a substantial value, it may be possible to lease them to help preserve your working capital. If you already own key assets, consider selling them to a leasing firm and leasing them back. This method of financing is often used with office buildings, trucks, land, office equipment, and machinery.

Leasing is like any installment purchase. You pay for the privilege of buying over time. To calculate the monthly cost of a lease, lessors figure a rate factor into the purchase price. For example, a three-year operating lease valued at $100,000 is calculated at approximately $35 per $1,000. Using an industrywide rule of thumb of $35, the monthly payments would be $3,500 ($35 × 100).

Leasing is not an option for every company. Most equipment lessors want to do business with established companies that have credit histories. Unfortunately, this can make leasing difficult for start-ups, the companies that can benefit most from the cash flow advantages.

SUMMARY AND CONCLUSIONS

The title of this chapter was "Creative Financing." We hope that by the time you were part way into the chapter material, you began to realize that creative financing is closely related to planned financing. If you properly plan for the financial requirements of your business, you can significantly increase the financing sources and options that are available to you. Without sources and options, you cannot get creative. We showed you how to prepare a basic financial plan before you begin your search for funding. Several sources of capital were covered along with suggestions to use when negotiating loan terms. Loan alternatives were also covered, and including equipment leasing and supplier credit.

Chapter 9

Organizing Your Business

WHAT ARE YOUR BEST OPTIONS?

One of the important decisions you will make when you set up a business will be choosing its legal form of ownership. With tax laws changing and increased concerns over business liability, you need to investigate the advantages and disadvantages of the different ownership forms. Each form has a different level of complexity to consider. Some may require the advice of a specialist, such as an accountant or attorney.

In this chapter, we'll cover several organizational options, insurance considerations, and employee issues. We'll also cover issues to consider when selecting a name and location for your company. The choices for a business form are sole proprietorship, partnership, and corporation. There are several questions you should ask yourself to determine the legal form that's best for your business.

> Are you going into business by yourself? Do you possess all the requisite skills and the funds to manage the business until it makes money?

> If you do not plan to go into business alone, how many partners or associates will you need, and how active will they be? Will your partners just provide financing and leave the operation of the business to you?

> What are your financial requirements for the first three to five years? How much personal liability are you prepared to accept? Are you willing to risk losing your personal assets if the business goes bankrupt?

> What degree of control over your business do you wish to retain? How much government regulation are you willing to tolerate?

> What will happen to the business if you are incapacitated for any period of time? Who will run the business while you are recovering?

Your answers to these questions will help you choose the legal business form that's best for you. Whatever you initially decide, your decision is not permanent. You can always change the organizational form of your business to accommodate its changing needs as it grows.

LEGAL FORMS TO CONSIDER

Different business forms may be under the jurisdiction of the city, state, or federal government, depending upon the form. Each form has different effects regarding personal liability, management, and taxation. There are five basic forms that a business can take:

1. Sole proprietorship
2. General partnership
3. Limited partnership
4. Corporation
5. Limited liability corporation

There are advantages and disadvantages to each of these legal structures, which we will cover. Examine the characteristics of all of them to determine which is best suited to your needs.

Sole Proprietorships

The sole proprietorship is the simplest business form to set up and is the oldest and most common form of business in the United States. It is usually capitalized by the one person who has sole responsibility for the business. Forming a sole proprietorship is simply a matter of contacting the local city or county clerk's office and obtaining a business license. A small registration fee is usually required.

If your business is engaged in interstate commerce, you may need a federal permit or license. For example, federal licenses are required for meat processing, interstate transportation, and investment advisory service businesses.

Of all the business forms, the sole proprietorship gives you the strongest control over your business. You have no partners to consult with on decisions or board of directors to satisfy. You may have employees with varying degrees of accountability, but the ultimate decision-making responsibility rests with you. In most cases, all of the business profits belong to you.

There are some disadvantages to the sole proprietorship. Banks and other financial sources are reluctant to lend money to sole proprietors. The sole proprietor may have a limited net worth and therefore may not have sufficient collateral to qualify for a loan. There is also the risk that if something were to happen to the sole proprietor, there would be nobody to manage the business.

The sole proprietor and the business are one and the same legal entity, which has liability and tax implications. The most serious drawback is unlimited personal liability. If the business incurs debts that it cannot pay, creditors can claim not only the business assets but the personal assets of the owner. In light of the high rate of failure among new businesses, liability considerations are important. If you have substantial personal holdings, you may want to consider another form of business that limits your personal liability. The advantages and disadvantages of the sole proprietorship are summarized in Figure 9-1.

The sole proprietor's business income is treated as personal income. You complete Form 1040 (Individual Income Tax Return), Schedule C (Profit or Loss

Figure 9-1
The Advantages and Disadvantages of a Sole Proprietorship

Advantages	Disadvantages
Low organizational start-up costs	Unlimited liability
Greatest freedom from government regulation	Lack of continuity if something happens to owner
Owner in direct control	Difficult to raise capital
Offers tax advantages to the owner	
The owner makes all the business decisions	

from Business or Profession), and Form 1040-ES (Declaration of Estimated Tax for Individuals). The IRS supplies you with four tax declaration vouchers that you submit in January, April, June, and September your with quarterly estimated tax payments.

General Partnerships

A general partnership is a business owned by two or more individuals. Like sole proprietorships, general partnerships are easy to form and are relatively free from government regulation. Most states do not require general partnerships to file formal partnership agreements, although these agreements are recommended. General partnerships are formed for a number of reasons:

- Partners can pool their capital to start or buy a business that is beyond the financial reach of any of the individual partners.
- Partners can pool their labor to share workload and the management of the business.
- Partnerships can be stronger because they combine individuals' skills that are strategic to the growth of the business.

Partnerships should not be formed through verbal or handshake agreements. With the help of an attorney, draw up a written partnership agreement. Partnership agreements are legal instruments that spell out the role of each partner in the business. The following are elements typically included in a partnership agreement:

- Name, purpose, domicile, and duration of the partnership
- Role and authority of each partner, clearly defined
- Financial contributions and obligations of each partner
- Business expense guidelines showing how expenses will be processed
- Identification of how much of the business each partner owns

- What accounting books and financial records will be maintained to run the business
- Identification of how profits and losses will be allocated among the partners
- Salary schedules of all partners
- Succession and buyout options
- Procedures for arbitration and the settlement of disputes
- Absence and disability policies for the partners

General partnerships are formed the same way a sole proprietorship is. In some states, if you wish to operate under an assumed name, you must file a "Certificate of Conducting Business as Partners" with the county or state. Like a sole proprietor, each partner is personally liable for all business debts. If a partner incurs a debt on behalf of the partnership, all the partners are responsible. Therefore, it is important to select individuals that you trust. The death of a partner, unless covered in the partnership agreement, automatically terminates the partnership. The advantages and disadvantages of general partnerships are summarized in Figure 9-2.

Figure 9-2
The Advantages and Disadvantages of a General Partnership

Advantages	Disadvantages
Low organizational start-up costs	Unlimited liability of each partner
Additional sources of financing available	Difficulty in finding suitable partners
Broader management and expertise base	Conflicts between partners and the need to resolve them
Limited government regulation	Trust factor between partners

The partnership itself is not a taxable entity. It does file a consolidated income tax return (Form 1065), but it is not itself subject to income taxes. The income of the business is taxed as partners' personal income. Each partner's share is reported on his or her individual tax return.

Limited Partnership

Most states allow for the formation of what is known as a *limited partnership*. A limited partnership is a business owned by two or more individuals in which some of the partners have limited liability. There must be at least one general partner who is personally responsible for all the partnership's liabilities. Because of their more complex formation and regulatory requirements, limited partnerships are more like corporations than like general partnerships.

The most common reason for forming a limited partnerships is to raise capital. Partners' contributions may include cash, property, or the performance of a service. Limited partnerships can raise capital by selling additional limited partnership interests in the business. A typical limited partnership includes a general partner who manages the day-to-day operations of the business and a group of limited partners. Limited partners do not exercise control over the general operations of the business. They invest capital in the partnership in return for a share in the profits (or losses) and are personally liable only up to the amount of their investment. The advantages and disadvantages of limited partnerships are summarized in Figure 9-3.

Figure 9-3
The Advantages and Disadvantages of a Limited Partnership

Advantages	Disadvantages
Limited liability of limited partners	Unlimited general partner liability
Additional sources of financing available	Limited partners must trust the general partner
General partner controls the business	Must comply with state regulations
Limited partnerships are not taxed in most states	Cost more than a general partnership to set up

Unlike a general partnership, a limited partnership must have a written agreement drawn up and filed with the state. For this reason, limited partnerships are more complex to set up than general partnerships. If you use a fictitious name for the partnership, you are also required to file a doing business as (DBA) form with the county clerk or with the state. The tax filing requirements for limited partnerships are the same as for general partnerships.

Corporations

A corporation is a legal entity that is separate from the people who create it. The corporation is owned by its shareholders and run by a board of directors elected by the shareholders. Corporations are created by filing articles of incorporation with the state. A corporation has a life of its own. Once formed, it can buy and sell property, file lawsuits, enter into contracts, merge, and buy other companies. Corporations pay taxes and are liable for all corporate debts.

State laws provide strict registration and taxation guidelines for the formation of corporations. State regulations vary in complexity. You should hire an attorney if you are thinking about incorporating. To set up a corporation, three or more individuals (depending on the state) file an application with the state office that grants corporate charters. This Certificate of Incorporation, also known as the articles of incorporation, spells out the names and addresses of the corporate shareholders, the scope of the company's business, and the amount of stock authorized.

There is a fee for filing an application. In addition, there is an annual state tax on the corporation's net income; the rate varies from state to state. Additional fees are charged if you want a permit to issue stock or other securities.

You can form your own corporation for a fraction of what an attorney will charge. There are a number of good "how-to" books on the market, including *Inc. Yourself,* by Judith McQuown. However, in most instances, you'll need professional help in setting up a corporation. It can save you a lot of problems during the start-up process.

The cost of incorporating is one of its disadvantages. Not only are costs incurred during the formation process, but the corporation pays annual taxes on corporate income and a host of other employment taxes. Once the corporation has been formed, its officers or directors must adopt by-laws that govern the operation of the business. Shareholder meetings must be held and minutes recorded. In certain cases, the corporate officers must sign incorporation agreements.

The primary benefit of forming a corporation is that the personal liability of the stockholders is limited to the amount of their investment in the company. Another advantage is the credibility corporations have with banks and other lenders. Lending institutions are more willing to make loans to corporations because of their broader investor base. However, lenders may require collateral and the personal signature of the shareholders.

Corporations can also raise capital by issuing stock, which represents ownership in the business. Stock may be issued in exchange for cash, property, or services rendered. The primary advantage of stock financing is that the corporation is not required to repay the principal or to pay interest. Instead, the shareholders acquire an ownership interest in the business and share in its future profits or losses. The advantages and disadvantages of a corporation are summarized in Figure 9-4.

Figure 9-4
The Advantages and Disadvantages of a Corporation

Advantages	Disadvantages
Limited liability of stockholders	Closely regulated by state and federal governments
Easier to raise capital	Extensive record keeping required
Can issue stock	Double taxation
A legal entity in itself	Most expensive form to organize

If you incorporate, your tax reporting requirements are more complex than if you form a sole proprietorship or partnership. As an employee of a corporation, you draw a salary and report it as income on IRS Form 1040. As a separate entity, the corporation completes Form 1120 (U.S. Corporation Income Tax Return). You therefore have two tax returns to contend with if you form a corporation.

Limited Liability Corporations

A limited liability corporation (LLC), sometimes referred to as an "S corporation," combines the tax benefits of a partnership with the liability benefits of a corporation. The differences between an LLC and a regular corporation are the formation requirements and the tax treatment. The LLC is a "hybrid" corporation. It enables the business owners to enjoy the limited liability that a corporation offers; however, it is not taxed as a separate entity. This can be an ideal corporate structure for new businesses.

In many ways, LLCs are like partnerships. They pay no federal taxes on net income. Instead, shareholders report their appropriate shares of corporation's profits or losses on their personal tax returns and pay taxes at their individual rates. Some states tax the income of LLCs, but in most cases, they escape state income taxes. LLCs must conform to the following requirements:

- It must be a domestic corporation, and all shareholders must hold residency in the United States.
- Only one class of common stock can be issued.
- The corporation is limited to thirty-five shareholders.

While the LLC has some significant advantages over the general corporation, the tax laws related to limited liability corporations are complicated. The advantages and disadvantages of a limited liability corporation are summarized in Figure 9-5.

Figure 9-5
The Advantages and Disadvantages of a Limited Liability Corporation

Advantages	Disadvantages
Limited liability of stockholders	Closely regulated by state governments
Easier to set up than a full corporation	Extensive record keeping required
Can issue limited stock	Form not recognized in all states
Single taxation	More expensive to form than a partnership

The limited liability corporation is a relatively new business structure, and not all states recognize it. Seek tax advice from your accountant before you form a limited liability corporation.

INSURANCE PLANNING

A sound insurance protection plan for your business is as important as a good organizational plan. It takes good planning to determine what insurance is necessary to minimize your risks and protect your business. The term "risk management" is often used of an insurance plan. Risk management is a planned approach by the business owners to avoiding losses of assets, lawsuits, or losses of earning power. General categories of insurance include property, liability, health, disability, workers' compensation, and life insurance.

Property insurance protects the business against the loss of assets. Insurance can be purchased that will pay the amount needed to replace lost assets at the current replacement value. Property insurance costs vary depending upon the type you choose.

Fire insurance covers losses from fires and can be extended to include damage from smoke, storms, hail, explosions, or vandalism.

Auto insurance covers damage to business vehicles caused by fire, theft, or collision, and damage the vehicle causes to others.

Theft insurance covers losses resulting from the unlawful taking of property owned by the business.

Fidelity insurance protects employers from losses resulting from employee theft. For example, cashiers in a jewelry store are likely to be covered by a fidelity insurance policy, which is often referred to as bonding. For any service that requires employees to enter customers' homes or offices, the employees should be bonded to cover potential theft.

Liability insurance protects business owners from lawsuits resulting from injuries to other people or their property. A customer slipping on a wet spot or an employee accidentally dropping something on someone are two examples of such injuries.

Product liability insurance protects businesses against claims for damages resulting from the use of the company's products. Every day, we hear about companies that have withdrawn a product or have been sued as a result of a product liability issue. Manufacturers, wholesalers, retailers, and service companies are all candidates for product liability insurance. Product liability has become a major issue, and every business owner should be familiar with product liability laws.

Professional liability insurance covers claims for malpractice and should be considered by anyone selling a service. Most of us are familiar with medical malpractice cases. However, psychologists, management consultants, and others selling advice might also wish to protect themselves from lawsuits claiming malpractice.

Health, disability, and life insurance are of concern not only for the owner, but also for employees. It is essential that you have health insurance to cover medical expenses and disability insurance to cover loss of income due to disability. Employee benefits may include group life, group health, and disability insurance. Providing health insurance for yourself and your employees is an expensive proposition. Many small businesses require employees to pay part of the insurance cost. Key person insurance (i.e., life insurance) is recommended to protect the business from loss in the event of death of a valuable employee or partner.

Workers' compensation insurance provides income and payments of medical costs if you or your employees are injured on the job. This insurance is governed by state laws and varies among the states. Workers' compensation rates depend on the amount of salaries covered, job hazards, and the company's safety record.

Business interruption insurance protects against loss of business income. It will cover specified expenses if a business is temporarily shut down—for example, in emergencies such as closure for remodeling following a fire, a strike by employees, or an interruption in utilities.

Insurance Agents

Insurance is a complex subject and requires professional advice. A qualified agent can explain the various options and recommend the right coverage for your business. Before you consult an agent, you should have an insurance plan in mind. Here are several issues to consider:

- Write a statement of what you expect insurance to do for your company. Determine how much insurance you need and can afford.
- Select an agent who can provide good, honest advice, and who knows the insurance needs of small businesses.
- Study insurance costs and investigate different coverage options. Once you purchase insurance, review it periodically to make sure that your coverage is adequate and your premium payments are competitive.

STAFFING PLAN

Once you have decided on the form of your business and your insurance needs, you'll need to determine the most efficient method for staffing your business. Start with an organization chart that shows the business functions and the delegation of responsibilities. Write out job descriptions that define the major responsibilities and tasks for each position.

Next, determine the job specifications by listing the knowledge, skills, abilities, and personal characteristics a person must have to perform each job effectively. Establish a performance evaluation system that will both be fair to your employees and reward them for their contributions to the business. Armed with this information, you are ready to start a recruiting campaign. There are a variety of methods for finding good employees:

Employment agencies offer a wide range of applicants, and most of them screen candidates effectively. However, their fees can be expensive.

Help Wanted ads can generate a large number of responses. Ads should be clearly written and provide enough information about the job to discourage unqualified respondents.

Educational institutions, such as area high schools, trade schools, and colleges, are excellent sources of part-time and full-time employees.

Walk-ins and write-ins are unsolicited applicants. They sometimes come along at just the right time.

Referrals from friends, business associates, and employees are often the best source of good candidates.

Employees vs. Contractors

As your business grows, you may decide to hire subcontractors to perform specific jobs on an "as needed" basis. The paperwork for contract labor is much easier to maintain than that for regular employees. However, if you incorrectly classify someone as contract labor, you could end up paying substantial penalties to the IRS and your state government.

Unfortunately, there are many state and federal laws that define employment relationships and are used to determine whether an individual is an employee or an independent contractor. The following subsections cover the general definitions of employees and independent contractors.

Employees

Employees are individuals who perform work that is subject to the control of an employer regarding what, where, when, and how something must be done. The working relationship between an individual and a business is important in determining whether someone is an employee or a contractor. If the employer has the legal right to control both the method and the results of the service being performed, then the person performing the service may be considered an employee.

Independent contractors

Persons who follow a trade, business, or profession, such as lawyers, accountants, or construction workers and offer their services to the general public are usually considered independent contractors. The single most important characteristic of independent contractors is their freedom to determine when, where, and how they will offer their services to a client (i.e., your business).

The IRS applies certain factors to determine whether a person is a contractor or an employee. The importance of each factor varies depending upon the type of business and the service that's being performed. Key IRS factors are summarized as follows:

- An employee is paid on a regular basis, whereas a contractor is paid by the job.
- An employee's business expenses are paid by the employer. A contractor pays his or her own business expenses and provides his or her own tools.
- An employee must comply with employer instructions and supervision. A contractor works without supervision according to a contract for the completion of a specific project.
- An employee works on the premises of the employer or at a location designated by the employer. A contractor may perform work at his or her own business location.
- An employee has an exclusive continuing relationship with an employer. The services of an independent contractor are available to the general public.

If you are not sure whether a worker should be classified as an independent contractor or an employee, contact the IRS and your state department of employment for an interpretation. Potentially, a person could be considered an employee by one agency and an independent contractor by another.

If your business is a sole proprietorship, your children can work for you and not be considered employees by most states and the IRS until they reach age eighteen, or until twenty-one if the business is conducted out of your home. Their wages may be subject to income tax withholding but they are not required to pay social security taxes (FICA).

Employee Selection

There are a number of procedures that you can use to select good employees. Application forms are a useful way of collecting background information, information about previous work experience, and references, which should always be checked. Standard forms are available at local stationery stores.

Interviewing is the most widely used selection technique. Interviews enable you to gather detailed information about the applicant's experience, abilities, and level of motivation. Interviews also help you determine how the candidate will fit in with your business.

Establishing a short tryout period is recommended. During this time, the new employee should be observed and frequently rated. It is easier to release a new employee after a few weeks than after several months if the employee doesn't work out to your satisfaction.

Training is vital to help ensure that new employees perform satisfactorily. Training helps to improve employee morale, increase productivity, reduce operational costs, and increase employee development.

Employee Compensation

The Fair Labor Standards Act (FLSA) is the federal law that governs employee compensation. The laws under this act are referred to as the "wage and hour laws." Employers are required to pay employees a minimum wage and a minimum overtime rate for hours worked beyond a forty-hour week. Most small businesses are covered by FLSA laws. Federal laws also govern small-business pension plans. Most employers are required to contribute to Social Security.

COMPANY NAME

One of the greatest pleasures in starting your own business is selecting the company name and logo. There are several points to consider when selecting a company name. Your company's name is one of its most frequently encountered advertisements and should say something about what the company does. This is one argument against using your own name for the company. For example, the name Smith and Associates doesn't tell anyone what the company does.

There are other reasons for not using your own name. What if you sell your company and it later gets sued? It could be embarrassing to have your friends ask, "Are you connected with the company that was indicted for polluting?" You can, of course, explain that you were, but not at the time of the pollution episode, but why put your name in the control of other people? However, if you are setting up a professional business, such as a legal, brokerage, consulting, or similar service business, and your name is well known (i.e., prestigious), then it may make sense to use it in the company name for its marketing advantage.

Company names consisting of initials tell prospective customers nothing about your company, its products, or its services. In most cases, these aren't appropriate names for new businesses. For names like IBM and 3M, it takes decades before name recognition sets in—which you don't have.

Names like Smith Enterprises don't do much for a company's credibility. The word "enterprises" suggests that you are trying out several different lines of business with the hope that one will work. This may indeed be the case, but you should try to conceal the fact from your customers and prospective investors. Also avoid using names like Smith & Associates. What are associates and who are they?

Again, your company name should convey to your customers an impression of what your company does. If you're setting up a high-tech operation, the use of technical buzzwords may be appropriate (The Byte Store for a computer store). Unfortunately, selecting a good name may be tough because many of the cleverest ideas have already been used. Come up with several good names and conduct a name search at your local library to make sure your name is not already in use. The research librarian can provide you with state and national directories of business names that are already in use.

SELECTING A LOCATION

One of the worst mistakes a small business can make is to locate in the wrong area. Small-business owners often locate their start-ups in their home town. Choosing a location can become an exercise in micro research that takes place in your own backyard. Finding the right location for a small business is a combination of science and art.

Whether you're launching a new company, moving an existing one, or opening a branch office, you'll need to draw on everything from market research to consumer psychology to find the optimal site. You can get some of the data you need to help you find the right location from sources like the chamber of commerce.

You may want to locate your business near your customers. Here's where demographic research can help. Start your search at the chamber of commerce, city planning commission, economic development agency, or local office of the U.S. Census Bureau. These organizations have valuable demographic data, such as average family income, length of residence, and average age. Much of this data is available free or at a nominal cost. When used properly, demographic research can function as a safety net.

Your first step is to learn all you can about your customers. Who are they, what are their buying patterns, and where do they come from? Find out everything you can about their basic demographics and habits so that you can find a location that they will prefer over your competitions'. For example, a hardware store might benefit from locating in a neighborhood in which relatively well-to-do young families are moving into older homes. The assumption would be that many of them will want to do major home renovations and therefore will use your store.

Once you have several locations in mind, begin the process of elimination. Visit the city hall or the planning office to see whether zoning regulations would prevent you from selecting a specific location. Pay particular attention to regulations governing business signs and types of businesses that are allowed at different locations. Find out if planned roads or developments could affect your choice. Rule out locations that your competitors already control.

When you have narrowed your search to a couple of choices, look at individual properties. Review commercial real estate listings in the classified section of your newspaper or use the services of a commercial real estate broker. If your business caters to the retail trade, where location is critical to sales, survey every available site before you make a decision. If you're a wholesaler looking for warehouse space, price and contract terms may be more important than the location.

After you open your business, set up a system that will help you to continue to find out where your customers are coming from. You can gather this information directly by asking customers to fill out a short questionnaire.

SUMMARY AND CONCLUSIONS

When you start your own business, you must carefully choose the appropriate legal structure. Examine the characteristics of each structure that we covered in this chapter to determine which one best meets your needs.

If you will be the sole owner of the business and do not require a great deal of capital, then the informality of the sole proprietorship may be appropriate. If you plan to go into business with others, the general partnership offers a means of pooling the partners' resources and sharing control of the business. Starting a limited partnership offers you the ability to acquire additional capital while maintaining control of the business. Sole proprietorships and partnerships do expose you to a significant amount of personal liability, which you must consider.

If you form a corporation, you can enjoy the benefits of protection from liability and the ability to capitalize the business by issuing stock. The required organizational formalities and organizational costs are considerably more than for proprietorships and partnerships.

We concluded the chapter by discussing other important organizational issues, such as insurance requirements, hiring employees, and selecting a name for your company, all of which are dependent upon the type of organization you set up.

Chapter 10

Getting Into Top Form

SET YOUR BUSINESS IMAGE WITH FORMS

Every time you send out a form, such as an invoice, a shipping document, or a purchase order, you have an opportunity to reinforce your company's image. Do your forms have the crisp, well-designed appearance one expects from a professional organization, or do they look amateurish? Are they set up in a way that makes them easy to fill out? Forms can reveal a lot about the quality of a business.

In this chapter, we'll show you how to create business forms that effectively combine function with professionalism. All of your business forms should adhere to a standard design. The closer you can come to an overall design standard and identity, the better.

COMPANY LOGOS

How do you create an identity for your business? The first design identity item is the company logo. A logo should be attractive, graphically pleasing, and consistently presented on your forms (see Figure 10-1). Your company's identity may extend beyond the logo to include the use of colored ink, like IBM's blue. You may also want to standardize your documents by using a particular typeface on all business forms.

Figure 10-1
Using the Company Logo to Establish Design Identity

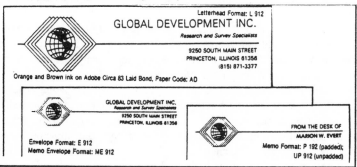

The hallmark of a successful logo design is its simplicity. You want a design that can be used repeatedly without becoming boring to your customers. A gimmicky design may generate a "gee-whiz" response, but does it have staying power? Study existing company logos that attract you and figure out what makes them effective.

One of the simplest and most effective strategies for creating a logo is to use distinctive line treatment, borders, and frame. Lines can be conceptually linked to your company's type of business. For example, a catering business may take a graphic "bite" out of the upper right corner of every form. A lawn sprinkler installation business might use a border of water beads along the left edge of its forms.

TYPEFACES

Use readable typefaces on all your forms—This includes headlines, descriptive labels, down to the smallest type on the form. Typeface refers to the design of the letters and symbols; many different typefaces are commercially available to the printing industry. As a standard, consider using the Times Roman typeface, which is one of the most common and easiest to read typefaces. Whatever typeface you decide to use, make sure it's legible and can be read at a glance.

Phrase the text on your form in clear terms printed in type large enough for humans to read (10-point or larger). If necessary, print the basic information in the body of the form and point the reader to an out-of-the-way location on the form where additional information can be found, in smaller print if necessary. Avoid using very fine print; it has the stigma of being filled with tricks and traps. That's what people will think, even if your fine print contains helpful information.

DESIGN CRITERIA

Lead the reader through your forms. That's an important concept to keep in mind even if there isn't a lot of text on the form. Organize the form as if it were a text page. Lead the reader from left to right and from top to bottom. Avoid designs in which readers must skip around the form to fill it out or to find the information they need.

When you design a form, draw arrows connecting the sections of the form in the order in which you expect the recipient to read them. Do the arrows progress from left to right and down the page? Is the starting text block at the top of the form? Left-to-right and top-to-bottom progression adds legibility and logic to your business forms. "Simply Better" was the theme that the Public Service Company employed to redesign its customer invoice in Figure 10-2.

To make form organization readily apparent, use lines and shading where appropriate. Use lines to indicate where you expect information to be entered, and use boxes to separate sections of your form. You can use bold lines to draw the eye to the beginning of each block. Limit yourself to two ruling-line weights. One thin line and a thicker line are adequate for creating visual areas on the form.

Shading can be used to draw your reader's eye to specific sections of the form, as illustrated in Figure 10-3. Boxes containing labels may be filled with a light shade to make them stand out and indicate that the shaded area is not a spot for writing. Only the areas you want filled in should be left white. When you complete a form, get others involved in the process. Show them the draft form and ask for their ideas for improvement.

Figure 10-2
An Illustration of a 'Simply Better" Form

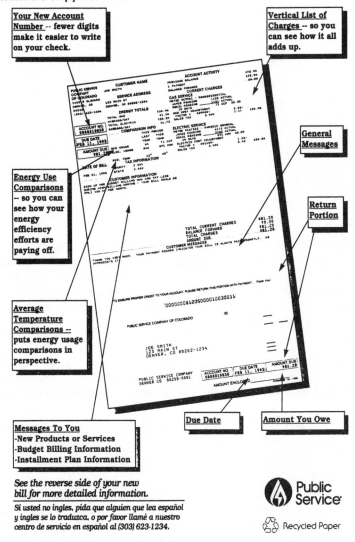

Your New Account Number -- fewer digits make it easier to write on your check.

Vertical List of Charges -- so you can see how it all adds up.

General Messages

Return Portion

Energy Use Comparisons -- so you can see how your energy efficiency efforts are paying off.

Average Temperature Comparisons -- puts energy usage comparisons in perspective.

Due Date

Amount You Owe

Messages To You
-New Products or Services
-Budget Billing Information
-Installment Plan Information

See the reverse side of your new bill for more detailed information.

Si usted no ingles, pida que alguien que lea español y ingles se lo traduzca, o por favor llamé a nuestro centro de servicio en español al (303) 623-1234.

Public Service·

Recycled Paper

Figure 10-3
Using Lines, Shading, and Boxes to Organize a Form

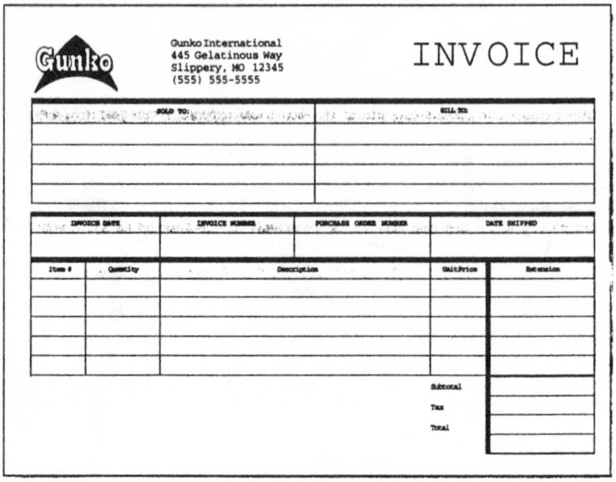

ILLUSTRATIONS

The human eye is more attracted to artwork and illustrations than to text. It's easier to look at a picture than to read the text surrounding it. If you decide to use artwork and illustrations in some of your forms, try to maintain a consistent style that has enough flair to be memorable. Think about size and perspective as ways of giving your illustrations a distinctive look. Using lots of tight close-ups, for example, can be a stylish way to do this.

PAPER STOCK

Using distinctive paper stock is another way to establish a design identity. Consider printing your material on paper with a subtle granite background or on blue-lined graph paper. There are a variety of colored, textured, and patterned papers available for use in laser printers or by commercial offset printers. A paper that's a light shade of gray or blue can make a powerful design statement and set your forms apart from the sea of white forms. Even a simple form can be sensational if it's reproduced on intriguing paper.

ENHANCE WITH COLOR

The use of color is another way to distinguish your company's forms. Examples include Coca-Cola's red and white and Kodak's warm orange. Printing with a second color does not have to be prohibitively expensive. There are standard-color inks that most commercial printers use routinely that might suite your purpose, and an infinite variety of custom-color inks can be also ordered. The cost of using colors isn't in the ink, it's in cleaning the press after running each color.

FORM DESIGN SOFTWARE

One of the major advantages of using personal computer software to design forms is the ability to revise and update these forms at minimal expense. You can use any good word processor or desktop publishing program, such as WordPerfect or PageMaker, to create almost any form you might need.

Figure 10-4
Example of a Window Interface to a Forms Design Software Application for a Personal Computer

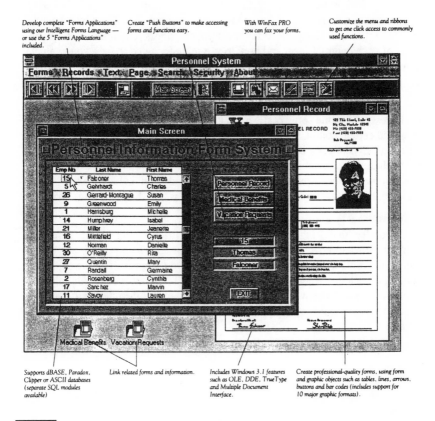

Develop complete "Forms Applications" using our Intelligent Forms Language — or use the 5 "Forms Applications" included.

Create "Push Buttons" to make accessing forms and functions easy.

With WinFax PRO you can fax your forms.

Customize the menu and ribbons to get one click access to commonly used functions.

Supports dBASE, Paradox, Clipper or ASCII databases (separate SQL modules available)

Link related forms and information.

Includes Windows 3.1 features such as OLE, DDE, TrueType and Multiple Document Interface.

Create professional-quality forms, using form and graphic objects such as tables, lines, arrows, buttons and bar codes (includes support for 10 major graphic formats).

If your business requires many different forms that must be changed frequently, consider purchasing software that's designed specifically to create business forms. In Figure 10-4, we show an example of a forms design interface window for PerFORM PRO, a forms design PC program that's available from

Delrina, 6830 Via Del Ora, Suite 240, San Jose, CA 95119. If you need only a few forms, you can purchase designer forms from a stationary store.

CONTRACT FORMS

A *contract* is an agreement that creates legally enforceable obligations between two or more parties. Each party named in the contract gives something of value to the other party. This is called the *exchange of consideration* and includes the giving of money or a promise to pay for a product or service in the future.

All of the forms in this section are contract forms that you can apply to applicable situations in your business. The forms in this chapter favor your business, so changes may be requested during the negotiation process. Check with your attorney to make sure that our forms meet your business requirements. Explanations of each contract form and how to use it are included to help you evaluate changes that may be required to support your business.

Oral Contracts

Although all the contracts in this section are written, contracts can also be oral. However, while some oral contracts are valid, a written contract is always best, and certain contracts should always be written, such as a contract for services that will take a significant amount of time and money to complete. Even people with the most scrupulous intentions do not always remember exactly what was said or whether a particular point was covered in an oral contract. Disputes and litigation are far more likely when a contract is oral than when it is written.

Letter Forms

If you feel that using a contract form will be irritating to the other party, the more informal approach of a letter form may be used. The last paragraph of the letter should read, "If the foregoing meets with your approval, please sign both copies of this letter beneath the words AGREED TO to make this a binding contract between us." The words AGREED TO, the name of the other party, and the company name would appear at the bottom of the letter as shown in the following example:

AGREED TO:
XYZ Corporation

Date_____

By_____
      John Doe, President

Two copies of the letter are sent to the other party, who signs both copies and returns them to you. When you receive them, sign one copy and return it to the other party. This gives the other party an opportunity to review the initial draft, but avoids a situation in which the other party may choose to delay signing.

Job Estimate Form

A job estimate form like the one in Figure 10-5 is completed after you have discussed an assignment with your client. Once they have agreed to the terms of the estimate, both parties sign the form. If your client gives you a purchase order, you may feel that this is sufficient documentation for the job if all points in our checklist are covered.

Figure 10-5
Job Estimate Form

Client Name: _____ Date: _____   Address: _____ Job #: _____
This estimate is based on the specifications and terms in this contract. It is understood that the work shall be performed by_____, herein referred to as Company, and that the work shall be performed for_____ , herein referred to as Client.
Job Description:
Due Date: The job shall be completed within _____ days after the Client's authorization to start the job.
Fees: The Client shall pay $_____ for the full job. Full payment is due _____ .   Expenses: The Client shall reimburse the Company for the following expenses: _____

The job estimate form should include only the terms that you feel are important. The form seeks to resolve issues that arise frequently. It is better to raise these issues at the outset of the assignment than to disagree about them later. The estimating form checklist is summarized as follows:

- Describe the assignment in as much detail as necessary. Attach another sheet to the form if more detail is required.
- Give a due date, which can be expressed either as a number of days after the client's approval or as a calendar date.
- Specify the fee and payment schedule, including fees for cancellation at different stages of the assignment.

- If expenses will be significant, provide for an advance against expenses. A schedule of payments is especially important for an extensive job.

Privacy Release Form

Companies often use photographs of people in their brochures or promotional materials. Both text and photographs can violate an individual's right to privacy. While these laws are intricate, this summary will help alert you to potential problems. State laws forbid the use of a person's name or picture without permission for advertising or trade purpose.

The public display of a photograph that shows or implies something embarrassing and untrue about someone could constitute a right to privacy violation. Photographs taken in a home or office that are used with an article can invade someone's privacy. On the other hand, use of people's pictures for newsworthy or editorial purposes is protected by the First Amendment. No releases need be obtained for photographs that serve the public interest.

Figure 10-6
Privacy Release Form

I, _____, do hereby give _____, his or her assigns, licensees, and legal representatives the irrevocable right to use my name (or any fictional name), picture, portrait, or photograph in all forms and media and in all manners, including composite representations for advertising, trade, or any other lawful purposes. I waive any right to inspect or approve the finished version(s), including written copy that may be created in connection with the approved form. I am over 18 years of age. I have read the release and am fully familiar with its contents. Signed: _____
Date: _____

If you plan to use an individual's photograph for commercial purposes you should obtain, a release. When signed, the privacy release form in Figure 10-6 allows you to use a person's image for advertising and trade. The release is intended to cover a single use and does not protect you against another use unless it is specified on the form. A minor must have a parent or guardian sign the form. The checklist for the release form is summarized as follows:

- Include the right to use the image for all business media, advertising, and trade uses.
- Include the right to make changed versions of the image.
- Allow advertising and trade uses of the image.

- Have the person waive any right to review any finished artwork and written copy pertaining to the image.
- Have the person state that he or she is over eighteen years of age.
- If the person is a minor, have a parent or guardian sign the release.

Permission Form

For some promotional projects, you may need to obtain permission from the owners to use materials that are protected by copyright, such as poems, articles, books, lyrics, illustrations, or artwork (see Figure 10-7). If the work is more than seventy-five years old, it is in the public domain of the United States, and no permissions are needed.

Figure 10-7
Permission Form

I, _____, do hereby give _____, his or her assigns, licensees, and legal representatives the irrevocable right to use the material specified in this Permission Form. The permission is for the following material: _____ Signed: _____
Date: _____

An obstacle to obtaining permissions is locating the person who owns the rights. Contact the publisher of the material and ask that its representative sign the permission form. If the author must sign the form, the publisher will provide you with the author's address. The permission form checklist is summarized as follows:

- Describe the material to be used and attach a photocopy of it.
- Obtain the right to use the material in the future, as well as in the present.
- Keep a log of all correspondence relating to the permission form.

Nondisclosure Form

How do you disclose an idea for a product or idea without risking the listener's stealing the idea? If the idea has commercial value, sharing it is often the first step in validating its potential. Ideas are not protected by copyright laws; they protect only the concrete expression of an idea. The nondisclosure form in Figure 10-8 creates an expressed contract between the party disclosing the idea and the party receiving it.

What should you do if a person refuses to sign your nondisclosure agreement? You have to evaluate the risk. Does the person have a good reputation, or is he or she notorious for appropriating other people's ideas? Are there other people that you could approach who would be willing to sign the nondisclosure

Figure 10-8
Nondisclosure Form

AGREEMENT, entered into as of this _____ day of _____, 19 ___, between _____, herein referred to as Company, located at _____, and _____, herein referred to as Recipient, located at _____. WHEREAS, the Company has developed certain valuable information, concepts, ideas, or designs, herein referred to as Information, which the Company deems confidential. WHEREAS, the Company wishes to disclose the Information to the Recipient and the Recipient is willing not to disclose this Information as provided in this agreement.

Disclosure: The Company shall disclose to the Recipient the information, which concerns:

Purpose: The Recipient agrees that this disclosure is only for the purpose of the Recipient's evaluation to assist the Company in its interest to commercially exploit the information.

Limitation on Use: The Recipient agrees not to manufacture, sell, deal in, or otherwise use or appropriate the disclosed information. The Recipient understands that the unauthorized disclosure of the information by the Recipient would cause irreparable damage to the Company.

IN WITNESS WHEREOF, the parties have signed this agreement as of the date set forth in this agreement. Company _____
Recipient: _____

agreement? If not, taking the risk may make more sense than trying to exploit the idea without the benefit of outside input. Disclosure checklist items are summarized as follows:

- Indicate what the information concerns without revealing away everything that is innovative.
- State that the recipient receives no rights in the use of the information and that you are disclosing the information to decide whether to embark on commercial exploitation.
- Require the person to keep the information confidential and state that disclosure of the information would cause irreparable damage to your company.

- If an appointment is made, confirm it by letter in advance and sign any visitors' logs. After the meeting, send a letter that covers what happened at the meeting.

Contractor Form

The contractor form in Figure 10-9 covers the contractors employed by your business. The form includes a price quotation section and specifications for the job. As always, seek more than one bid to make sure you're getting a competitive price.

Figure 10-9
Contractor Form

AGREEMENT, entered into as of this _____ day of_____, 19 ___, between _____, herein referred to as Company, located at ____ , and _____, herein referred to as Contractor, located at _____. WHEREAS, the Contractor will provide services, herein referred to as Work, that are needed by the Company and described in this agreement.

Work Specifications:

Delivery of Work: The Contractor agrees to deliver the Work on or before _____ to the following location _____ under the following terms _____

Price and Quantity: The price for the Work shall be $ _____ for _____ quantity. The price shall be payable within _____ days of the delivery of the Work.

IN WITNESS WHEREOF, the parties have signed this agreement as of the date set forth in this agreement. Company _____
Contractor:_____

The checklist for the form is summarized as follows:

- Fill out the job specifications in as much detail as necessary.
- Specify a delivery date and location, and the terms of delivery. If time is of the essence, specify delivery dates and penalties if these dates are not met.
- State that the risk of loss during the delivery is borne by the contractor and that the contractor shall pay the expense of returning any defective materials supplied.
- State the price for the quantity ordered and when payment will be made.

Sales Representative Form

The sales representative form in Figure 10-10 covers the key issues when you retain a sales representative. The types of accounts and the territory to be covered are carefully documented on the form. If the sales representatives are paid commissions on net receipts, any items that will be subtracted from the gross receipts to arrive at the net receipts upon which the commission will be paid are specified.

Figure 10-10
Sales Representative Form

AGREEMENT, entered into as of this _____ day of _____, 19 ___, between
_____, herein referred to as Company, located at _____, and _____,
herein referred to as Representative, located at _____. WHEREAS, the
Representative will provide services, herein referred to as Sales, that are
needed by the Company and described in this agreement.

Scope of Sales Representation:

Term: This agreement shall have a term of _____ months but can be terminated
by the Company upon _____ days' written notice to the Representative.

Commissions: For the services of the Representative, the Company agrees to
pay the Representative a commission of _____ percent of the net receipts from
all sales made by the Representative. Net receipts are defined as follows:
_____

Payment: Commission shall be paid to the Representative on the _____ day of
the month.

IN WITNESS WHEREOF, the parties have signed this agreement as of the date
set forth in this agreement. Company _____
Representative: _____

The term of the agreement should be closely tied to your right to terminate the agreement. If a sales representative does not perform to your satisfaction, you need the right to terminate the contract immediately. Checkpoint issues are summarized as follows:

- Specify the territory to be covered by the sales representative.
- Identify the types of accounts to be covered and any accounts that will not be covered by the representative.
- Specify a term for the contract and the commissions to be received by the sales representative.

- Define net receipts or the amount upon which commissions will be paid and the time of payment.
- State that no commissions shall be paid for bad debts and returned merchandise.

Distributor Form

The rights granted to a distributor of your products and services are covered in Figure 10-11. Grant only those rights that can be effectively exercised by the distributor. If the distributor sells to stores in the western United States, that should be the distribution territory granted.

Figure 10-11
Distributor Form

AGREEMENT, entered into as of this _____ day of _____, 19 ___, between _____, herein referred to as Company, located at _____, and _____, herein referred to as Distributor, located at _____. WHEREAS, the Distributor will provide services, herein referred to as Distribution, that are needed by the Company and described in this agreement.

Scope of Distribution:

Term: This agreement shall have a term of _____ months but can be terminated by the Company upon _____ days' written notice to the Distributor.

Sale: The Company agrees to sell the following products at the indicated discount price to the Distributor.

Consignment: The Company agrees to consign products to the Distributor under the following terms: _____
The Distributor agrees to the following payment terms: _____

IN WITNESS WHEREOF, the parties have signed this agreement as of the date set forth in this agreement. Company _____
Distributor: _____

Both you and the distributor may actively promote your products. The contract allows you to define the promotional responsibilities in whatever way will make the promotional campaign most effective. For example, will the distributor do more than place your products in its catalog? Will the distributor have booths at trade shows and advertise in appropriate media? Checklist items to consider are summarized as follows:

- Specify what products and services the contract covers. Limit the grant of rights to those items you want the distributor to sell.
- Specify a term for the contract. Allow termination of the contract by either party on thirty days' written notice. After termination, require that all consigned products be returned to you at the distributor's expense.
- State whether products are being sold or consigned to the distributor and seek the highest unit price possible. Specify payment dates and charge interest on late payments.
- For consigned products, do not allow the distributor to make sales at more than a certain discount from retail price.
- Require that consigned products be kept separate from the distributor's products in an area marked to show that the products belong to your company. This protects your products from the distributor's creditors.
- State that the distributor shall undertake, at its own expense, an annual physical inventory of your consigned products in accordance with accepted accounting procedures.
- Require the distributor to use its best efforts to sell your products and specify the kinds of promotional activities that the distributor will pay for.

Copyright Form

To register a written work such as a brochure or a catalog, you must send a completed Form TX (see Figure 10-12), a nonrefundable filing fee, and a nonreturnable copy or copies of the written work to

Register of Copyrights
Copyright Office
Library of Congress
Washington, DC 20559

The instructions for filling in Form TX are provided by the Copyright Office. The Copyright Office also makes available a free copyright information kit, which includes copies of Form TX and other Copyright Office circulars. It will allow you to submit your materials using reproductions of Form TX.

Register any work that you feel may be infringed upon. Registration has a number of advantages, the most important of which is proving that you had created a particular work as of a certain date. Both published and unpublished works can be registered. Unpublished works can be registered in groups for a single application fee. One complete copy of unpublished material and two copies of published materials are required.

A copyright registration is effective as of the date the Copyright Office receives the application fee and the materials to be copyrighted. It may be several months before the certificate of registration is sent to you. To ensure that the Copyright Office receives the materials, send your application by registered or certified mail. You can request information on the status of your application at any time. The Copyright Office charges an additional fee for this service.

Summary and Conclusions

Forms are an important part of the operation of your business. Not only can properly designed forms save you time, they can also give the business a professional image. In this chapter, we talked about several basic concepts to take into consideration when you design forms. Design identity and ease of use were emphasized. Numerous examples were included to help illustrate the forms design process. The importance of contract forms was also covered, and several actual forms that you can use in your business were provided.

Figure 10-12
Copyright Form

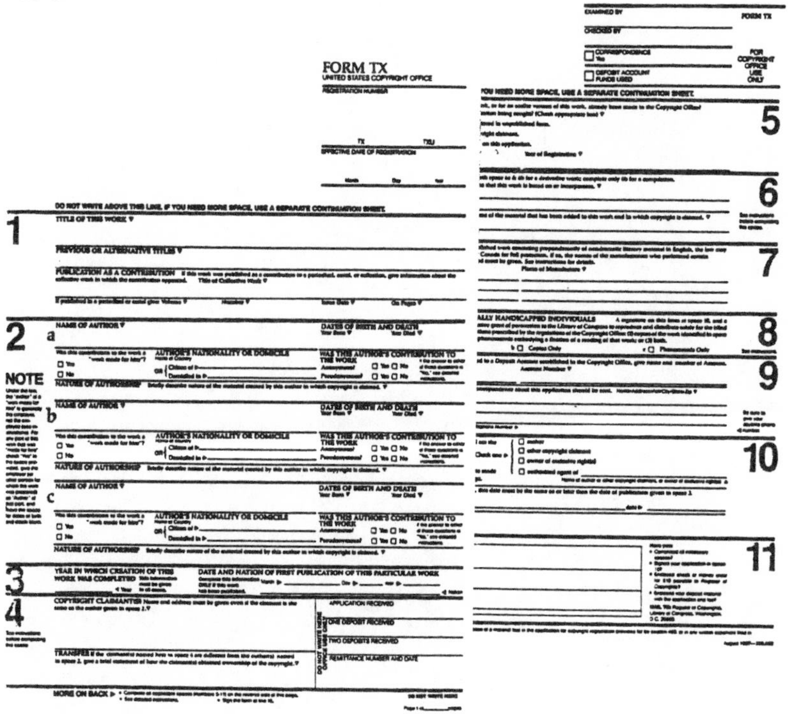
FORM TX
UNITED STATES COPYRIGHT OFFICE

1

2 a

NOTE

b

c

3

4

5

6

7

8

9

10

11

Chapter 11

The Perfect Office

PRODUCTIVITY IS THE NAME OF THE GAME

In this chapter, we'll consider what office furniture, equipment, and computer tools you need in order to compete effectively in today's business environment. When you set up your office, consider the options that make sense for your particular situation.

There are three ways to get started. There is the basic setup for someone who is just starting or who is working from home part-time and doesn't want to invest a lot of money. The basic start-up items include a telephone, an answering machine, and stationery. A more advanced setup may be appropriate for someone one who is starting out full-time and requires more equipment to push the work out. Finally, a person who needs more equipment because of the type of business he or she is in or the volume of business he or she is doing may require a high-tech setup.

However you decide to configure your office, look for equipment that is compact, affordable, easy to use, and reliable. Financing or leasing options may be available at your local office equipment outlet. Your accountant can tell you if financing or leasing is advisable.

TELEPHONES

No matter how big or small your office is, choosing the right phone is important. Just because something is called a feature phone does not necessarily mean that it's suitable for your business. Feature phones include a speaker for hands-free conversation, memory for one-touch dialing, automatic redial, and conference call capabilities. Additional features to consider include the following:

> *Call waiting.* A soft beep alerts you when another call is on the line. This feature allows you to accept important calls even when you are on the phone. You can switch back and forth between callers as often as you like.

> *Call forwarding.* This is a convenient feature that allows you to keep in touch while you're on the move. When you leave your office, you enter a telephone number at which you can be reached; all of your incoming office calls are automatically transferred to that number. This allows you to come and go as you please without missing calls.

Conference calling. This feature is useful if you want to hold meetings on the phone. It allows you to connect your phone with more than one local or long distance location to conduct a telephone conference.

Speed calling. This is useful if you frequently place calls to the same telephone numbers. it saves you time in dialing and eliminates reaching wrong numbers because of dialing errors. For frequently called numbers, you enter a short code and the phone completes the dialing process. You don't have to look up the phone number for your routine calls. Just store the short numbers on a card next to your phone.

Ident-A-Call. This feature gives you additional telephone numbers on your regular line. Each number has its own distinctive ringing pattern so that you can identify important calls that you want to answer personally. You can give different numbers to members of your family or key business associates. Call your local telephone business office to get more information and costs in your area. Costs will vary depending on the level of service you need.

Separate line. This is useful if you are operating out of a home office. You can use one line and number for your business and have a separate line for your family to use. A separate line adds an element of professionalism to your business. As your business grows, you can always install more lines or dedicate a second line to a fax or computer modem.

ANSWERING SERVICES

You may want to hire an answering service to take your calls when you are out of the office. This can be a good alternative if you are concerned about your telephone image and prefer to have your clients talk to a person rather than to a machine. However, today many companies use voice mail systems and sophisticated answering machines, and this has greatly reduced the image problem. Answering services generally charge on a per call basis, and some charge you a flat monthly service fee. Services that operate during business hours are less expensive than those operating twenty-four hours a day, seven days a week.

ANSWERING MACHINES

If you decide to use an answering machine, buy a reliable brand with as many features as you can afford. A cheap machine can have reliability problems and may not offer the voice quality you need. If you anticipate that your answering machine will be accepting a large volume of calls, make sure that you get one with sufficient capacity. Capacity is typically rated in terms of the number of minutes of messages that a machine can store.

Voice Mail

Voice mail is a computer-based system that records voice messages and stores them for later retrieval. Voice mail allows you to send and receive messages twenty-four hours a day, broadcast messages to several phones at once, and save or replay messages. You can activate voice mail from a remote touch-tone phone to retrieve messages when you are away from the office. There are three basic voice mail options to consider: You can develop a custom system from commercially available voice boards using your personal computer and voice mail software, you can buy a system from a voice mail vendor, or you can use the services of a voice mail service bureau.

What you get out of a voice mail system depends largely on what you do with it. Knowing exactly what voice mail can do and how to use it to your best advantage can give you an advantage over your competition. Determine in advance what voice mail features you need given the types of calls you get and the types of messages your callers need to hear before you contact a voice mail subcontractor.

Make sure your system is caller-friendly. You don't want to lead callers on a wild voice mail chase. If it takes customers more than a minute to reach the right person, they'll hang up. Make sure that callers are greeted by a friendly human voice and that they have a minimum amount of numbers to press. Here are things that you should understand when you select a voice mail system:

> *Port size* is the number of ports, which determines the maximum number of calls that a system can handle simultaneously.

> *Message storage* is the total number of hours of stored messages a system can handle. If you have several salespeople who are out of the office most of the time and who rely on storing messages for later retrieval, you should consider a system with a large storage capacity.

> *Mailboxes* are used to store messages and greetings. They are activated by the people calling into the office. Each extension receiving messages is assigned a mailbox. However, not all mailboxes have associated extensions or even receive messages; examples of those that don't are company greeting mailboxes or information mailboxes used to give callers information. For this reason, the number of mailboxes may exceed the number of telephone users in your company.

> *User capacity* is at most equal to the number of mailboxes, since each user has an assigned mailbox.

> *Price range* is that of the basic voice mail system; it generally covers the equipment costs. Installation costs are separate. Cost factors will vary depending on your current phone system and the features you order.

As a business owner, you undoubtedly want your business to grow. Protect your investment by purchasing a voice mail system that can grow with your company. That way, when your business and communication needs expand, you won't have to go through the aggravation of installing a new system and training people to use it.

FAX MACHINES

The explosive growth in the number of fax machines is fueling the market for enhanced fax services, aided by rapidly dropping prices for faxes, rising costs for printing and postage, and the labor required to transmit information either by mail or by phone. Millions of businesses have fax machines, opening up new channels of communication and new marketing opportunities.

An office without a fax machine will soon become almost as rare as one without a computer. Companies are using faxes to send sales, technical, pricing, and other information to customers. They can make information instantly available when interest is highest and avoid the labor cost of making telephone calls or stuffing envelopes.

Fax machine choices abound. In recent months, computer-based faxes and modems have become popular. These are stand-alone fax machines that can fax documents as well as computer files. Some faxes double as photocopy machines. Considerations when buying a fax machine include whether you want your fax and voice phone to share one phone line. Faxes come with paper sheet feeders of various sizes. If your fax will operate unattended for long periods of time, you may need a large sheet feeder.

On-Demand Faxes

On-demand faxes provide information on request on a wide range of subjects. For example, if customers request product information, on-demand faxes automatically send the information requested and produce sales follow-up messages at the same time. On-demand faxes can record who's calling for information and produce reports that show when they called and what their phone numbers were.

Broadcast Faxes

Broadcast faxes can be an integral part of any sales and marketing program. They are used to distribute the latest pricing, product, promotional, or other information to customers on a frequent basis. Fax broadcasting is popular in travel, real estate, or any business that communicates frequent changes in prices or sales information to a network of customers or associates.

You can send a fax to customers announcing a new product, then, after the fax is sent, follow up with a phone call or another fax to reinforce the original message. Faxes' perceived level of importance will help get your message past the secretary to the decision maker's desk. They enjoy a much higher delivery rate than do their bulk mail counterparts. Over 50 percent of faxes reach their destination, and in most cases, they are cheaper to process than brochures.

Computer Faxes

Inexpensive fax boards can be installed in a personal computer. They work with companion software that lets your computer function as a fax machine. Some marketing forecasters predict that sales of computer faxes will surpass those of traditional fax machines in the near future.

There are advantages and disadvantages to computer faxes. Computer faxes are sharper and clearer than copies sent by a traditional fax machine because they avoid the distortions caused by the machine's scanner. They can also send information to multiple receivers at much faster rates than traditional faxes, saving line charges.

However, a computer fax can transmit only characters from a computer file unless you have a scanner to digitize hard-copy material, whereas a standard fax machine can send anything from newspaper clippings to handwritten notes, drawings, and photos. Before you buy a computer fax, seek the advice of a technical person whose judgment you trust.

PHOTOCOPIERS

If you don't have a copier, you may be wasting time making trips to your local copy shop. There are only a handful of personal copy-machine manufacturers, including Sharp, Canon, Xerox, and Mita; however, they offer a wide range of small and inexpensive machines. In the past few years, a number of copiers have been developed specifically for small businesses. They have matured from slow, poor-quality machines to units that have paper trays, automatic feeders, enlargement and reduction functions, and high-quality copying features. You can find a good copier for as little as $300 and full-featured units that cost less than $1,000.

If you live in an area where copy shops are everywhere, spending a few hundred dollars for a once-a-week, in-office convenience may not be worth it. However, if you are making numerous copy trips a week, leasing or buying an office copier may save you time and money. Low-end personal copiers print about eight pages per minute.

POSTAGE EQUIPMENT

What is small and can save you a lot of money in a very short period of time? The answer is a postage meter or scale. Sticking excess postage on an envelope to cover your best guess as to what you think that envelope should cost to mail is a waste of money. A postage scale can be purchased from an office supply store for as little as $10, and you'll eliminate the postage guessing problem.

Scales weigh mail items in ounces. Once you know an item's weight, you look up the postage amount in the Post Office's Postage Rate Information brochure, which is available free from any post office. Postage meters are more sophisticated and calculate the correct postage amounts automatically. The postage scale or meter that is right for your business will depend upon the amount of mailing that you do.

FURNITURE AND EQUIPMENT

If you know where to look, you can find bargains when you shop for office furniture and equipment. This is an area where you don't want to overspend during the start-up stages. A desk is a desk, and it doesn't function any better if it's made out of mahogany rather than pine. Many small-business bankruptcies can be traced to top-heavy investment in capital assets.

We do recommend that you buy comfortable and functional furniture. An uncomfortable office chair will cost you in the long run in back pain and loss of productivity. Your desk should have sufficient storage and filing areas for most of your work materials to be easily accessible. There is no economy in a limited-capacity-desk that requires you to constantly get up to find what you need.

Office furniture and equipment can often be found at bargain prices through the following sources:

Auctions provide closeout sales for businesses that either have gone out of business or are upgrading to new furniture and equipment.

Office equipment stores often maintain warehouses to store used or slightly damaged merchandise. In many cases, they are anxious to get rid of surplus merchandise that's taking up warehouse space.

Classified ads offer furniture and office equipment bargains. Look under the heading "Office Furniture" or "Office Equipment." Consider placing your own ad, since many businesspeople have furniture that they want to sell, but haven't had time to place an ad.

FILING SYSTEMS

The average small-business owner has thirty-six hours of work on his or her desk at any one point in time and, on average, wastes ten hours a week searching for files. You know you've got a filing problem when people start putting correspondence on your chair because that's the only place you'll notice it.

Successful businesspeople maintain filing systems that allow them to quickly find anything they need. As a result, their desks are clean when they leave the office. Here are some filing concepts that will help you get started:

Remove everything from your desk when you leave your office with the exception of personal items like photographs.

Create files for correspondence, work in progress, and reading in a hanging-file system in your desk. If it takes more than a second to get to the files, you won't use them.

Designate a to-be-done file and write down in your calendar the day you'll do each item. Avoid using multiple calendars where you can miss several action items if you forget to look at the right one.

PERSONAL COMPUTERS

Not too many years ago, few companies could consider computerization until they were large enough to afford a mainframe computer and the data processing department that supported its operation. Computerization was out of the question for most small businesses. Since the advent of the personal computer, all that has changed. Today, any small business can afford a personal computer.

The advantages that personal computers offer to the small business are numerous. We'll cover only a few of them in this section. If you are not familiar with personal computers, now is the time to learn. Our computerization rule is, do it early if you are going to do it at all. If you are one of the die-hards who is content to run your business the old-fashioned way, you can skip this section under one condition: Recognize that your competitors have computerized their business systems and that your manual systems will have to compete with them. We wish you the best of luck!

One of the major advantages of computerizing early in the business start-up stage is that it allows you to expand later. For example, you may initially set up a simple accounting system on a low-end personal computer. If your business suddenly doubles or triples in size, you can accommodate the growth by acquiring a faster computer to run the same accounting applications.

Hard Disk

The hard disk on a personal computer is its warehouse for storing programs and data. The storage size of a hard disk is quoted in megabyte, or MB. One MB is the approximate equivalent of one million characters of storage. The more sophisticated an application is, the more space (i.e., MB) it requires.

Floppy Disk Drives

Before hard disk drives became popular, programs and files were stored on removable "floppy" disks. Floppies no longer serve as primary storehouses, but they remain essential for installing programs and as for storing old or infrequently used files. They're also a convenient way to carry information from one PC to another. Floppy disks come in 5.25-inch and 3.5-inch sizes, and each requires its own disk drive. Most modern floppy disks will store about 1.2 MB of data.

Computer Monitors

The kind of monitor you need depends on the type of applications you use. Early computer monitors displayed green or amber characters against a black background on what was called a *monochrome* display. Color graphics array (CGA) monitors brought limited color to personal computing; however, their resolution was even lower than that of their monochrome counterparts. Today, enhanced graphics array (EGA) monitors offer higher resolution than either monochrome or CGA monitors. Vector graphics array (VGA) and Super VGA monitors offer even higher color resolution.

Avoid monochrome monitors unless you will use your computer only for short periods of time. Using them for lengthy periods can lead to eyestrain. CGA monitors are seldom sold with new systems but are available as replacements for old computers. Should you buy a VGA or SVGA monitor? A VGA monitor will meet the needs of most businesses, although SVGA's superior resolution and color capabilities make it ideal for graphics applications and desktop publishing. A new class, XGA (extended graphics array) monitors, offers even higher resolution, but they are expensive.

Networks

If you buy more than one computer, you can network them together so that information can be shared. Networks offer a low-cost way for employees in small offices to share files. Leading networks include LANtastic, Novell Lite, and Windows for WorkGroups. Client-server networks are more expensive but offer more services. Leaders include Novell NetWare, Microsoft LANman, and Banyan Vines.

Computer Security

As with any other business asset, you need to protect your information from loss, vandalism, and theft. Tape backup drives allow you to make a copy of your entire hard disk on a cassette tape that can be removed and stored for safekeeping. Antivirus software can identify and purge files that have been "infected" by viruses that destroy files and programs. These are just a few of the options to consider. There are a number of good books that cover computer security in detail.

COMPUTER PRINTERS

We could have covered computer printers in the personal computer section, but we chose to cover them in a separate section for several reasons. Computer printers can cost as much as or more than the personal computer that runs them. The selection criteria for a printer that's right for your business can be different from those you applied to your personal computer. Printers can be upgraded independent of the computer that you select, which offers you some flexibility in your initial selection criteria.

Like that of personal computers, computer printer technology is changing daily. For this reason, we'll cover only some of the basic issues that you will need to consider when selecting a printer. There are three basic types of printers to consider: (1) dot-matrix, (2) ink-jet, and (3) laser printers. Dot-matrix printers are at the low-end of the price range. Ink-jet printers are in the middle of the range, and laser printers are at the high end. As you would expect, print quality increases in direct relation to the price of the printer.

Dot-Matrix Printers

Dot-matrix printers are designed to print a series of dots, arranged so as to form letters and numbers. The advantages of dot-matrix printers are that they are relatively fast and inexpensive. The disadvantage is that the print quality is below that of ink-jet and laser printers. It's acceptable for printing draft documents. However, some dot-matrix printers include a "near letter quality" print feature that allows the printer to print characters at about seventy-five percent of the quality of a typewriter.

Ink-Jet Printers

Ink-jet printers print a series of micro ink dots (jets), arranged so as to form characters. Because the dots are significantly smaller than their dot-matrix printer counterparts, the quality of the printed document is substantially better, which is the primary advantage of the ink-jet printer. One of the disadvantages of the ink-jet printer is that the ink must dry on the paper and therefore can be smeared if the paper is handled before it dries.

Laser Printers

Laser printers are at the high end of the computer printer options. They use laser beam technology to create images on the print medium. Print quality is quoted in dots per inch (DPI). A low-end 300-DPI printer prints characters and images that are about the same as their ink-jet counterparts. The print quality is more than acceptable for business correspondence and business brochures. The more you are willing to pay for a laser printer, the higher the DPI and print speed rating of the printer. High-end laser printers are capable of printing in excess of 1,000 DPI and at speeds of several hundred pages per minute. Low-end laser printers print at about six pages per minute.

SOFTWARE

The computer industry uses the term "software" to distinguish computer programs from the computer hardware that runs them. Software is divided into two major categories: applications and operating systems. Applications are programs that actually do things, such as print letters or store and retrieve information. The most common business applications are word processors, databases, spreadsheets, graphics programs, accounting programs, and desktop publishing programs.

Operating Systems

Before you can run a personal computer application, you need operating system software to translate commands from the application program into commands that the computer can understand. The applications you choose will determine your operating system. The dominant operating system is known as the Disk Operating System, or DOS: it is packaged with virtually every personal computer sold. A few years ago, the majority of personal computer programs were written to work directly with DOS.

Microsoft has introduced a product called Windows, a graphical user interface that sits on top of DOS. Windows' principal advantage is that it allows users to switch quickly between an application appearing in one "window" on the monitor and an application in another window. If you want to run Windows and DOS applications together, then your best option is IBM's OS/2 operating system, which resembles Windows but can run Windows, DOS, and its own OS/2 applications. OS/2 also permits two or more programs to run simultaneously. If you need to use a word processor while sorting information in a database, OS/2 will let the database run in a background window while you type in the foreground.

Applications

Accounting

Accounting programs keep track of business income and expenditures, including accounts receivable, accounts payable, operating expenses, cash flow, and payroll. Popular accounting programs include QuickBooks, DacEasy Accounting, Peachtree Accounting, Profit, One-Write, and Paciolli 2000.

Electronic mail

As a company grows, more people need access to company data. You could share a quarterly spreadsheet, for example, by printing out two copies and passing one on to a coworker, or you could use electronic mail software, which allows personal computers to send files to and receive them from other computers and employees. Electronic mail can also be used to set-up and notify people of a meeting, transmit company news and announcements, and to communicate by electronic bulletin boards with other people.

Sales presentations

If your business depends on your ability to pitch a product, presentation software can help you create colorful, animated demonstrations called "electronic slide shows." Software presentation products include Persuasion and CorelDraw.

Word processors

Word processors are used to create and store documents. Users can insert and delete words, sentences, and paragraphs at will. Nearly all include spell checkers. Some come packaged with electronic thesauruses and grammar checkers. Word processing also allows the computer to double as a typewriter with the added features of spell checking, electronic filing, and more efficient text entry, among others.

Databases

Databases are the backbone of business computing. They are used to store and retrieve information such as customer lists, inventories, and notes. They can also be used in sorting information, letting users do things like search a customer list for customers in a given zip code. A database application can store and connect such diverse information as customer addresses and numbers, employee files, company policies, supplier phone numbers, office inventory, and insurance claims. Popular databases include dBASE, Paradox, FoxPro, Professional File, access, and Q&A.

Spreadsheets

Spreadsheets are used to keep track of financial information, inventories, and other information. They are particularly useful for business forecasting. For instance, you can use a spreadsheet to calculate how a change in material costs will affect your bottom line. Spreadsheet software also allows for "what if" analysis of such things as pricing alternatives, profit maximization, and a variety of other business problems. The most popular spreadsheets are Lotus 1-2-3, Quattro Pro, and Excel.

Graphics programs

Graphics programs are used to create graphs and drawings for use in newsletters, posters, advertisements, and other documents. Some allow users to import photographs into documents or create animated pictures for use in multimedia presentations. Popular graphics programs are PC Paintbrush, Professional Draw, IntelliDraw, Illustrator, Persuasion, and CorelDraw.

Desktop publishing

Desktop publishing programs are extremely sophisticated word processors that can incorporate word processing, graphics, and image files to create newsletters, manuals, fliers, advertisements, magazines, and newspapers. Desktop publishing software can also be used to design business forms, brochures, newsletters, and fliers to support your marketing and sales efforts.

Most of today's DTP programs come with predesigned layouts for fliers, brochures, and catalogs. Insert your company logo, your text copy, and some graphics, and you can quickly create a sales document. Popular desktop programs include Microsoft Express Publisher, Aldus PageMaker, Ventura Publisher, and Quark XPress.

Integrated software

Integrated programs include three or four different functions such as a word processor, a database, and a spreadsheet, in a single package. Some include communications software that will allow you to send files to and receive them from other computers. The most popular integrated packages are Microsoft Works, WordPerfect Works, ClarisWorks, GeoWorks Pro, and Lotus Symphony.

Specialized software

There is specialized application software to meet virtually every business need. For example, personal information managers (PIMs) help busy entrepreneurs keep track of their personal schedules, and project planners enable them to keep group projects moving on schedule. If you can imagine a problem that a program could solve, the program probably exists.

OFFICE SUPPLIES

To make a good impression, you should have well-designed stationery on good-quality paper. You will need some or all of the following: first- and second-page letterhead, business cards, #10 envelopes, large mailing envelopes, mailing labels, report covers with the same design as your letterhead, memo pads, invoices, receipts, purchase orders, catalogs, and brochures.

OFFICE TAX DEDUCTIONS

Tax deductions are among the rewards of self-employment. Under the right circumstances, you can save as much as half the purchase price in taxes when you buy office furniture and equipment. How you use the equipment will determine whether you can take full advantage of the tax breaks.

Always consider the tax code before you buy or lease equipment. Businesses can deduct up to $10,000 in the year in which they buy equipment if certain tax code conditions are met. This deduction can save you significant amounts of money. If you're in the 28 percent tax bracket, live in a state with a 7 percent income tax, and are subject to the 15 percent self-employment tax, your business tax bracket is 50 percent. Purchase a $4,000 computer and take the tax deduction, and you will in effect save $2,000 on your purchase.

There are a number of limitations for you to consider. The IRS allows only one $10,000 deduction per family. So a husband and wife who have separate businesses get just one $10,000 equipment deduction per year. You can't use the equipment tax deduction if you aren't making money. Your deduction is limited to the amount that your business makes in a year.

If you bought $10,000 worth of equipment but only recorded $7,000 in business income, you would only be able to take a $7,000 deduction. However, you don't lose the rest of the deduction. You can carry the remaining $3,000 over to the next year. You'll still be limited to a $10,000 deduction next year.

Car phones, computers, videotape equipment, and similar items are called *listed property*. They are on an IRS list of equipment that can easily be used outside of your business. The list was created to make sure that you don't take business deductions for equipment for personal use. If you are using any office equipment for both business and personal use, you have to prove that you use it for your business at least 50 percent of the time to take any business tax deductions. The percentage of the equipment's cost that you can deduct is limited to the percentage of the time the equipment was used in the business. Log books are commonly used to prove the percent of use for the business to the IRS.

The IRS exempts from the listed-property test any equipment such as computers that you keep at your place of business. However, if you keep your computer in your office and use it to maintain personal as well as business files, a visiting IRS agent could disallow the whole office as a deduction as well as the computer. If you deduct the cost of tape recorders, telephones, and other equipment that has mixed use, you are subjecting yourself to more pages of IRS formulas and tables. The safest approach is to use your office equipment exclusively for your business.

SUMMARY AND CONCLUSIONS

This chapter presented you with a smorgasbord of office equipment, furnishings, and computer hardware and software to choose from when you set up your office. Running a highly efficient, well-equipped office is one of the major advantages over their larger business counterparts that small businesses can enjoy.

We started with a discussion of the basic tool, the telephone, with all of its modern-day features. Next, we talked about the proliferation of fax machines and presented you with a number of ways to use these incredible machines to support your business. We exposed you to the rapid drop in photocopy machine prices before we moved on to a basic discussion of office furniture and filing systems.

Personal computers dominated the last half of the chapter, and for good reason. Personal computer hardware and software technology is changing as you read this paragraph. Our intention in this section was to introduce you to the basic hardware components and software applications in the interest of making you a more informed computer buyer.

Chapter 12

The Strategic Business Plan

IT ALL COMES TOGETHER IN THE STRATEGIC PLAN

A well-written, well-thought-out business plan is an essential tool for any business. The business plan brings together all the goals, plans, strategies, and resources of the business. A good plan can dramatically increase your chances of succeeding and can help you define your business concepts, evaluate the competition, estimate costs, predict your sales, and control risks. You can use it to help launch new products and services, rejuvenate your business with new ideas, or analyze marketing opportunities. In addition, a business plan can

- Focus your attention and ideas on the primary goals and objectives of the business.
- Create a track for you to follow during the start-up stages of the business.
- Create benchmarks against which you can measure business progress.
- Provide a vehicle for attracting capital to help finance the business.

This chapter will show you how to develop and write a business plan. A number of examples from Computech's business plan are included to illustrate the process.

WHAT'S IN A BUSINESS PLAN?

A business plan is a written statement that includes details about your business concepts, plans, goals, and objectives. It explains why, how, and when you plan on achieving strategic business goals. When you develop a business plan, you should have a clear understanding of what you want to accomplish. What is your target market, and who are your customers? What are your market strengths and weaknesses? Who are your competitors? What are your production and distribution plans? Who are your suppliers? How much money will you need to start the business and keep it running over the next several years? At what point in time will your business make a profit? These are the basic questions that are addressed and answered in a business plan.

A solid plan is practical, pragmatic, and specific. It emphasizes implementation and the achievement of measurable objectives. A business plan is also a living document that, over time, is marked up, modified, and relied upon to run your business. Don't fall into the trap of evaluating the adequacy of your business plan by its length. Ten to thirty pages should be sufficient for most plans, and each page must mean something to you. If it doesn't add value to your business, delete the page.

BUSINESS PLANNING BASICS

A business plan should reveal where your business stands at any moment in time, where it plans to go, and how you plan to get there. You measure your progress by comparing actual results to planned results. Financial projections are an essential component of the plan. A comparison of projections and actual results should show in dollars and cents how well your business is doing. The plan therefore becomes a critical document that helps prospective investors gauge your potential and determine if they want to invest in your company.

Financial projections follow the same format as your financial statements. Revenue projections are reported with supporting data that shows how you plan to meet these projections. Anybody reviewing your plan should be able to clearly understand how the numbers were derived and whether the numbers present a valid assessment of your company's growth potential.

To illustrate the importance of detailed revenue projections, let's assume that Computech plans to sell $1 million worth of products in its first year of operation, and this lump-sum figure is all that is stated in the sales forecast section of Computech's business plan (see Figure 12-1). This is hardly sufficient for planning the year's production. The absence of quantitative information makes relying on the projections impossible. Prospective investors will lack the solid information they need to make an intelligent business decision, and so will you.

Figure 12-1
The Sales Forecast in Computech's Business Plan

All too often, sales forecasts are little more than theoretical projections based on the total size of the market and the assumption that a business can command a certain percentage of that market. All revenue and cost projections must be substantiated in the business plan. Investors will want to know what evidence supports your market share predictions and how solid the company's market research data is. Unless investors are confident that your plan addresses these and other questions, your company will not qualify for a loan. If you cannot answer these questions to your satisfaction, you should seriously question the viability of the business that you are about to enter.

For plan projections to serve their purpose, sales must be broken down into verifiable categories, such as market segments or customer groups, for which estimates can be made. Detailed revenue projections are also used to accurately forecast your costs based upon sales estimates. The interrelationships between sales and cost forecasts are a critical component of a good business plan. The guidelines in the sections that follow will help you to develop a credible plan.

Market Segmentation

In every company, sales are made in different categories or segments. Similarly, revenue projections should be structured by first calculating the basic components of each segment, then adding the segments together to produce the company's sales forecast. Sales numbers can be segmented by a wide range of characteristics, including product lines, geography, and customer profiles. The last works best when the customer base falls into identifiable groups, such as retail and wholesale customers.

Reality Checks

Do your financial projections make sense? Review your numbers in the context of the projected time period. What percent of today's market do they cover? For example, if you are projecting 200 percent annual growth, is that feasible? Is your industry growing at a 200 percent annual rate?

As a general rule, changes in sales levels should result in corresponding changes in profits. Test this assumption in your plan. What impact does a 5 percent sales increase have on the profitability of your product lines? If profits increase markedly, chances are that your cost estimates are out of line. Most likely, you have failed to capture the interrelationship between sales and costs.

Shrewd investors are both wary of and attracted by substantial revenue and profit projections in a business plan. They are concerned when the reasoning and strategies that give rise to big numbers have not been thoughtfully developed. Providing supplemental detailed analysis for projected revenues demonstrates your insight into the financial performance of your business. This is critical to the credibility of your business plan and will increase your chances of attracting partners and capital.

CREATING A PLAN

There are seven basic sections that make up of a business plan. All plans start with an executive summary and include financial projections for at least three to five years out. Although no two business plans are alike, most follow a standard outline:

1. Executive summary
2. Company summary
3. Product and service analysis
4. Market analysis
5. Strategic plan
6. Management profile
7. Financial analysis

The executive summary is by far the most important section in the plan. It should be written last, after you've completed the other sections. It summarizes everything that the plan covers in sections 2 through 7.

Company Summary

The first question your business plan must address is who you are and what your qualifications are. The company analysis section should include

- The business name and the owner's name
- A brief background of the owner and other key employees
- A short history of the business
- Business goals and objectives

Here's an example of an excerpt from Computech's company summary:

Computech was founded last year by David Crosby to develop, produce, and market personal computers, and related services. A brief outline of David Crosby's background follows. . . . The company has designed two prototype computers and has received letters of interest from two major distributors and the largest specialty department store chain in the state (see Attachment A for letter copies). The goal of the company is to become the premier producer of personal computer products and services.

Computech's company summary tells the reader that the company had two major distributors indicate their interest, which is an important business issue. To provide proof of that statement, the reader is told that copies of the distributors' letters are included in Attachment A of the plan. The use of this "proof technique" adds credibility to Computech's business plan.

Product and Service Analysis

Your next task is to describe in detail the products or services you intend to offer. The goal here is to differentiate yourself from your competitors. Start with a summary paragraph that clearly and concisely describes your products or services. It should emphasize the following points:

Benefits. Show why your products and services are unique, distinct, or of considerably better quality than others that are available.

Costs. Show all expenses, including the costs of raw materials, component parts, equipment, labor, and overhead. Show where you plan to get your materials. If yours is a service company, how much will it cost to fulfill your service obligations?

Location. Provide details of where your business will be located and why you chose that particular location. What is the cost of your facilities?

Technology. If your product or service is based on a unique technology, show why the technology is unique and important to your business. Is it protected by a patent, copyright, or trademark?

Future. If you will be offering a family of products or services at a future date, what are they? Investors are particularly interested in entrepreneurs who understand that long-term success favors businesses with several related products more often than those with a single offering.

An abbreviated summary of Computech's product and service analysis is shown in Figure 12-2. This section of the business plan relies on information that you have collected and incorporated into your marketing and financial plans.

Figure 12-2
The Product and Service Analysis in Computech's Business Plan

BENEFITS: Computech manufactures a premier personal computer that features a three-year unconditional warranty. The computer will sell at a retail price that is 20 percent below that of competitive personal computers.

COSTS: The average production cost for a Computech computer is about $675 per unit. A detailed explanation of all costs and price quotes is given in Attachment B.

LOCATION: The geographical location of Computech is not considered to be a critical factor, since most consumers are willing to travel a reasonable distance to a high-quality computer store. Computers will be shipped to the distributors by UPS. To minimize Computech's location cost, the company has a six-month lease on 800 square feet of retail space in Denver, Colorado.

TECHNOLOGY: Computech's personal computer has been named Computech 1 and is covered under a U.S. patent (see copy in Attachment C).

FUTURE: Following the successful release of Computech 1, Computech is in the process of developing Computech 2, a personal computer that will include advanced multimedia features.

Market Analysis

Most businesses fail because they don't perform an adequate market analysis. There are precious few businesses that wouldn't benefit from an in-depth market analysis. In this section, summarize what you have already learned from the chapters covering marketing, sales, and promotion. As with all sections in your plan, start with a summary paragraph so that your readers will know what the section is about. Then make sure to include the following points:

Industry analysis. Present an overview of your industry. Is it growing or declining? What have been the historical business cycles? Is the industry seasonal, and how long will the market need your products or services?

Competitors. List all of your known competitors. Are they big companies with massive budgets, or are they small companies? What are their market shares and are they profitable? What advantages and disadvantages do they have over your business? How do you plan to leverage your advantages and neutralize your disadvantages?

Customers. Identify who your most likely customers are. How many are there? Is it a highly targeted market? What common traits do your customers share?

Market fit. Describe how you will fit into the market. How does your product or service meet market needs? How do you compare with the competition in terms of features, location, distribution, price, quality, and other factors?

An abbreviated summary of Computech's product and service analysis is shown in Figure 12-3. This section of the business plan relies on information that you have collected and incorporated into your marketing and sales plans.

Figure 12-3
The Market Analysis in Computech's Business Plan

COMPETITORS: There are only two personal computer models in the Denver market area that competes against Computech's personal computer (Computech 1). The competitor's only offer a one-year warranty on their computers.

CUSTOMERS: The customer prospects for Computech's personal computer will be the 50,000 Denver area residents who currently uses personal computers at home or work.

MARKET FIT: Computech will be the only computer retailer in the market that offers a three-year unconditional warranty, an in-store service department, and a complete line of educational seminars.

Strategic Plan

In the strategic plan section, you lay out your business' plan of action. It shows how you plan to implement your strategies based upon the information presented in the previous sections. Important points to cover are summarized as follows:

> *Marketing.* Identify the major parts of your marketing program and how they fit together.

> *Pricing.* Summarize your pricing rationale, and state how it was determined and why it will work.

> *Distribution.* Describe the distribution channels that are available to you and those that you will be using. Many small businesses fail because they have not established adequate distribution channels.

> *Sales.* Outline how you plan to sell your products or services. Will you have a sales force or use contract representatives?

> *Promotion.* Show how you plan to promote your business. What free publicity is available to you? How will you advertise, and what will it cost?

> *Forecast.* Include charts showing estimated sales for the next three to five years.

In this section, do not combine all sales into a single number. Separate your total sales into categories and show subtotals on a monthly basis in dollars and units, if applicable. The most common method of segmentation is by product or line of business. Charting sales by product line often will highlight trends, such as seasonal variations. For example, you can project the seasonal fluctuation in one product line while planning for more steady growth in another product line.

Alternatively, geographic regions could be the basis for segregating sales. You may be using this information to track the performance of sales representatives or distributors. The use of a computer database system or a spreadsheet program to record sales by major customer can be helpful in preparing sales projections.

How you segment your revenues will be determined by the projections you want to make. Once you decide, you can design an information system to capture this information on an ongoing basis. An abbreviated summary of Computech's strategic plan is shown in Figure 12-4.

Management Profile

The backgrounds of the key players, including yourself, are covered in the management profile section of the plan. Include the following information:

- An organization chart showing who reports to whom and what function each person performs

Figure 12-4
Computech's Strategic Business Plan

MARKETING: Computech's computers will be marketed and promoted through trade shows and advertised in the business sections of the major newspapers.

PRICING: The Computech 1 computer will be sold for $955, which is 20 percent below the average price of competitive computers. At this price, Computech believes that it can capture a significant portion of the competitors' market.

DISTRIBUTION: Over 60 percent of the distribution of computers will be handled through Computech's two retail stores.

SALES: Computech will hire a sales force. The company has elected to pay sales representatives a base salary plus a commision.

- Resumes of the principal owners and managers showing their accomplishments and experience
- Professionals such as attorneys, accountants, business advisers, or industry experts whose advice you plan to use
- A personnel plan that explains in detail the employment needs of your business and how you plan to hire the right people

Financial Analysis

The financial analysis converts the material covered in the other sections into dollars. It is a recap of what you have already learned in the accounting and financial chapters. Explain where the money to run your business will come from and show projections for everything from accounts receivable to expenses. This section also includes a break-even analysis to show how much you will spend before you become profitable. Your financial analysis should include the following:

> *Balance sheet.* Show where your business assets, liabilities, and equity will be quarterly for a minimum of a three-year time period (see Figure 12-5).

Figure 12-5
The Balance Sheet for Computech's Business Plan

Account	Current	Year 1	Year 2	Year 3
Assets	$95,600	$119,424	$175,480	$248,123
Liabilities	$20,600	$25,000	$25,000	$25,000
Owners' Equity	$75,000	$94,424	$150,480	$223,123

Income statement. Show your net profits or losses for a three- to five-year time period (see Figure 12-6).

Figure 12-6
The Income Statement for Computech's Business Plan

Account	1st Quarter	2nd Quarter	3rd Quarter	4th Quarter	Year 1	Year 2	Year 3
Sales							
Computers	$95,000	$95,000	$68,500	$38,900	$297,400	$380,600	$425,000
Services	$30,000	$30,000	$26,500	$16,250	$102,750	$77,555	$106,445
Total sales	$125,000	$125,000	$95,000	$55,150	$401,500	$458,155	$531,445
Costs							
Cost of goods sold	$52,500	$52,000	$40,000	$19,695	$164,195	$191,825	$220,159
Operating expenses	$46,650	$50,000	$35,800	$22,300	$154,750	$190,542	$215,010
Other expenses	$1,000	$1,200	$1,000	$1,000	$4,200	$1,900	$3,600
Total expenses	$100,150	$103,200	$76,800	$42,995	$323,145	$384,267	$438,769
Net profit (loss)	$24,850	$21,800	$18,200	$12,155	$78,355	$73,888	$92,676

Cash flow schedule. Reconcile where and when cash will be spent and collected over the next three years. Project how much you will owe and when each installment will be due over the next three years. Many businesses suffer from cash flow problems simply because you must spend money before you make it (see Figure 12-7).

Figure 12-7
Computech's Three-Year Cash Flow Requirements Budget

Cash Flow Item	1st Quarter	2nd Quarter	3rd Quarter	4th Quarter	Year 2	Year 3
Beginning cash balances	$2,500	$12,456	$29,515	$51,598	$78,023	$147,163
Net sales	$90,170	$96,758	$103,785	$111,296	$425,000	$440,000
Other income	$550	$675	$900	$875	$3,200	$52,000
Total available cash	$93,220	$109,889	$134,200	$163,769	$506,223	$639,163
Cash disbursements						
Payroll	$12,115	$12,056	$12,390	$12,862	$53,790	$67,238
Advertising	$2,062	$2,045	$1,765	$1,750	$35,000	$43,750
Sales commissions	$5,038	$6,019	$8,230	$10,500	$18,675	$23,344
Cost of goods sold	$22,180	$23,094	$24,275	$21,437	$98,555	$123,194
Interest expense	$4,038	$4,019	$4,130	$4,287	$14,300	$17,875
Taxes	$8,076	$8,037	$8,260	$9,970	$35,435	$44,294
Equipment leases	$8,884	$8,841	$9,086	$9,432	$37,430	$46,788
Building rent	$15,345	$15,271	$15,694	$15,517	$65,875	$82,344
Total cash disbursements	$77,738	$79,378	$83,830	$85,746	$359,060	$448,825
Cash after disbursements	$15,482	$30,511	$50,370	$78,023	$147,193	$190,338

Break-even analysis. This is the bottom line of your business plan. Now that you have estimated sales and expenses, you can plot the point in time at which the two will be equal, or the break-even point. The break-even point is reached when total costs equal total sales. You'll start making a profit when total sales are greater than total costs (see Figure 12-8).

Figure 12-8
Computech's Break-even Point

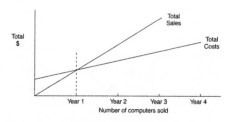

176

Executive Summary

As we stated earlier, the executive summary appears at the beginning of a business plan. It summarizes the high points of everything you are including in your business plan and therefore should be the last section of the plan that you write.

The purpose of the executive summary is to quickly convince readers that your business has merit and encourage them to read the remaining sections of your plan. The executive summary should be written in an enthusiastic but realistic tone and take up one or two pages. It should include the following:

Purpose. State what the intention of your business plan is, such as to clarify your ideas, find financial backing, establish partnership interest, or all of the above.

Definition. State your business idea, clearly explained in thirty words or less. Here's an excellent opportunity to see if you have a sharp focus on your concept.

Overview. Provide an overview of the market and its potential, summarizing who your competitors and your customers are.

Features. Show what makes your product or service unique and qualified to compete in the market.

Financial. Quantify what it will take to put your business plan into action.

Growth. Outline your expectations for your company. How will it grow, and why?

Make sure that your executive summary is as perfect as you can make it. The executive summary is sometimes all that potential investors or lenders will read, so it must be written to capture their attention. An effective summary will properly position your company and help to distinguish your concepts from the competition. It must be concise, persuasive, and no more than two pages in length. If the executive summary fails to motivate the reader to read the rest of your plan, then it has failed to do its job. Excerpts from Computech's executive summary are shown in Figure 12-9.

PUTTING IT TOGETHER

Writing a business plan is much easier if you divide the elements into sections. Critique your plan carefully. Is it a true representation of the facts as you know them? And, most important, is this the business you want to commit time and resources to for the next several years? Before drafting your final version, show your business plan to trusted colleagues. Ask for their opinions and incorporate valid suggestions into your final draft.

When you create a document as important as your business plan, you want it to look as professional as possible. Produce the final draft of your plan on high-quality paper. The quality of the paper you choose can dramatically affect the look of your document. When it's time to print the final copy, use twenty-pound

Figure 12-9
The Executive Summary for Computech's Business Plan

PURPOSE: Computech's business plan has been prepared to clarify our business ideas and to obtain financing to support the growth of the company.

PRODUCTS & SERVICES: Computech manufactures and services personal computers. Our initial computer (Computech 1) is already on the market.

MARKET OVERVIEW: Our target market for Computech 1 will be the 50,000 people in the Denver metropolitan area who use personal computers. Only two other competitive personal computer models are currently being sold in our market area.

FEATURES: Our computer is covered by a three-year unconditional warranty, an option that is not available from our competition. The retail price of Computech 1 is 20 percent below the price of our competitors' computers.

FINANCIAL: Computech has sufficient working capital to fund the release of our next computer (Computech 2). The company reached its break-even point within the first 12 months of operation.

GROWTH: Computech has to develop a comprehensive seminar program in the near future. We believe that such an offering will encourage people to buy Computech computers.

bond paper. You can further enhance the look by choosing paper with a laid finish or other high-quality textured paper.

Include a cover, a table of contents, headers, and footers in your plan. A table of contents allows the reader to move around the document easily. Headers and footers help the reader find the sections that they are interested in and shows them that this is a carefully constructed and complete plan. Headers and footers should have the same format throughout, and the use of indents, tabs, and headings should be consistent. Consistent business plan elements show that you are building a consistent and reliable business.

To make your plan more readable, use bold, underlining, italics, or different font sizes to highlight important elements. Add borders to separate text from financial charts, graphs, and illustrations. Use bullets and numbered lists when appropriate.

Most good word processors can handle these formatting and style recommendations and give your plan a professional look. If you do not have access to the appropriate software, consider buying a desktop publishing program or having a professional desktop publisher produce the final draft for you. The final draft should be printed on an ink-jet or laser printer. Even though dot-matrix printer output has improved dramatically, it cannot match the print quality of ink-jet and laser printers.

If you don't have an appropriate printer, find an office supply or computer shop that will rent you one. Once you have a master copy, you can make duplicates on high-quality paper. Always retain an extra copy for your files and record the name of anyone who has a copy of the plan. Insert the final draft in a high-quality binder. In addition to keeping your copy clean, binders will give your plan extra weight and presence.

BUSINESS PLANNING SOFTWARE

A business plan is an invaluable tool. It helps you understand where you are and where you want to go. You can revise it whenever you want to reevaluate your business options, add a partner, or introduce a new product. However, putting it all together can be a headache.

Major corporations often hire expensive consultants to help with this process. Small-business owners can get some of the same advice from relatively inexpensive software packages. Two of the most popular are BizPlan Builder from Jian Software and Business Plan Toolkit from Palo Alto Software (see Figure 12-10). Both were created by experienced business planning consultants and offer guidelines for writing a business plan.

Most business planning software packages support DOS, OS/2, Microsoft Windows, and Apple computer operating environments. They work under the assumption that it is easier to edit existing text than to write new text from scratch. Many provide a series of boilerplate text templates for the business plan sections that we have covered. Some of these packages include spreadsheet templates and charting options to facilitate the presentation of financial and marketing information. Most will accept text files from word processors as input.

Many of the planning software packages include helpful sample phrases that you can use to fill in the blanks. Worksheets also use a fill-in-the-blanks approach. For example, when preparing the sales forecast, you enter your first month's projected sales and an annual growth rate or a flat monthly increment. The planning software then generates the sales data by month and year. Some of the better programs will generate graphics and charts from your data.

SUMMARY AND CONCLUSIONS

Preparing a sound business plan requires an investment of a substantial amount of time and resources. You may need the assistance of qualified professionals to complete your plan. To assure that your plan is effective in guiding your business and attracting investors, follow the suggestions in this chapter.

As you complete a section, ask impartial third parties to review it and give their perspective on its quality, clarity, and thoroughness. Many of the Small Business Administration's regional offices (see Appendix C) offer free business plan counseling and advice. If you intend to use your plan to attract capital, honestly ask yourself if you would invest in the business after reading the plan. If you can't answer yes, then the plan needs more work.

Figure 12-10
BizPlan Business Planning Software

Business Power Tools™

Software to Turn Business Projects You Hate Into Results You'll Love!

The Street Smart Executive's Guide To Leveraging Time And Technology: Software To Run A More Efficient And Profitable Business

The less effort, the faster and more powerful you will be. — Bruce Lee

TOOLS FOR SALES, INC.

Chapter 13

Running Your Business Right

SURVIVAL TACTICS TO ASSURE YOUR SUCCESS

No matter what kind of business you start, it is important that you maintain control over your operation from the beginning. You must be able to assess your personnel needs, manage costs, and attract and hire good people. The action plans in this chapter will help you run your new business right, from the beginning.

Operational requirements will vary depending upon the type of business that you start. Retail, manufacturing, and service businesses must maintain good relationships with suppliers. Obtaining favorable credit terms, dependable deliveries, and good-quality merchandise is essential if any new business is to function effectively.

RECOGNIZING SUCCESS

What is success, and how will you know if you are successful? This is a question that all business owners must deal with on a regular basis. There will be times when you will question whether the time and energy you spent building the business was worth it. Are you making enough to justify hiring an assistant? Will your business qualify for a bank loan? Can you afford a new computer? Are you on track with your strategic business plan? These are some of the questions that all new business owners face.

Self-assessment is a crucial part of the start-up process. Unless you know how you're doing, you won't know what to do next. Realistic self-appraisals will help you build a stronger business and beat back self-doubts. Financial numbers that indicate that you're doing fine are a potent weapon against the discouragement that can develop on a bad day. On the other hand, discouraging financial numbers can lead you to renew your effort to improve your financial position. That might be just what your business needs.

Self-Assessment

Perform a self-assessment of your business every three months. Measure your performance against your personal goals. Analyze the trends and compare your business with other businesses similar to yours. Start your review with a clean desk and a clear head. If you are worrying about your bills, pick a different day for the review.

If your business is new, go easy on yourself. The standards for someone who's been in business for less than a year for someone who's been in business for several years. There are several tests you can put your business through to find out how you're doing.

Bill-paying test

Are you covering all business expenses? If you are covering all your expenses in the first year, you are better off than most first-year businesses. The test gets harder the longer you're in business. By the time you've been in business for a few years, your self-employment income should cover a comfortable lifestyle, vacations, nights out, insurance premiums, and a retirement plan.

The job test

How much could you demand on the open job market? How much is the person who has your old job making? How much do the help-wanted ads offer people with your skills? Several magazines publish annual surveys of salaries for positions in your field. How does the money you're making in your business compare with what you could be making working for someone else? For many of us, it's worth a premium to work for ourselves. However, if you are working sixteen-hour days, seven-day weeks, and not making what you could in a 9 to 5 job, it may be time to reconsider your career options.

The investment test

If your business was a publicly held company, would you be better off investing in it or in another investment option (stocks, bonds, etc.)? This key financial indicator tells you how well your business is using your money. First, figure out how much money you spent to set yourself up in business. Then determine how much profit you made in your first year. If you didn't draw a salary, subtract what your salary would have been from the amount of money left at the end of the year, after expenses. If you are a sole proprietor and your profit is commingled with your salary, go back to the job test to figure out what portion of your earnings is a comparable salary and what part is profit.

Divide your profit by the money you spent to set up the business. Your return should be equal to or greater than the prevailing interest rate or average investment rate. If it's less than the prevailing rates, you might want to consider putting your money in an alternative investment and finding a job.

The numbers test

There are rules of thumb for recognizing a healthy businesses. One of these uses a numbers test called the *quick ratio*. The quick ratio is calculated by dividing current assets excluding inventory current liabilities. A 1-to-1 ratio is considered acceptable. Anything above 1-to-1 is considered good. Another useful calculation is the *current ratio*, which compares the company's total current assets to current liabilities. Divide current assets by current liabilities to determine the current ratio. A 2-to-1 or better current ratio is considered good.

The debt-to-equity ratio compares the total debt of your business with its net worth. Total debt is divided by net worth. Although debt adds risk, a debt-free business may not be able to grow fast enough. The whole reason for using debt is to help grow the business and increase the owners' return on capital. A debt-to-equity relationship lower than 1 is considered good for a business.

The sales test

Compare your sales and profit for like periods of time (last year to this year). Are your sales moving in the right direction? Growth company investors like to see sales and earnings growing at 15 percent or more a year. Is your business approaching or exceeding the 15 percent standard? At the very least, you should be keeping up with the inflation rate.

The comparison test

Comparisons are among the most accurate measures of success. Many trade associations and professional groups track their numbers' progress by taking surveys. How does your business compare with the business and operational trends in your industry? Where does your business fit in the rankings? Are you in the upper 25 percent?

The profit test

Break down your sales by individual product and service categories. What categories make you the most money, and how much of your time do you spend on these categories? Who are your most profitable clients? Review the data to determine if you're focusing your attention in the right sales areas. Are you putting more marketing energy into one service or product than is justified by its profits?

The inside test

Are you self-employed for reasons that aren't all financial, such as spending more time with your family or enjoying the freedom of working your own hours? If so, how well are you meeting your personal goals? You need to determine how you define success for yourself in terms of income, liquidity, free time, and the quality of life.

Ask yourself how it all feels inside of yourself. If your business is growing, with new clients, it is moving in the right direction, and you feel comfortable, then you are a success. In the final analysis, you have to feel good about what you're doing.

MISTAKES TO AVOID

Many small-business owners find the business end of their operation a chore. For example, calling on past due accounts may be a task they don't like. They would rather pursue a more exciting task, like developing new markets. But watch out! The better you are at what you like to do, the more likely you are to commit a basic business mistake. You may tend to focus solely on what you like to do and ignore what you should be doing.

Contract Mistakes

Failing to have a written contract is a common mistake. About half the business partnerships in the country operate without a formal written contract or under an outdated contract. A partnership without a contract is like a common-law marriage: It has most of the advantages of a marriage but enjoys few of the legal protections of the fully sanctioned union. In most states, if one partner leaves, your partnership technically ceases to exist. Leases could be canceled, your bank could call in your loans, and you might have to pay off the departing partners or, worse yet, take legal action. Any business partnership that doesn't have a formal written agreement is asking for trouble.

If you are going into business with other people, sit down with your associates and analyze your business in detail. First, decide whether a partnership or a professional corporation is the best structure for your business. Many firms and practices become professional corporations because the owners do not want to be personally liable for the acts or debts of their associates. Partnerships, by contrast, are generally easier to set up and dissolve than corporations, and they have certain tax advantages.

Draft an agreement that is acceptable to all of the partners. No matter which structure you select, you will need to specify how new employees will be added to the business, how they can become partners or stockholders, and what will happen if one of you leaves, retires, dies, becomes disabled, or must be let go.

"Find Me" Mistakes

"The customers will find me" is a common start-up mistake. Maybe that was true in the past, but not anymore. In today's competitive environment, any business that doesn't have a constant flow of new customers is probably shrinking. One way to bring in new business is to advertise. Consider building relationships with other businesses with complementary specialties to which you can refer customers and from which you can get referrals in return.

Become active in local groups and associations. Look for opportunities to publicize yourself by giving speeches at civic or professional meetings. Write for professional periodicals or lend your expertise to local journalists who cover your field by being quoted in a newspaper or featured on television. All of these activities will help you find customers.

STRATEGIES TO FOLLOW

Emphasize Customer Satisfaction

Give customers a reason to come back. It takes more than a good deal to make a satisfied customer. You'll find that your most loyal customers keep coming back not because of your competitive price but because they like doing business with you. So how do you increase your stock of customer goodwill? We've said it before and we'll say it again: Gather as much information as you can about your customers. Get to know them better and find out what they like and don't like. Incorporate their likes into the way you do business, and avoid their dislikes.

Call them with tips that will save them money. Tell them about unadvertised specials that you are about to announce and about any seasonal discounts you offer. Do everything you can to make sure they value their relationship with you.

Take Advantage of Tough Times

Tough times are good times to get noticed. At the first hint of a bad economy, many small businesses panic and run for cover. They slash their advertising and sales budgets and try to sit out the downturn. At times like these, you can practically have the field to yourself. As your competitors make themselves invisible, grab the chance to stand out and be noticed.

Businesses that advertise during tough times almost always take market share away from businesses that don't. Tough times may be the best time to launch an advertising blitz to gain market share. Advertising agencies are eager to get whatever business they can, so you may be able to negotiate better rates and terms. At the same time, explore less expensive and perhaps more cost-effective advertising alternatives.

Introduce New Offerings

Always look for opportunities to expand your area of operation. Proceed with caution and obtain some marketing intelligence before you proceed. Check out the most likely prospects in the expansion areas that interest you, and find out if you can compete with existing suppliers.

A smart marketer knows that a product or service has greater consumer appeal if it is perceived as new. You can add newness to already existing products and services by adding such features as extended warranties, free installation, and consultations. Always be thinking of ways to differentiate your products and services from your competitors'. Start by experimenting with several variations on a small scale until you hit upon the right combination. Test the new derivative on a sample set of your customers to see if they like it. If they do, introduce the new product or service to increase your sales.

Increase Productivity

Increasing productivity does not mean working harder. Chances are that you're already doing that. Increasing productivity means working smarter. Analyze your business on a product and service basis to see which elements contribute most to your costs. Identify and eliminate excess costs. For example, you might sell idle equipment, inventory, or property or sublease empty warehouse space. Follow the time-honored strategy of taking a sharp red pencil to all your costs, including entertainment and travel costs.

Accelerate Collections

To keep money flowing, streamline your billing process. The ideal billing approach is to collect payments when goods and services are delivered. If, for competitive reasons, you have to bill your customers, send invoices out the day the product or service is delivered. Follow up with a reminder bill two weeks later. If you don't receive payment in thirty days, get on the phone and make a collection call. Talking to customers may be far more effective than sending letters. To encourage early payments, offer customers a discount (1 to 3 percent) for payments made within fifteen days.

If you can't supervise collections, assign someone to do the job for you. If you don't have anybody for that the position, consider hiring a commercial collection company to manage your past due accounts. They are listed in the Yellow Pages.

Delay Payments

Delay all of your payments whenever possible. However, aggressive use of this strategy is best reserved for companies in a cash flow crunch and should be undertaken only with the consent of your creditors or suppliers. Review your supplier requirements and find vendors who will let you stretch out your payments. Many vendors will advance you goods on consignment. Treat your suppliers as partners in your business, and ask them to work with you to develop an acceptable payment plan. You will probably get more help from suppliers that consider your business a major account. Delay payments as long as you can without damaging your credit. If your suppliers lose faith in your company, they could require you to pay in advance, which could put you in a difficult cash bind.

Advertise

The best way to expand your marketing opportunities is through advertising. One of the biggest mistakes small businesses make is not aggressively pursuing new markets. You can have the best product or service in your industry and still go out of business if people don't know you're there. Keep your company in the public eye by developing an effective advertising campaign.

Talk to other business owners to find out what works for them. Talk to your customers to learn what types of advertising appeal to them. Evaluate the features of your company and its products and services to determine which offer advantages over your competition. Implement a coordinated advertising program that exploits the best features of your business. The cost will vary widely depending on the market you're in, the medium you choose, and how often your ads run. Consider advertising jointly with other businesses to reduce cost.

Barter Goods

Trading goods and services directly with other businesses for something those businesses have that your business needs rather than for money can preserve precious cash. Most barter deals are worked out informally between businesses. For example, if you own a camera shop and your accountant is looking for a camera, you might negotiate a trade of one of your cameras for accounting service hours.

Bartering also takes place more formally under the auspices of organized nationwide barter exchange organizations. There are over 400 barter organizations in the United States today. For a list of the ones near you, call the International Reciprocal Trade Association (IRTA) at 703-759-1473.

Membership in one of these groups can cost as much as $500 the first year, plus annual fees of 4100 to $200. Members agree to provide their products and services to other members at their regular price. You are paid in credit or trade dollars, which you can use to purchase goods or services from other participants.

Don't Waste Time

Time is money. Study after study shows that most businesses waste 25 to 50 percent of the time it takes to produce a product or a unit of service. Even the best-run companies spend a significant amount of time performing tasks that add no value to their end products or services. Lost and wasted time can prevent your company from becoming a major competitor.

Time management is a relatively easy concept to grasp and exploit. Start by separating all your activities into two categories: Those that add value to your business and those that don't. Tasks like assembling product parts or shopping for a more competitive insurance policy clearly add value. Tasks like writing a sales report or carrying a part from one end of the factory to another may not add any value. These tasks should become the target of your efficiency analysis. If you don't need them, get rid of them.

Another time-saving technique is called *process flow mapping*. To map your business processes, start with a big sheet of paper and some Post-it notes. Tape the paper to the wall. Write every step involved in your business, from making a sales call to filling orders, on a Post-it note (one step per note). Stick the notes on the paper and draw lines connecting the steps in the order you perform them. Find wasted time by looking for steps that add no value, that are duplicated, or that can be combined. Can you speed up the process by having two activities go on concurrently rather than sequentially?

Opportunities to save time are painfully obvious once you start looking for them. Many operations are in such deplorable condition that there's plenty of low-hanging fruit to pick. No matter how many hours your business may have wasted today, the most critical time wasted is the time between now and when you start looking for ways to save time. A time management strategy will enable you to fuel new product development and new technology.

ADDING PEOPLE

Before you add employees, partners, or associates to your business, make sure that the increase in head count is justified by the workload and fits into your long-range business plan. Explore the alternatives. Write down the tasks that need to be done. Could you hire an assistant to do the job instead of a full-time employee or partner? Can you hire a temporary employee to get you through a short-term workload increase instead of hiring a permanent employee? People are expensive and add an additional dimension of management complexity to the business.

Equal Employment Laws

If you think you can hire and fire whomever you choose, think again. Although the doctrine known as employment at will is still a powerful influence in employment laws, it has been substantially weakened over the past decades by equal employment opportunity legislation. Designed to prevent discrimination, this legislation requires employers to base their hiring, wage, promotion, and firing policies solely on the needs of a particular job, not on a person's race, color, sex, national origin, or religion.

To avoid any problems, model your hiring practices on guidelines provided by the Equal Employment Opportunity Commission. You can order an EEOC hiring manual from one of the agency's regional offices. The EEOC also holds seminars on hiring practices, at which you can learn everything you need to know about affirmative action and discrimination. Contract your regional EEOC office for more information.

Job Analysis

Before you hire any employee, make sure you understand the requirements of the job you are filling. What kind of personality, experience, and education are needed? Perform a thorough job analysis before you start looking for candidates. Your analysis should answer the following questions:

- What are the mental and physical tasks involved in the job, such as judging, planning, managing, or lifting.
- What methods and equipment will be used to perform the job?
- Why does the job exist and what are its objectives? How does it relate to other positions in the company?
- What are the qualifications needed for this job, including training, knowledge, skills, and personality traits?

After you have analyzed the job, write a job description. This is an outline of how the job fits into the company. Start by writing down the job title and who the person will report to. Next, develop a job statement and summarize the job's goals, responsibilities, and duties. Finally, define how the job relates to other positions in the company. You can now create the recruitment material for the job ad campaign.

Wage Scales

You should consider the competitive aspects when you set a salary level for a job. If your salaries are not competitive, your employees will lack motivation, which can lead to high turnover rates. If you pay too much, you'll have to raise your prices, which could limit your competitiveness.

To determine what a competitive salary should be in your area, conduct a salary and benefits survey. Call personnel managers in other companies, recruiters, industry associations, labor organizations, and management consultants. Find out salary levels for the position you're filling, as well as any benefits offered, such as bonuses, health insurance, retirement plans, or life insurance plans.

Recruitment Ads

When developing recruitment ads, focus on selling the job and the company to prospective applicants. Your ads should be concise, yet make the job and company sound exciting. Include company descriptions, such as "fast-growing" or "dynamic." Tell the applicant about the excitement and challenge of the job, the money, and what he or she will get out of the job.

Many people who respond to recruitment ads are unqualified. You need to weed these people out before setting up interviews. One way to screen applicants is by asking for a resume in the ad. While resumes are not entirely reliable, they help you narrow the field of applicants. If you want to narrow the field further before you conduct face-to-face interviews, conduct phone interviews. Your goal is to eliminate people without the necessary experience by asking questions related to the job you want filled.

Before the interview, have candidates fill out an employment application. It should ask for specific information, such as educational background and work experience. You can buy generic application forms at an office supply store, or you can develop your own to meet your specific needs. Make sure the application form you use conforms to EEOC guidelines. Employment application forms cannot ask about arrests, race, sex, religion, marital status, pregnancy, child care, or sexual preference.

Testing Applicants

Be careful when testing applicants. Tests that demonstrate a key ability required for the job, such as typing, are perfectly legitimate. Personality and intelligence tests may violate EEOC regulations. If a certain group of minorities is rejected at a greater rate than other groups based on the test, or if it cannot be demonstrated that the test predicts probable success on the job, you could be in violation of EEOC regulations.

The interview is the true face-to-face test. One of the keys to a good interview is to put the prospective employee at ease. Most people are nervous during an interview. To help break the ice, you should begin the interview by explaining the job and describing the company, its business, its history, and future plans.

During the interview, observe the person and his or her dress, mannerisms, and words. Let the person talk freely so that he or she can reveal important information. For example, if a person complains about bosses he had in the past, it may be an indication that he has problems taking direction from others. When asking interview questions, keep the EEOC guidelines in mind.

Employee Records

After you interview an applicant, create a file containing the resume, the application, and your interview notes. If you hire the applicant, that file will become the person's employee file. Federal law requires that a job application be kept for at least three years after a person is hired. If you do not hire the applicant, keep the file for at least one year after the decision not to hire has been made. In today's legal climate, applicants sometimes sue an employer who has not hired them.

EMPLOYEE MORALE

One of the best ways to boost employees' morale is to increase their self-esteem. Improved productivity is also a byproduct of self-esteem. When employees have high self-esteem, they're much more productive. Self-esteem is one of the best single indicators of excellence in job performance. If you choose to ignore self-esteem issues, which is common practice in large corporations, you will be undercutting one of the biggest potential advantages small businesses have over their larger corporate counterparts.

The price of poor self-esteem among employees is obvious: It can cripple productivity. Workplace conflicts, tardiness, lying, absenteeism, high turnover, and poor attitudes about getting the job done are all correlated with low self-esteem. Where organizational esteem is low, employees spend work time reading help-wanted ads and daydreaming about other opportunities. Their commitment to the business goes no further than the next payday.

Another sign of poor self-esteem is an employee's reluctance to take risks. If you feel good about yourself, it's much easier to take risks. A company that's mired in an ultra-cautious risk avoidance posture rarely prospers in today's economic climate. Companies whose employees have high-self-esteem are usually the industry leaders. A case in point is Wal-Mart, which has meticulously concerned itself with self-esteem issues. The discount operation has grown from a single five-and-dime store into the nation's premier retailer. Wal-Mart employees are so proud of where they work, that they even have a company cheer. Go into a Wal-Mart and you know instantly that the employees are glad to be there.

How do you create a company climate that encourages high self-esteem? The first step is to create an environment in which you always have motivated employees who want to come to work. Set up guidelines for employees that establish the parameters necessary for the success of the business, such as always being on time. Draw up a list of guidelines and ask employees to sign the list, indicating that they understand the rules and will abide by them while they remain a part of your company.

If employees break the rules, they have no one to blame but themselves. They have to take charge of their own lives, and that's where self-esteem starts. When self-esteem is low, we blame others, including customers, coworkers, the economy, and management. When self-esteem is high, the employees bear the responsibility for the results they get.

COMPANY MISSION

Every company should have a clear mission statement that every employee can relate to. Significant increases in productivity can be achieved just by having this statement. Too often, employees see a business merely as a vehicle for making money for its owners. A mission statement clarifies the business's more fundamental objectives. Here are some examples of small-business mission statements:

> For a motel: To create hospitality that brings guests back.

> For a florist: Expressing deep feelings to others through the symbol of flowers.

> For a cleaning service: To be the best there is at everything we do.

When you develop a mission statement, keep it short and make sure your employees are involved in drafting it. Every employee should have a sense of ownership and be committed to achieving the goals and objectives of the company's mission.

Knowing the business's mission is the first step. Every person in your organization needs to know exactly what he or she can do to contribute to the company's mission. Employees need to know what their contribution means to the company and to them personally. If people believe that their work makes a difference, it boosts their self-esteem enormously. They need to know how their effort contributes to the overall success of the business.

Employee Communications

People in authority have a tendency to talk at their employees, not with them. When employees aren't listened to, they stop valuing their own opinions, and their self-esteem suffers. Listen to your employees when they talk to you. Diplomatically turn down bad ideas or those that are impossible to implement. Don't discourage the communication process, and always be looking for good ideas.

Employees respond best when their efforts are praised by management. Praise not only enhances self-esteem but also builds loyalty, which is the greatest single workplace motivator. Developing employee loyalty is a process that takes a committed effort. When you make the effort, you'll see and enjoy the benefits.

Employee Suggestions

All successful business owners are constantly looking for business improvement ideas. Your employees are one of the best sources of good ideas you have. They are often the people closest to the operations of the business. They are the ones who really know what the problems are and how to solve them.

Taking advantage of employee suggestions also increases morale. To get the most from your employee suggestion program, conduct regular meetings to discuss employee ideas. You can offer rewards to employees who come up with ideas that help the company become more efficient, but this may not be necessary. Employees are often satisfied with the feeling that they're contributing to the company.

Reward Programs

A good way to improve your staff's performance is to create incentives for superior work. You might establish a bonus system to reward people for more or better work. One way is to set a companywide goal, such as increasing sales. Offer rewards to employees if the goal is met to your satisfaction. If your employees help the company meet the goal, then everybody wins.

If you can't afford raises or bonuses, try to increase productivity by taking advantage of the fact that many employees grow bored or dissatisfied with the same job. Offer them the opportunity to switch into new areas where they can learn fresh skills. As employees become more enthusiastic about their jobs, their productivity will increase. Above all, remain flexible and always look for new ways to increase employee productivity. That's what gives small companies their competitive edge against larger and better capitalized firms.

PERFORMANCE PROBLEMS

Few business owners would admit that they condone incompetent employees. After all, employees who don't pull their weight will drag your company down. Unfortunately, most business owners talk a good game, but when it comes to disciplining marginal employees, they will often back down.

That can be dangerous to your business. Employees who don't perform up to standards hurt your business. If you don't confront their performance, it will inevitably worsen and threaten the morale of other employees. Confront undesired behavior as soon as it occurs. Don't let things build up until you're angry. Keep a cool, level head when talking to the employee. The last thing you want to do is embarrass the person.

Conduct the conversation in a private place where you cannot be overheard. When discussing the behavior in question, be as specific as possible. Define the problem in the context of what it means to the employee's effectiveness or the company's bottom line so that the employee understands the impact of this behavior.

Once you've stated the problem and are sure the employee understands your concerns, outline a plan for improvement. The plan should include detailed steps with measurable determinations of success. When the employee improves, be sure he or she knows it. If the employee doesn't improve, dismiss him or her and document the reason for the dismissal in his or her presence. Ask the dismissed employee to read and sign the dismissal form. If the employee refuses to sign, indicate that on the form.

HEALTH INSURANCE

In a recent poll conducted by *Money* magazine, small-business owners cited rising insurance costs, including those for health coverage, as their major expense concern. Health insurance is the fastest-growing small-business expense. Premiums for many small businesses have risen 70 percent in the past four years.

The size of small-business work forces compounds the problem. Some insurance companies don't like dealing with small companies because of the high administrative costs that result from the higher employee turnover rates. Small businesses also represent a greater risk. For example, one catastrophic expense, such as saving the life of a premature baby, can wipe out the insurance company's profit on a small business for years. For these reasons, most small companies do not qualify for lower group rates and pay considerably more per employee for coverage than their larger corporate counterparts. Here are some options to consider to reduce your medical insurance costs:

- Check into the availability of COBRA coverage. COBRA was an act passed by Congress that allows former employees of a company with at least twenty employees to keep their company health plan for at least eighteen to thirty-six months after leaving the company. Under the COBRA plan, a former employee retains the exact policy he or she had while working for another company. The individual must pay the premium to receive coverage. It may be cheaper for you to pay for an employee's COBRA coverage than to add the employee to your own policy.

- Find out if health insurance is available from any organization to which you belong or for which you are eligible. Many religious, fraternal, and professional organizations provide health insurance for their members at competitive rates. If your business is eligible for membership in an association, find out which ones offer health insurance coverage.

- Check with the local chamber of commerce. Many of them offer MEWA (Multiple Employer Welfare Arrangements) health insurance coverage to small businesses and the self-employed. Since several employers are bunched together under the same plan, this coverage allows employers with few employees to benefit from the cost savings of a plan with many members. Some local business organizations also provide MEWA coverage.

Shop carefully for individual coverage. If none of the options mentioned works for you, your only course may be to purchase individual health insurance. This is not difficult, but can be expensive. Individual policies are the most expensive type of health insurance available. Call every available insurance agent to find the best price and coverage. The insurance market is extremely competitive, so it pays to shop for any insurance policy.

One way to reduce the cost of health insurance is to raise the deductible on your policy, particularly if you are in good health and rarely see a physician. If you purchase new health insurance, be aware of the fact that most preexisting conditions may not be covered for a period of time. The health insurance industry is promoting reforms that would remove the preexisting condition stipulations, but for now they remain in force on most policies.

Blue Cross and Blue Shield are required to insure all people without regard to most of the criteria commercial insurers normally use. Blue Cross often charges more because it can't refuse to cover those with prior problems or those who live in high-risk areas. A one-person business can expect to pay even higher rates, but if you can afford it, Blue Cross is readily available.

Some states, such as Hawaii, Vermont, Oregon, and Florida, are implementing their own universal health plans. Minnesota has started Minnesota Care, a comprehensive program of state-subsidized health care. New York has passed legislation that will force commercial insurers to take all applicants. New Jersey has passed a subsidized insurance plan. If your business is located in one of these states, you may be able obtain affordable coverage.

With all these possibilities, which way should you go? First, eliminate insurers that make you feel uncomfortable for any reason. Second, consult a knowledgeable third party and use his or her judgment to help narrow the field. Talk to industry colleagues and incorporate their judgments into your decision-making process. Subject the surviving plans to a financial test. How much are you willing to pay for monthly premiums and actual medical expenses? Consider the out-of-pocket expenses, the deductible, and copayments as well as the monthly premiums.

RETIREMENT PLANS

In this section, we'll cover the major retirement plans and show you how they work. We'll also discuss the advantages and disadvantages of the different plans and what it takes to set them up. The costs for the plans vary depending on how you implement them and which type you select.

Salary Employer Plan (SEP)

SEP retirement plans are popular with companies that have ten or fewer employees. You simply open an Individual Retirement Account (IRA) for each employee and yourself. SEP plans are available through mutual funds, banks, and insurance companies. Many of these companies offer multiple investment options.

You set contribution amounts, which can be as much as 15 percent of each person's income, up to a maximum of $30,000 an employee. The percentage must be the same for all employees, but you can change it yearly. Employees cannot contribute to the SEP directly, but they do pay yearly a custodial fee to the company administering the plan. They also decide where the funds in their account are to be invested.

If the simplicity of a SEP appeals to you but you don't want to make all the contributions yourself, look into a salary reduction SEP. Like a regular SEP, it's basically a collection of employee IRA accounts. However, the contributions are made by the employees and not you unless you elect to participate. Fifty percent or more of eligible employees must participate in the plan to pass IRS rules. In addition, you must have no more than twenty-five employees to qualify for a SEP.

Profit Sharing

If your profits fluctuate from year to year, you might benefit from a profit-sharing plan. Under this arrangement, you can choose how much of your company's profits to invest on your employees' behalf each year. You may either specify the investment account the money goes into or leave that decision up to the employee. You can reward people by giving them a larger percentage as long as you treat all employees equally. If your company has a bad year, you can cut or eliminate the contribution.

Profit sharing can be used to motivate employees and associates. For example, you might promise that if your employees meet a certain sales goal, you'll add an amount equal to some percentage of their pay to their profit-sharing plan. In effect, you are conveying the message, "If the company makes money, then those that helped make it happen will also make money."

Money Purchase Plan

If your company's profits are stable, you could choose a money purchase plan. You promise to set aside a fixed percentage of payroll every year for the employees' retirement, regardless of your profit or loss position. The annual contribution can be as much as 25 percent of their salary, up to $30,000 per employee. The disadvantage of the plan is that you must contribute in both good and lean years. The retirement outlays become part of your overhead. If you can't make the payment, you have to seek a waiver from the IRS or risk paying a 10 percent penalty. The advantage of the plan is that you can set aside more money per employee than is allowed under a profit-sharing plan.

Target Benefit Plan

A target benefit plan allows you to decide how much annual income each employee should get after retirement. You work with an actuary to allocate your contributions to meet your retirement goals. Certain employees, including yourself, can have a larger sum set aside for them each year. Target plans are popular with companies employing older people. The annual contribution limit is 25 percent of a person's salary with a $30,000 annual limit per employee.

401(k) Plans

If you want employees to contribute to their own retirement plan, consider a 401(k) plan. This is by far the most complex of the contribution plans and is suitable for companies with twenty or more employees. If you're competing against big companies for new hires, a 401(k) may be a necessity, since 40 percent of large businesses have them.

Your employees can contribute up to 20 percent of their salaries to the plan. Your company can match all, some, or none of the employees' contribution as long as the total does not exceed 25 percent of a person's salary or $30,000 per employee. Even a match as small as 10 cents on the dollar is usually enough to encourage employees to participate.

Workers' Compensation

Worker's compensation was created as an equitable, no-fault system of ensuring that workers receive adequate care in the event of a work-related injury. The costs associated with workers' compensation have increased significantly over the years. Employer premiums have tripled in recent years, and the average cost per claim climbed 200 percent in the same period. Medical costs now account for 40 percent of the total compensation costs.

In response to the cost crisis, some states have undertaken sweeping workers' compensation reforms and have been successful in curtailing some of the excessive costs of the program. The best model of workers' compensation reform is that in Oregon, where employers have seen a 30 percent reduction in workers' compensation rates since the state passed new laws in 1990.

Implementing a strategy for trimming costs depends on your company's safety track record. If you've had a number of claims over the years, focus on promoting workplace safety and accident prevention. A commitment to safety starts at the top. There is a tendency to blame the employee. However, as the business owner, you have to take responsibility for changing the safety record at your company.

Start by drafting a comprehensive set of safety guidelines that make sense to every employee. If you already have guidelines, and you're still having more than your share of accidents, review the current safety guidelines with everybody. If your safety program is inadequate, adopt new measures to decrease the incidence of worker accidents. Review your safety files to identify unsafe areas or practices that prompted claims in the past, and update your safety guidelines accordingly.

A new safety policy is meaningless unless your employees are aware of it and support the program. Be sure that the new policy is communicated to every employee and that employees understand how it works. Distribute safety handbooks to emphasize that safety is a top priority. You can reduce workers' compensation costs by improving the way you treat employee claims. Early intervention is extremely important. All interaction with an injured employee should be open and supportive.

Legitimate interest on your part not only lets the employees know that you're concerned about their welfare, but also helps get expectations out in the open. Your primary goal should be to get the employee back to work. If an employee can't yet return to his or her old job, offer a temporary light duty assignment. Employers who make an effort to get employees back to work as soon as possible generally spend less on workers' compensation. Insurance companies use the number of workdays lost to calculate your premiums.

The estimated amount of workers' compensation fraud perpetrated by small-business employees is relatively minor. However, you should be aware of some of the warning signs of fraudulent claims. Here are some of the indicators:

- The claimant has a history of injuries and lost time.
- The claimant is never home when called.
- The claimant has checks mailed to a post office box.
- The claimant hires a lawyer immediately.
- The claimant fails to keep doctor's appointments.
- There were no witness to the accident.

Although these factors don't always indicate fraud, be on the alert to irregularities in an employee's claim. The rising cost of workers' compensation will not be stemmed any time soon, but at least state insurance officials and legislators are aware of the need for reform. Keep abreast of the status of workers' compensation in your state. Your insurance agent or trade association can provide you with information or direct you to the most appropriate source. Your state's department of insurance should also be a good source of information.

As a business owner, you can't totally control your workers' compensation costs. But that doesn't mean you shouldn't try to make changes where you can in your own company. By preventing workplace injuries and taking an active approach in dealing with employee claims, you can save money on workers' compensation. In the process, you'll create a safer and more productive workplace.

SUMMARY AND CONCLUSIONS

This concludes the last chapter in the book. A number of business operating issues were discussed to assure the ongoing success of your business. We went through several self-assessment tests that you can use periodically to determine how your business is doing. Next, we talked about techniques you can employ to assure that you have satisfied customers and can continue to grow your business. A number of cost reduction strategies to help you improve the competitiveness of your business were discussed. Several pages were devoted to the important issues of hiring people. This led us into a discussion of employment and business-related insurance and retirement programs. We wish you and your business venture the best of luck and all the success in the world. Go for it!

Appendix A

New-Business Ideas

Many of the new-business ideas that are listed in this section were obtained from *Entrepreneur* magazine's Small Business Development catalog. This catalog includes business start-up guides that you can order direct from the Entrepreneur Group, the publishers of the catalog. For further information, write:

> Entrepreneur Group
> P.O. Box 2072
> Knoxville, IA 50198-2072
> 1-800-421-2300

Our alphabetical directory of business ideas gives you a brief overview of what it takes to set up and run each type of business. Use it to develop your ideas for a personal business and to create a list of viable options that fit with your abilities and style.

ADVERTISING AGENCY

This is a tough, competitive business, but if you are looking for excitement and creativity, it's a business to consider. Every business needs to develop a successful advertising program. It is a competitive industry, but if you prove that you are good, it can be very profitable.

ADVERTISING SPECIALTY

Businesses, organizations, schools, and sports teams spend almost $4 billion a year to have their names, logos, and messages printed on pens, key chains, hats, T-shirts, and other objects that can be printed on at relatively low cost.

ANTIQUE SALES AND RESTORATION

The profits to be made by collecting and restoring are well known. Businesses that restore old furniture and collectibles represent a multimillion-dollar industry that continues to grow.

APARTMENT PREPARATION SERVICE

If you're handy with tools, this could be a business for you to consider. Rather than employ full-time maintenance people, many apartment owners and managers hire outside services to clean, paint, and repair vacant units before the next tenant moves in. With an unusually low investment, you can cash in on the need to bring rental units up to rentable condition.

AUDIO BOOKSTORE

Get in on a ground-floor opportunity to own an audio bookstore, one of the fastest-growing businesses of the decade. Many retail businesses suffer from reduced consumer spending in their first two years of operation. The average audio bookstore grew by 30 percent per year in its first two years of operation. Audio bookstores are just like regular bookstores, except that the inventory is all books on audio cassettes.

AUTO DETAILING

This vital part of the huge automotive aftermarket can be extremely profitable. On a volume basis, detailers "prep" new and trade-in used cars for dealers. The highest profits come from doing maintenance on autos owned by private individuals.

BAKERY (SPECIALTY)

Freshly baked breads, bagels, cakes, and cookies are universally loved and appreciated. That's why people are flocking to specialty bakeries today to savor the exotic breads, coffees, and pastries.

BALLOON DELIVERY SERVICE

All around the country, people are giving bouquets of balloons instead of flowers. With an almost universal market and only small amounts of start-up capital needed, this business is relatively easy to start.

BAR/TAVERN/NIGHTCLUB

What other business offers an over 800 percent return? When you sell drinks, a $20 gallon of wholesale liquor sells for $1.50 or more an ounce. Your profit is $1972 a gallon. What's more, your business is almost recession-proof since, in bad times, bar activity increases. If you're friendly, outgoing, and sociable and have good business and accounting sense, consider the bar business.

BEAUTY SUPPLY STORE

Americans spend $1.3 billion on beauty supplies annually. Women are leading the explosion, making almost 80 percent of all beauty supply purchases. But you'll also find a growing male market.

BED AND BREAKFAST INN

What does it take to be the owner of a bed and breakfast inn? Innkeepers come from all walks of life and all parts of the country. Proper preparation and realistic goals are essential to the success of this business.

BODY CARE BOUTIQUE

All over the country, boutiques specializing in lavish personal products, including herbal shampoos, floral soaps, and perfumes made from natural products, are making this a profitable business.

BOOKSTORE (USED)

The secret to this business is that you deal only in books with established track records. Unlike new book stores, you know which books sell and which don't. With high new book prices, customers are flocking to bargain book outlets.

BUSINESS BROKERAGE

With the average business selling for $100,000, a business broker can make sizable profits. If you enjoy a challenge, have strong sales and financial skills, and can take rejection in stride, you can rise to the top in this demanding field.

CARPET CLEANING SERVICE

With a small amount of up-front cash and some knowledge of the industry, you can get in on this booming service business. You can quickly expand to the point where you are bringing in up to $1,000 per day using the right marketing and management practices.

CAR WASH

There are more than 100 million cars, vans, and pickups on the road today and only 22,000 car washes to serve them—there's plenty of room for growth in this industry.

CHECK CASHING SERVICE

This business has nothing to do with banks. It's not federally regulated, doesn't make loans, and doesn't offer checking or savings accounts. It simply cashes checks. An estimated 20 percent of Americans have no formal banking relationship, and that's a lot of people.

CHEMICAL LAWN CARE/MAINTENANCE

There are two low-budget ways to enter the lawn care field: maintenance and chemical lawn care. The cheapest way is lawn maintenance, and the second is the chemical part of the business, where you help limit lawn pests, weed, and fertilize lawns.

CHILDREN'S BOOKSTORE

Children's bookstores are one of the last areas of bookselling that hasn't been swallowed up by the big chains.

CHILDREN'S CLOTHING STORE

With the current "baby boom" promising to continue through the 1990s, this should be one of the hottest retail businesses for years to come. You don't need any technical knowledge, and manufacturers will help you establish your inventory. If you hire the right people and learn how the market works, you don't need prior retailing experience.

CHILDREN'S FITNESS CENTERS

Budget-cutting schools are eliminating exercise and fitness programs, and yet the need for children's fitness is greater than ever. Children's fitness centers are filling this the need across the nation. Both profit potential and personal rewards are high in this growing industry.

CHILD SERVICES

With so many parents working, child services are very important. The five most popular are diaper delivery, nanny placement, day care, children's camp, and creative dance programs.

COFFEE AND TEA STORE

Gourmet coffee and tea stores are currently making good money, with consumers willing to pay $6 to $9 a pound for fancy coffee blends. You need top-quality gourmet coffee beans and teas, a prime location with plenty of foot traffic, and a friendly atmosphere to make it in this business.

COLLECTIBLES BROKER

Collectibles brokers buy, sell, and appraise anything collected—from sports memorabilia and historical documents to rare coins and movie posters. You can start this business from your home with a computer, a fax machine, and a telephone.

COLLECTION AGENCY

Many businesses have a hard time collecting money. There's plenty of room for collection agencies, but you must know what you're doing before you go up against the established collection businesses.

COMPACT DISC STORE

Today, CD players are found not only in many American homes, but also in many new cars and anywhere you find music lovers. The market is still relatively new and provides tremendous opportunities for stores that specialize in selling CDs.

COMPUTER CONSULTING AND TEMPORARY-HELP SERVICE

This is a temporary agency that offers a complete range of computer services, from data entry, computer operations, and systems analysis to programming in high-level languages.

COMPUTER LEARNING CENTER

Computer learning centers are multimedia learning facilities using the latest computer technology, CD-ROM information, and on-line services to enhance the educational experience.

COMPUTER REPAIR SERVICE

Businesses today don't have time to send computers to manufacturers for repair. Many rely on independent computer specialists to deliver the service they need. You need some computer background and employees who know how to service and repair computers.

CONSIGNMENT/RESALE CLOTHING STORE

This is a low-investment, high-margin business. It's recession-proof and ideal for absentee ownership. Selling high-quality preowned clothing is ideal if you have a knack for dealing with people and good negotiating skills. You don't need any retail apparel experience to start this business.

CONSULTING

Many entrepreneurs are discovering how to turn their most marketable skill into a profitable consulting business. It takes at least a year to start up a consulting business.

CONVENIENCE FOOD STORE

Sound business management is the key to success in this $10 billion industry. The average start-up cost for a convenience store is $200,000.

COUPON MAILER SERVICE

Small businesses are always looking for ways to save on advertising. Coupon mailers allow many different companies to group promotional coupons and ads in one envelope to reduce costs. Several large companies handle coupon mailers on a national basis. However, there is still a demand for mailings that serve small businesses and local markets.

CRAFTS

If you have a talent for working with your hands and an ability to recognize a salable handicraft, you can start this business from your home. Craft people sell through flea markets, swap meets, retail stores, and direct mail, and through consignment stores.

DATING SERVICE

There are several ways to get into this business, from the one-on-one personal matchmaker service to an expanded video or computerized matching service.

DAY-CARE SERVICE

Within the next ten years, there will be about 11 million children in the United States under the age of six. There are presently only 1.2 million spaces available in preschools. This is a business you can start in your home or in a preschool center. Many states have strict licensing requirements for day-care centers.

DESKTOP PUBLISHING

With today's page-composition software and laser printers, you can turn your personal computer into a profitable desktop publishing center. You can make camera-ready typeset pages (e.g., brochures, fliers, etc.) for your customers at a good profit.

DIAPER DELIVERY SERVICE

Cotton diapers are the very best for your child, and people are concerned about the effect on the environment of plastic diapers. As a result, thousands of parents are turning to diaper delivery services. The demand for reusable diapers is growing, and diaper delivery services are meeting that demand.

DRY CLEANING

You can be the owner of a successful dry cleaning business if you know the right techniques. The key to the business is location and volume.

ENVIRONMENTAL SERVICES

Tough new federal regulations have environmentally unfriendly companies reeling. They are being forced to clean up their act and are turning to environmental services for consultation and training. Environmental services for which markets exist include everything from indoor air quality testing to paper and plastics recycling.

EVENT PLANNING SERVICE

Corporate meetings and conventions, reunions, fund raisers, weddings, and other social events have one thing in common—they require planning. If you are good with details, have an imagination, and enjoy people, an event planning business might be for you.

EXECUTIVE RECRUITING

Executive recruiters are more specialized then employment agencies and concentrate on filling executive positions. Regional recruitment firms can efficiently tap into the needs of the executive market.

FAMILY HAIR SALON

Family salons cater to the hair care needs of the whole family. You don't have to be a beautician or barber to take advantage of this opportunity. There are plenty of qualified people out there to fill these jobs. You need to be a manager with a flair for promotion.

FINANCIAL AID SERVICES

Financial aid services are making college affordable for students by offering them choices they never thought they had. They combine their expert knowledge of the financial aid system with databases full of alternative financial aid sources. These businesses charge a fee to assist students in obtaining educational loans.

FINANCIAL BROKER

Success as a financial broker lies in knowing some basic financial principles being able to promote a highly competitive business. You work with clients that need money and lending institutions to put together loans. This profession demands skill and long hours to start up.

FLAT-FEE REAL ESTATE AGENCY

You charge a flat-fee commission to do the detail work of writing appraisals, helping with negotiations, financing, and closing. You save your clients thousands of dollars, and make a good profit in the process.

Flower Shop

Over the past ten years, retail flower shops' annual sales have blossomed from $2.3 billion to $4.3 billion. It's a great business if you like customer contact.

Food and Party Catering Service

Thousands of people start catering services with no more than a kitchen and a few favorite recipes. This is a great business for a couple.

Food Court Restaurant

As the number of shopping centers grows, so does the food court restaurant business. Food court restaurants are often located in shopping malls and can make higher profits than their freestanding counterparts.

Food Delivery Service

Many people today are so busy that they have their food delivered to them. In this business, you contract with a local restaurant to deliver food for a small fee, which is paid by the customer in addition to the menu price. You pocket the change and a percentage of the food bill.

Freelance Writing Business

Freelance writing is a low-investment business you can run from your home. To be successful, you must be able to market your writing abilities. The freelance writing business is 30 percent writing skills and 70 percent selling skills.

Frozen Yogurt Shop

Frozen yogurt tastes great and has about half the calories of its counterpart ice cream and one-fifth the fat. The industry is maturing and is highly competitive.

Gift Baskets

Here is a job where you can use your creativity, control your work hours, and work at your home creating gift baskets for every occasion to make excellent money.

Graphic Design

Every business needs a recognizable image, used in everything from letterheads to logos, to proclaim its separate identity. Businesses need graphic designers to create these images. If you have a graphics design background, consider this business.

Health Food/Vitamin Store

Here's a way to capitalize on the demand for natural foods and health products. This is a stable growth business.

Herb Farming

Herbs are gaining popularity in America. Gourmet restaurants and families are seeking out year-round sources for herbs. Herbs are also used for medicines and cosmetics. These are just a few examples of the overall potential in herb farming.

HOME COMPUTER

There are hundreds of ways to make money at home with your personal computer. Doing contract work for small businesses and overflow work for large businesses are two examples.

HOME HEALTH-CARE AGENCY

Home health-care agencies deliver quality care to patients at home for a fraction of the cost of hospital care. It is the wave of the future.

HOME INSPECTION SERVICE

With the high cost of homes today, people are using home inspection services to help ensure that they are getting a good investment. To meet the demand, the number of home inspectors has been growing rapidly. Membership in the American Society of Home Inspectors (ASHI) has grown significantly.

HOME REMODELING SERVICE

Americans spend over $100 billion a year on home remodeling. You can specialize in a particular area or offer the entire spectrum of remodeling services.

HOUSE PAINTING

Interior and exterior house painting is one of the least expensive businesses to get into because tools and equipment are minimal. You can run this business from your home.

ICE CREAM STORE

Entrepreneurs all over the country are succeeding with small ice cream stores featuring super-premium or gourmet ice creams and the nostalgia of old-fashioned parlors. According to the International Ice Cream Association, the market for gourmet ice cream is growing annually.

IMAGE CONSULTING

Image consulting can be a very profitable business. You can help individuals enhance their personal appearance and communication skills or teach corporate employees to project the desired corporate image.

IMPORT/EXPORT

Top import/export agents make a lot of money by matching buyers and sellers in different countries. You need initial contacts before you start this business.

INFORMATION BROKER

If you have a computer, modem, printer, and some research skills, you can join this industry. Information brokers locate information requested by clients for a fixed or variable fee.

INSTANT PRINT

Everyone needs copying and printing services. Business clients with an ongoing need for printed forms, promotional materials, and invoices dominate your customer base. You need a good location for this business.

INSTANT SIGN STORE

Computerization has revolutionized the sign industry. You don't need sign-making experience, because the equipment is easy to use. You need creative skills, because the client will often ask you to create the finished sign artwork.

INSURANCE RESTORATION SERVICE

Insurance restoration businesses specialize in helping clients repair properties damaged by floods, earthquakes, fires, vandalism, or other catastrophes. You get paid by the insurance company.

INTERIOR DESIGNER

If you have basic drawing, conceptual, and interior design skills, a flair for decorating, and a good eye for details, you can make money at this business.

JANITORIAL SERVICE

With low start-up costs and little experience required, a janitorial service is an extremely simple business. Every business needs janitorial services.

LANGUAGE TRANSLATION SERVICES

If you are bilingual or can hire bilingual employees to work for you, you can make outstanding profits. Language translation services are in high demand by individuals, organizations, heads of state, and local governments.

LAUNDROMAT

This business runs itself. You can net a profit as an absentee owner if you have the right business location and the start-up capital.

LIMOUSINE SERVICE

Aside from making a nice income, you will mingle with some of the most influential people in your city. However, the cost of a new limousine may be prohibitive. Look for good used vehicles.

LINGERIE SHOP

Lingerie sales have recently increased by more than 30 percent, and continue to rise. This is a specialized retail market that demands a perfect location and an upper-class client base.

LIQUIDATED-GOODS BROKER

The key to this business is finding sellers and buyers of distressed merchandise. You deal with retail merchandise, but there are no specific location needs and no costly facilities or equipment. Start-up costs are minimal, overhead is light, and you can start part-time from home.

LIQUOR STORE

Liquor stores are recession-proof and can be very profitable. However, watch out for the chain stores. Even a store in the right location can be destroyed if a chain moves in across the street.

LUBE SHOP

Americans spend about $8 billion a year on oil changes. Convenience and economy are the main reasons for the success of lube shops.

MAID SERVICE

Maid service is predicted to be one of the hottest business prospects through the 1990s. Low overhead, high profit potential, and low start-up costs make this an easy business to get into.

MAIL ORDER

With more people shopping through the mail, this is a growing industry. You can start a small mail-order business with a few hundred dollars and can work from home. There are a lot of books out on the subject, so research the industry well before you get started.

MARKETING A FAMILY RECIPE

Entrepreneurs are creating specialty foods by creating retail food products from unique recipes—everything from sauces and sandwiches to condiments and cheeses. According to the National Association for the Specialty Food Trade, this is a multibillion-dollar industry.

MEDICAL CLAIMS PROCESSING

A medical claims processor helps clients fill out claim forms and get the benefits they rightly deserve. As the population ages and their medical needs increase, the demand for this service can only grow.

MICRO BREWERY

Micro breweries combined with restaurants and bars are being discovered by Americans who like freshly brewed beer. This is an expensive business to start. The brewery equipment alone can cost in excess of $300,000.

MOBILE AUTO INSPECTION

High new car prices are encouraging a lot of people to buy used cars. Mobile auto inspectors inspect used cars for the potential buyer. Instead of taking the car to an auto service shop, the auto inspector drives to the car the buyer is considering. The service is convenient for both the buyer and the seller.

MOBILE AUTOMOTIVE WINDOW SERVICES

Over 75 percent of windshield damage is repairable. Most people would rather pay you $35 to $55 to fix the windshield than pay a glass shop $200 to $1,000 to replace it. Auto window repair equipment is relatively inexpensive to obtain, and with a minimum amount of training, it's easy to use.

MOBILE DISC JOCKEY

If you enjoy music and have good management skills, this business may be for you. Some of the most profitable DJ businesses are operated by people who hire DJs to work the shows at clubs and special company events.

MOBILE FROZEN YOGURT

Frozen yogurt is a hot item, and sales figures prove it. According to market research, frozen yogurt mobile sales are a $1 billion annual business.

MULTILEVEL MARKETING

If you'd like to start your own business with a minimum investment, work out of your home, and keep your job, then multilevel marketing may be just the opportunity you're looking for. The goal of multilevel marketing is to sell products through a network of distributors. The distributors are allowed to recruit other distributors to sell directly to customers, as well as to other distributors. With a small initial investment, the potential for income can be significant.

NANNY PLACEMENT

A nanny placement service helps families find qualified, reliable nannies. It charges a finder's fee for the service.

NEWSLETTER PUBLISHING

If you're looking for a business that can net you a sizable return on your time, newsletter publishing is worth considering. Over the last ten years, this industry has grown by more than 130 percent.

ONE-HOUR PHOTO

If the location is right, with less than 1,000 square feet and a good marketing plan, your one-hour photo store can be very profitable. The equipment is expensive.

OPERATING A 900 NUMBER

Pay-per-call services have exploded into a billion-dollar industry in the last decade. Services offered include everything from stock tips to astrological forecasts to opinion polls.

PACKAGING AND SHIPPING

There is plenty of opportunity to make money helping people and businesses who need to have items packed and shipped. These one-stop shops package and send just about any item, using one of the many national carriers. It doesn't take much to get started in this business.

PARKING LOT CLEANING

Parking lot cleaning has become the latest service to come out of the diverse cleaning industry and make it big. Your market is not only apartment complexes but also, for example, hospital parking lots, school grounds, and shopping center lots.

PERSONAL SHOPPING SERVICE

This business has an extremely low start-up cost and high profit potential. All one needs is a phone, an answering machine, and some business cards to get started.

PERSONALIZED CHILDREN'S BOOKS

Personalized children's books are a $14 million industry. Using a personal computer and laser printer, personalized book entrepreneurs add the child's name, home town, friends, and favorite activity to the prewritten copy of one of many exciting titles. The result is a custom book featuring the child's experiences.

PET SHOP

There are 60 million pet-owning households in America. Pet shops offer one of the highest net profit percentages in retailing.

PET SITTING

Pet sitters go to people's homes and care for their pets while the owners are away. And because many pet owners still don't know pet sitters exist, they're as grateful for your service as you are for their business, and will pay for it.

PHYSICAL FITNESS CENTER

This recreational/sports business has excellent profit potential. It doesn't require any technical knowhow and allows you to help people feel better about themselves.

PINBALL AND VIDEO ARCADE

Video game rooms are one of the hottest businesses today. If you are interested in a business with high profit and no bookkeeping problems, this is a good cash-only business to consider.

PIZZERIA

This business takes a lot of hard work, but it can be very lucrative. You need a good product, lots of creativity, business smarts, and determination to start one.

POOL CLEANING AND REPAIR SERVICE

To get started in this field, you need a truck, some general equipment, and repair tools. Many people who have pools do not want to be bothered with pool cleaning and maintenance.

PRIVATE INVESTIGATOR

Most of today's private investigators don't work at finding hardened criminals, but work on civil cases for private parties or corporate clients. They investigate cheating spouses or fraud cases, track down missing people, and perform background checks on prospective employees. Many states have strict licensing requirements for private investigators.

PROFESSIONAL ORGANIZER

Professional organizers typically charge individuals and businesses $40 to $125 an hour to help them become more efficient and organized. With a minimal investment, individuals can turn their organizational strengths into cash.

PROPERTY TAX CONSULTANT

About 30 percent of the population are paying more than they should in property taxes. Armed with an arsenal of property tax weapons, the property tax consultant negotiates tax adjustments and refunds for clients who have been overcharged on their property tax. They get paid a fee plus a percentage of the refund.

REAL ESTATE INVESTMENT

No other investment offers the advantages, income return, and increase in value that real estate does. Many Americans have made fortunes in real estate, either by themselves or by putting deals together for clients.

RECYCLING CONSULTANT/BROKER

As a broker, you analyze office waste and implement recycling programs for businesses, cities, counties, and municipalities. Most recycling consultants have a background in recycling.

REFERRAL SERVICE

People are so busy today that they do not have time to research their options when they need a dentist, doctor, mechanic, or other service provider. This is where the referral service comes in. You do the research necessary to fine a reputable provider for your customers' needs.

RESTAURANT

Americans spend close to $175 billion a year dining out, and that number just keeps growing. This business is not risk-free and is highly competitive.

RESUME-WRITING SERVICE

Even educated people often don't have the necessary skills to effectively write a persuasive and promotional resume. To start this business, you need a good command of the English language, a computer with word processing software, an interest in people, and the ability to market your services well. You can run this business from home.

SANDWICH AND DELI SHOP

Sandwich shop owners all across the country are doing well with these businesses. You need a good location and excellent product that keeps people coming back.

SECRETARIAL AND WORD PROCESSING SERVICE

With good technical and marketing skills, you can start small and upgrade when your business volume increases. More businesses are using independent secretarial and word processing services to reduce their overhead.

SELF-IMPROVEMENT AND AWARENESS SEMINARS

If you're a good public speaker, enjoy dealing with people, and have a drive to help others, the personal improvement business is worth considering. Organized seminars and workshops have proliferated across the country. These seminars pull in crowds all across the nation, offering everything from relaxation to habit control, marriage enhancement, and business self-analysis.

SENIOR DAY CARE

By the year 2000, the number of Americans over seventy-five will nearly double. The cost of convalescent homes and private nurses for the elderly is skyrocketing. The market for senior day care can only expand. These centers offer a variety of health, social, and other related services, including leisure activities, exercise classes, and companionship.

SILK PLANT SHOP

Entrepreneurs across the nation are opening retail and home-based silk plant and flower shops, selling to the millions of homeowners, apartment residents and businesses looking for beautiful, trouble-free silk plants. You can run this business from your home or open your own retail store. Your investment is dependent upon the size of the operation you want to start.

SPECIALTY GIFTS

Stores specializing in gift items are opening in urban centers across the country. Specialty gift stores sell everything from teddy bears to specialized footwear to chocolate novelties.

SPORTS MEMORABILIA

The sports memorabilia business really started to grow about ten years ago. Today, it's a multibillion-dollar retail industry and one of the most dynamic retail enterprises of the decade.

STREET VENDING

With smart promotional skills, the right location, and the right inventory, you can make high profit margins in this business, which covers a variety of products.

TELEPHONE ANSWERING SERVICE

Small businesses are growing at a rapid rate. Because of their size, many need answering services to cover them outside of business hours.

TEMPORARY HELP SERVICE

Nine out of ten U.S. companies use temporary help. In the temporary help business, you have no stock to buy or inventory to maintain. When the economy gets tough, more businesses cut back on staff and fill in with temporary help.

TRANSPORTATION FREIGHT BROKER

As a freight broker, you arrange freight transportation for your clients. You need to know about the freight business and interstate freight laws before you can start this business.

TRAVEL AGENCY

If you love travel, this is the ideal business to be in. Airlines, cruise ship operators, hotels, and tour promoters will invite you on free trips. They know that if you enjoy yourself, you will be much more inclined to recommend the trip to your customers. Travel agents book over 90 percent of all foreign travel and 60 percent of all domestic travel.

T-SHIRT SHOP

You can make good money, no matter where you're located. Everyone buys T-shirts, from tourists to movie companies, college professors to teenagers. There's minimal investment, few equipment requirements, and good absentee ownership potential. This business offers high profit margins once you're up and running.

UNPACKING SERVICE

Some people think that low start-up costs mean low profits. In unpacking services, low investment means high earnings. With nearly 43 million Americans moving each year, unpacking services are very much in demand in the moving industry. They unload boxes, organize belongings, hang paintings, put dishes away, and arrange furniture.

USED AND CONSIGNMENT FURNITURE

You show merchandise provided by the owners and pay them for it after it is sold. You are an independent sales agent for the person supplying the goods. All you need is a knack for dealing with the public.

UTILITY BILL AUDITING

Utility bill auditors look for billing errors in water, sewage, gas, telephone, and other utility bills. Auditors are paid a percent of the overpayments that they find.

VENDING MACHINES

Vending machines are a $22 billion annual industry. Route size and the number of machines one owns determine an owner's profit potential. A soda machine in a good location can move 1,200 cans a month.

VIDEOCASSETTE RENTALS

This business offers numerous advantages, and profit potential as well. You get a lot of help from video manufacturers and distributors. Your equipment needs are minimal.

VIDEO SERVICES

Part- and full-time video service specialists are using common video cameras to start video filming businesses in major metropolitan areas. They film everything from weddings to special business events.

WEDDING PLANNING SERVICE

Wedding planners work with the bride and groom and their families to create an exciting, memorable occasion. You'll help the couple stay within their budget and select a location, caterer, florist, music, cake, and much more. You need to plan ahead, hire the best talent for the best price, cultivate good community contacts, and have good organizational skills.

WEDDING SHOP

Wedding shops offer everything people need for weddings, including tuxedo rentals, photography service, bridal services, food catering, and everything else necessary to put on a wedding.

WELCOMING SERVICE

People moving into large communities today often find it hard to acclimate themselves to their new surroundings. To ease the moving process, start a welcoming service. Local businesses pay welcoming service operators to introduce their products and services to area newcomers.

WOMEN'S CLOTHING STORE

The secrets to this business are location and knowing the tastes of your market. With the right combination of these ingredients, plus smart pricing and advertising, you can build a profitable women's clothing store.

Appendix B

The Best of the New Franchises

Franchising is a multibillion dollar annual industry. With more than 3,000 companies offering franchise opportunities, it might appear that there is no chance for newcomers to find a viable franchise opportunity. Nothing could be further from the truth. In addition to all the familiar franchise names, smaller companies are continually turning to franchising as a means of expanding their businesses.

Appendix B lists several hundred relatively new franchise companies along with their addresses. Write to those that interest you and ask for a free brochure describing their franchise offering. A complete list of every franchise company in the country—and the world, for that matter—is available at the research desk of any good public library. Ask for the national or international *Franchise Directory*.

AUTOMOTIVE

Airchek
6600 Southwest 62nd Avenue
Miami, FL 33143
Automobile air conditioning service and repair

American Brake Service
935 Brighton Avenue
Portland, ME 04102
Brakes and auto service

American Fluid Technology
239 Littleton Road
Westford, MA 01886
Mobile on-site antifreeze recycling service

American Turbo Wash
4517 Northwest 31st Avenue
Fort Lauderdale, FL 33309
Self-service car wash

Auto Accents
6550 Pearl Road
Cleveland, OH 44130
Cellular phones, car accessories, and alarms

Batteries Plus
2830 North Grandview Boulevard
Pewaukee, WI 53072
Batteries and related items

Carmerica Tire and Service Center
101 Westpark Drive, #150
Brentwood, TN 37027
Tires and automotive services

Colors On Parade
P.O. Box 1549
Conway, SC 29526
Automotive appearance services

Dents "Or" Us
7801 West 63rd Street
Overland Park, KS 66202
Paintless dent removal

Ever Vision Inc.
235 Hunters View
Atlanta, GA 30075
Windshield washer fluid service

Hometown Auto Service
2062 West Main Street
Jeffersonville, PA 19403
Automotive services

Leaverton Auto Inc.
827 South 9th Street
Joseph, MO 64501
Mufflers, brakes, shocks, alignment, and quick lube

LemonBusters
603 West 13th Street, #1D
Austin, TX 78701
Mobile used-car inspections

Oil Butler International Corp.
1599 Route 22 West
Union, NJ 07083
Mobile oil change and quick lube

BEAUTY AND HEALTH

Boca Beauty Club
210 University Drive, #402
Coral Springs, FL 33071
Full-service beauty salons

E-Z Tan Franchise System
21073 Powerline Road, #63
Boca Raton, FL 33433
Indoor tanning salons

Goodebodies The Natural Investment
1001 South Bayshore Drive, #2402
Miami, FL 33131
Natural skin, hair, and body care

Hairline Creations Studios
5850-54 West Montrose Avenue
Chicago, IL 60634
Hair replacement

Inches A Weigh
P.O. Box 59346
Birmingham, AL 35259
Weight loss program

Joe Weider Fitness Gyms
15375 Barranca Parkway, Suite B210
Irvine, CA 92718
Fitness and gym facilities

BUSINESS SERVICES

Advertising Services

The Bride's Club
P.O. Box 654
Nesconset, NY 11767
Wedding and related marketing services

Images
2827 Treat Street
Adrian, MI 49221
Printing and advertising specialty items

Information Displays Franchise Corp.
3276 Kitchen Drive
Carson City, NV 89701
Custom information displays

Kidder Advertising
P.O. Box 135
Berwick, LA 70342
Billboard advertising

The Premium Shopping Guide
P.O. Box 44
Windsor, CO 80550
Direct mail coupons and display advertising magazine

Welcome Host of America Inc.
13953 Perkins Road
Baton Rouge, LA 70810
Direct mail welcoming services

Personnel Services

Computemp Inc.
4401 North Federal Highway, #202
Boca Raton, FL 33431
Technical temporary personnel services

1st Agency Professionals
511 Wilson N.W.
Grand Rapids, MI 49504
Temporary medical staffing services

Sitters on Site Inc.
210 Abbott Road, #44
East Lansing, MI 48823
Child care placement and referral agency

Miscellaneous Business Services

Advanced Technology Specialists
Route 9, Box 534
Crossville, TN 38555
Computer and electronics supplies

The Business Connection
4155 East Jewel Avenue, #600
Denver, CO 80222
Computerized matching of buyers and sellers

The Lite Office
3901 MacArthur Boulevard, #200
Newport Beach, CA 92660
Office support services

Magis Fund Raising Specialists
845 Heathermoor Lane, #10A
Perrysburg, OH 43551
Fund-raising services for nonprofit organizations

Mobile International Marketing
621 Northwest 53rd Street, #160
Boca Raton, FL 33487
Telecommunications systems

Nacomex
301 Route 17 North
Rutherford, NJ 07070
Computer brokerage

Parcelway Courier Systems
3122 North Third Avenue
Phoenix, AZ 85013
Messenger and courier delivery system

People Helping People
3101 North Central Avenue
Phoenix, AZ 85012
Business referral and networking service

Postal Plus Services
70 East Beaver Creek Road, #29
Richmond Hill, Ontario, Canada, L4B 1J6
Postal, packaging, shipping, and business supplies

PostNet Postal and Business Centers
2225 East Flamingo Road, #310
Las Vegas, NV 89119
Postal, business, and communications centers

Signs and More in 24
1739 St. Mary's Avenue
Parkersburg, WV 26101
Signs and awnings

Trade Labor
P.O. Box 70661
Nashville, TN 37207
Barter network system

CHILDREN'S PRODUCTS AND SERVICES

CompuQuest Educational Services Inc.
6600 Busch Boulevard, #101
Columbus, OH 43229
Computer education

Friday Nite Live
601 White Hills Drive, #500
Rockwall, TX 75087
Youth services

Fun Works
3216 Power Boulevard
Metairie, LA 70003
Indoor entertainment center

Jabbawokki
2640 Golden Gate Parkway
Naples, FL 33942
Children's activity center

Kiddie Academy Int'l
108 Wheel Road, #200
Bel Air, MD 21025
Child care center

Kids Praise
6987 North Oracle Road
Tucson, AZ 85704
Personalized Christian children's books

The Little Gym
150 Lake Street South, #210
Kirkland, WA 98033
Child development and fitness center

Play Go Round
9877 Pines Boulevard
Pembroke Pines, FL 33024
Indoor playground and party facility

Pre-Fit Franchises
10336 South Western Avenue
Chicago, IL 60643
Preschool fitness program

Safe-T-Child Inc.
401 Friday Mountain Road
Austin, TX 78737
Child security and identification program

Toddlin' Time
8631 Point of Woods Drive
Manassas, VA 22110
Parent and toddler play gym

ENVIRONMENTAL SERVICES

American Recycling Franchise Sales Inc.
533 North State Street
Elgin, IL 60123
Nonferrous metals recycling facility

Envirobate
1020 Old Long Lake Road
Wayzata, MN 55391
Environmental services

Environmental Biotech Inc.
1390 Main Street, #510
Sarasota, FL 34236
Biological grease, oil, and sugar removal process

Professional House Doctors Inc.
1406 East 14th Street
Des Moines, IA 50316
Environmental and building science services

FOOD
Baked Goods

KelKea's Cookie Oven
2660 Mountain Industrial Boulevard, Suite F
Tucker, GA 30084
Mobile cookie store

Philly's Famous Soft Pretzel Co., Inc.
6557 Las Flores Drive
Boca Raton, FL 33433
Gourmet soft pretzels

Pretzel Time
5285 Devonshire Road
Harrisburg, PA 17112
Hand-rolled and soft pretzels

Mexican Fast Food

Salsa's Gourmet Mexican
13610 North Scottsdale Road, #10-352
Scottsdale, AZ 85254
Gourmet Mexican food

Tasty Tacos
1420 East Grand Avenue
Des Moines, IA 50316
Quick-service Mexican food

Zuzu Handmade Mexican Food
2651 North Harwood, #200
Dallas, TX 75201
Quick-service Mexican food

Oriental Fast Food

China Run
740 South Military Trail
West Palm Beach, FL 33415
Chinese food takeout and delivery

Mark Pi's Express
3950 Lyman Drive
Hillard, OH 43026
Chinese fast food

Rickshaw Restaurant
1230 El Camino Real, Suite D-4
San Bruno, CA 94066
Quick-service Chinese restaurant

Pizza

Edwardo's Natural Pizza Restaurants
4415 West Harrison Street, #510
Hillside, IL 60162
Chicago-style pizza restaurant

La Pizza Loca
7920 Orangethorpe Avenue, #202
Buena Park, CA 90620
Pizza

The Original Gino's East of Chicago
4415 West Harrison Street, #510
Hillside, IL 60162
Pizza restaurant

Pizza Chef Gourmet Pizza
525 Metro Place, #485
Dublin, OH 43017
Pizza, salads, and subs restaurant

Miscellaneous Fast Food

The Box Lunch Inc.
P.O. Box 666
Truro, MA 02666
Rolled pita bread sandwiches

Cafe Bresler's
999 East Touhy Avenue
Des Plaines, IL 60018
Salads, sandwiches, and bakery

Cafe Salads Etc.
4300 North Miller Road, #143
Scottsdale, AZ 85251
Salads, pastas, sandwiches, soups, and desserts

Charley's Steakery
1912 North High Street
Columbus, OH 43201
Grilled sandwiches, fries, and salads

Coney's World Famous Hot Dogs
102 Dunlap, P.O. Box 1137
Batesville, MS 38606
Hot dogs, hamburgers, chicken, and sausage

Congress Rotisserie
231 Westmont
West Hartford, CT 06117
Sandwiches and rotisserie chicken

Heros Simply Subsational
P.O. Box 21676
Billings, MT 59104
Submarine sandwiches

Juice Club
17 Chorro Street, Suite C
San Luis Obispo, CA 93405
Smoothies, juices, and snacks

L.A. Smoothie
700 Canal Street
New Orleans, LA 70130
Smoothies, health foods, and vitamins

Mike Schmidt's Philadelphia Hoagies
800 Bustleton Pike
Richboro, PA 18954
Hoagies and steaks

WallyBurger Express Drive-Thru
4305 North State Line Avenue
Texarkana, TX 75501
Fast food hamburgers, fries, and drinks

Miscellaneous Food Stores

Always Open
1130 Wabash
Chicago, IL 60605
Convenience store, deli, and market

Bourbon Street Candy Co. Inc.
420 South Third Street
Jacksonville Beach, FL 32250
Bulk candy store

Candyland
3522 Charlotte Street
Pittsburgh, PA 15201
Bulk candy store

Hot N' Fast
5180 Park Avenue, #310
Memphis, TN 38119
Electronic fast-food serving equipment

Jerky Hut
Hamlet Route 934
Seaside, OR 97138
Beef jerky and smoked meats

Oodles Home Ready Foods
19580 Telegraph Drive, Box 348
Surrey, British Columbia, Canada V3T 5B6
Frozen-food store

Quix Systems Inc.
4 North Third Street
Temple, TX 76501
Convenience food store

Miscellaneous Full-Service Restaurant

Blazers All American Barbecue
13610 North Scottsdale Road, #10-352
Scottsdale, AZ 85254
Barbecue restaurant

BW-3 Franchise Systems Inc.
2634 Vine Street
Cincinnati, OH 45219
Buffalo-wing specialty restaurant

Cami's Seafood Place
6272 South Dixie Highway
Miami, FL 33143
Seafood and pasta restaurant

Chick's Franchising Ltd.
11494 Sorrento Valley Road, Suite G
San Diego, CA 92121
Rotisserie chicken restaurant

Empire Kosher Restaurant
100-19 Queens Boulevard
Forest Hills, NY 11375
Kosher chicken restaurant

The Front Page Cafe
1101 South Caraway
Jonesboro, AR 72401
Full-service restaurant

Hubb's Pub
7738 Industrial Street
West Melbourne, FL 32904
Draft beer, sandwiches, and salad

Jack's Hollywood Diner
8230 Calumet Avenue, #100
Munster, IN 46321
Hollywood movie theme restaurant

Lisa's Tea Treasures
1213 Lincoln Avenue, #102
San Jose, CA 95215
Victorian tearoom and gift boutique

The Loop
One San Jose Place, #3
Jacksonville, FL 32257
Restaurant

Mark Pi's China Gate
3950 Lyman Drive
Hillard, OH 43026
Gourmet Chinese restaurant

Mark Pi's Feast of the Dragon
3950 Lyman Drive
Hillard, OH 43026
Chinese restaurant and buffet

Moxie Java
199 East 52nd Street
P.O. Box 2526
Boise, ID 83702
Espresso bar

Red River Bar-B-Que Franchising Inc.
5700 Corporate Drive, #235
Pittsburgh, PA 15237
Full-service restaurant

Spaghetti Jack's
1861 North Rock Road
Wichita, KS 67206
Italian restaurant

HOME IMPROVEMENT SERVICES
Carpet Sales

America's Carpet Gallery
4395 Electric Road
P.O. Box 21737
Roanoke, VA 24018
Carpet and home decorating store

Carpet Network
109 Gaither Drive, #302
Mt. Laurel, NJ 08054
Mobile floor covering sales

Carpet Sculptures International Inc.
510-A Central Avenue
Brea, CA 92621
Carpet sculptures

Lifestyle Mobile Carpet Showrooms
P.O. Box 3876
Dalton, GA 30721
Carpeting

Window Treatments

Progressive Window Fashions
201 North Front Street, #604
Wilmington, NC 28401
Custom interior and exterior window treatments

3 Day Blinds
2220 East Cerritos Avenue
Anaheim, CA 92806
Hard window coverings

WindoWear Inc.
770 North Main Street, Suite B
Orange, CA 92668
Window coverings

Window-olgy
141 South Amberwood Street
Orange, CA 92669
Mobile window coverings

Miscellaneous Home Improvement Products and Services

Comprehensive Painting
4723 North Academy Boulevard
Colorado Springs, CO 80918
Home painting services

Furniture Medic
277 Southfield Parkway, #130
Forest Park, GA 30050
Furniture touch-up and repair services

LumaDome Franchise Inc.
10360 72nd Street North, #808
Largo, FL 34647
Custom lighted ceilings

Precious Places
8321 Linden Oaks Court
Lorton, VA 22079
Shop-at-home service for decorating children's rooms

Pro-Mat
5180 Park Avenue
Memphis, TN 38119
Entry mats

SilkCorp Plant and Tree International Factory Outlet
P.O. Box 820
Hillside, IL 60162
Silk plants, trees, and arrangements

HOTELS AND MOTELS

Bed and Bath Mini Motel
1414 West Randol Mill Road, #104
Arlington, TX 76012
Motel

Knights Lodging System
26650 Emery Parkway
Cleveland, OH 44128
Hotel

MAINTENANCE SERVICES

A-Pro Services
Grubb Road
P.O. Box 132
Newfield, NJ 08344
Carpet and upholstery cleaning, restoration, and sales

Bath Fitter
27 Berard Drive, #2701
South Burlington, VT 05403
Acrylic bathtub liners

Blind Cleaning Express
3728 Overland Avenue
Los Angeles, CA 90034
Blind cleaning, repairs, and sales

Clean Team
210 University Drive, #402
Coral Springs, FL 33071
Window cleaning services

Ductbusters Inc.
29160 U.S. Highway 19 North
Clearwater, FL 34621
Duct cleaning

The Grout Doctor Inc.
1875 Diesel Drive, #10
Sacramento, CA 95838
Ceramic tile grout repair

Racs International
931 East 86th Street, #101
Indianapolis, IN 46240
Commercial cleaning services

Re-Bath Corp.
1055 South Country Club Drive, Building 2
Mesa, AZ 85210-4613
Acrylic liners for tubs and showers

WorkEnders
P.O. Box 810455
Boca Raton, FL 33481-0455
Residential cleaning

PHOTOGRAPHIC/VIDEOTAPING SERVICES

Action Sports Photos
4526 Northwest 1st
Oklahoma City, OK 73127
Sports photography

Elegant Images
15 Engle Street, #302
Englewood, NJ 07631
Glamour makeover and photography sessions

Freeze Frame
5000 Birch Street, #3000
Newport Beach, CA 92660
Fashion photography

Portrait Masters
114 High Country Drive
Cary, NC 27513
Preschool and youth sports photography

ProVideo Productions
8040 East Morgan Trail, #8
Scottsdale, AZ 85258
Video production services

Special Delivery Photos Inc.
P.O. Box 34905
Bartlett, TN 38134
Newborn-baby in-hospital photography service

PUBLISHING

Auto Show Weekly
5180 Park Avenue
Memphis, TN 38119
Auto sales magazine

FaxToday Franchising Inc.
1200 Network Centre Boulevard
Effingham, IL 62401
Faxed daily newspaper

RECREATION

Golf

Amateur Golfers Association of America
One Civic Plaza, #270
Newport Beach, CA 92660
Golf tournaments

Great Golf Learning Centers Inc.
1001 Lower Landing Road, #201
Blackwood, NJ 08012
Golf training

MacBirdie Franchise Corp.
5250 West 73rd Street
Minneapolis, MN 55439
Novelty golf gifts, apparel, and accessories

MetaPro Golf
330 Versailles Road
Frankfort, KY 40601
Custom golf equipment and accessories

Washington Golf Center
2625 Shirlington Road
Arlington, VA 22206
Golf store

Miscellaneous Recreation Products and Services

A.J. Barnes Bicycle Emporium
14230 Stirrup Lane
West Palm Beach, FL 33414
Full-service bicycle store

BikeLine
1035 Andrew Drive
Westchester, PA 19380
Bicycles and fitness equipment

Dek Star Dek Hockey Centers
1106 Reedsdale Street, #201
Pittsburgh, PA 15233
Outdoor non-ice hockey recreational facility

Jillian's Billiard Club
3350 Southwest 27th Avenue
Coconut Grove, FL 33133
Billiard parlor and cafe

Second Wind Sports Consignment Inc.
879 Hanover Street
Manchester, NH 03104-5419
Sports equipment

Strictly Shooting
25702 Pinewood Drive
Monee, IL 60449
Firearms and ammunition store

RETAIL STORES

Aaron's Rent-To-Own
3001 North Fulton Drive, N.E.
Atlanta, GA 30363
Rent-to-own furniture, electronics, and appliances

Art Avenue
242 Great Northern Mall
North Olmstead, OH 44070
Original oils, posters, prints, and framing

Bestseller Audiobooks
2300 North Scottsdale Road
Scottsdale, AZ 85257
Audiobook sales and rentals

Candleman
424 Northwest Third Street
P.O. Box 731
Brainerd, MN 56401
Candles, candle holders, and accessories

Easy Spirit Shoe Stores
15 Engle Street, #302
Englewood, NJ 0731
Comfort footwear shoe store

Express Pawn and Jewelry
909 Northeast Loop 410, #500
San Antonio, TX 78209
Pawnshop

Field of Dreams
72-027 Desert Drive
Rancho Mirage, CA 92270
Sports memorabilia

Gabbriele
P.O. Box 158
Oakton, VA 22124
Leather goods and accessories

Greg Sound and Communication
14200 Sullyfield Circle
Chantilly, VA 22021
Mobile electronics store

La Bride d'Elegance
2120 North Woodlawn, #364
Wichita, KS 67208
Bridal apparel and services

One Accord Inc.
3116 East Shea Boulevard, #247
Phoenix, AZ 85028
Christian bookstore

Puppy Hut Franchising Inc.
5201 Monroe Street
Toledo, OH 43623
Pet restaurant and gift center

Reading Glasses To Go
9131 King Arthur Drive
Dallas, TX 75247
Retail reading glasses store

Successories
919 Springer Drive
Lombard, IL 60148
Self-improvement and motivational tools

The Treasure Cache
44-F Jefryn Boulevard West
Deer Park, NY 11729
Arts and crafts rent-a-shelf store

Vend-A-Video
4155 East Jewell Avenue, #600
Denver, CO 80222
Automated video rental store

SERVICE BUSINESSES

Advanced Electronic Tax Services
3000 North Market Place, #110
Shreveport, LA 71107
Tax preparation and electronic filing

Coachman Dry Cleaning and Laundry
One Tower Bridge, #800
West Conshohocken, PA 19428
Dry cleaning, pickup, and delivery service

Door 2 Door
1240 West 14 Mile Road
Clawson, MI 48017
Restaurant delivery service

4-Sale Hotline
5921 South Middlefield Road, #200
Littleton, CO 80123
Audio-enhanced real estate sales

Home Services Alliance
4799 Olde Towne Parkway, N.E.
Marietta, GA 30068
Home improvement referral service

Mobile Container Service
5180 Park Avenue
Memphis, TN 38119
Waste container service and repair

1-Day Resume
5180 Park Avenue
Memphis, TN 38119
Resume preparation and consultation

Out of Harm's Way Inc.
35 International Boulevard
Etobicoke, Ontario, Canada M9W 6H3
Personal protection training and products

The Para-Legal-Office
3116 East Shea Boulevard, #247
Phoenix, AZ 85028
Computerized legal document preparation

Physician Dispensing Systems Inc.
One Logan Square, #1601
Philadelphia, PA 19103
Physician drug dispensing

Rental Referral Pros, USA
6040-A Six Forks Road, #407
Raleigh, NC 27609
Rental listing service

Service Center Inc.
7655 East Gelding Drive, Suite A3
Scottsdale, AZ 85260
Business management services

Star Cleaners Inc.
2502 Rocky Point Road, #655
Tampa, FL 33607
Full-service dry cleaning

Tailor, Needle and Thread
500 Park Boulevard
Itasca, IL 60143
Alterations services

Temptco A-1 Wholesale Copy Service and Supply
4214 East Broad Street
Columbus, OH 43213
Wholesale copy service for the printing trade

United Check Cashing Co.
325 Chestnut Street, #1005
Philadelphia, PA 19106
Financial services

Waiters on Wheels International
425 Divisadero Street, #305
San Francisco, CA 94117
Dinner delivery service

X-Bankers Check Cashing
1155 Main Street
Bridgeport, CT 06604-4407
Check cashing and financial services

TRAINING CENTERS

Atheneum Learning Corporation of America
500 108th Avenue, N.E.
Bellevue, WA 98004
Training, change management, and team building

Com-Cep Learning Centers
9700 Rodney Parham Road
Little Rock, AR 72207
Adult multimedia video learning center

Crestcom International Inc.
7150 East Hampden Avenue, #304
Denver, CO 80224
Video-based management training

LearnRight
1315 West College Avenue, #303
State College, PA 16801
Supplemental educational services

New Horizons Computer Learning Center Inc.
1231 East Dyer Road, #140
Santa Ana, CA 92705
Computer training

Vide-O-Go Tape Learning Centers of America
Market Hall, Princeton Forrestal Village
Princeton, NJ 08540
Cassette learning programs

Appendix C

The Small Business Administration Directory

The United States Small Business Administration (SBA) was created by Congress in 1953. Its mission is to encourage the formation of new enterprises and to nurture their growth. SBA services include providing information, offering financial backing, and speaking on behalf of small businesses on Capitol Hill and informing Congress of the needs of small businesses. The SBA also provides a wide variety of free or relatively inexpensive publications and consulting services as well as loan guarantee programs. To learn more about the SBA, contact one of its offices in your state.

SBA OFFICES BY STATE AND CITY

Alabama

908 South 20th Street, Room 202
Birmingham, AL 35205
(205) 254-1344

Alaska

1016 West 6th Avenue, Suite 200
Anchorage, AK 99501
(907) 271-4022

101 12th Avenue, Box 14
Federal Building & Courthouse
Fairbanks, AK 99700
(907) 452-1951

Arizona

3030 North Central Avenue
Suite 1201
Phoenix, AZ 85012
(602) 241-2200

301 West Congress Street, Room 3V
Tucson, AZ 85715
(602) 762-6715

Arkansas

320 West Capitol Avenue
Savors Federal Building
Little Rock, AR 72201
(501) 378-5876

California

1229 "N" Street
P.O. Box 828
Fresno, CA 93712
(209) 487-5189

350 South Figueroa Street, 6th Floor
Los Angeles, CA 90071
(213) 688-2956

1515 Clay Street
Oakland, CA 94612
(415) 273-7790

2800 Cottage Way, Room 2535
Sacramento, CA 95825
(916) 484-4720

880 Front Street, Room 4-S-29
San Diego, CA 92188
(714) 293-5440

450 Golden Gate Avenue
P.O. Box 36044
San Francisco, CA 94102
(415) 556-7487

211 Main Street, 4th Floor
San Francisco, CA 94105
(415) 556-7490

Colorado

1405 Curtis Street, 22nd Floor
Denver, CO 80202
(303) 837-5763

721 19th Street
Denver, CO 80202
(303) 837-2607

Connecticut

One Financial Plaza
Hartford, CT 06103
(203) 244-3600

Delaware

844 King Street, Room 5207
Wilmington, DE 19801
(302) 573-6294

Florida

400 West Bay Street, Room 261
P.O. Box 35067
Jacksonville, FL 32202
(904) 791-3782

2222 Ponce De Leon Boulevard, 5th Floor
Miami, FL 33134
(305) 350-5521

700 Twiggs Street, Suite 607
Tampa, FL 33602
(813) 228-2594

701 Clematis Street, Room 229
West Palm Beach, FL 33402
(305) 659-7533

Georgia

1375 Peachtree Street, N.E., 5th Floor
Atlanta, GA 30309
(404) 881-4943

1720 Peachtree Street, N.W., 6th Floor
Atlanta, GA 30309
(404) 881-4325

Hawaii

300 Ala Moana, Room 2213
P.O. Box 50207
Honolulu, HI 96850
(808) 546-8950

Idaho

1005 Main Street, 2nd Floor
Boise, ID 83701
(208) 334-2200

Illinois

219 South Dearborn Street, Room 437
Chicago, IL 60604
(312) 353-4528

One North, Old State Capital Plaza
Springfield, IL 62701
(217) 525-4416

Iowa

210 Walnut Street, Room 749
Des Moines, IA 50309
(515) 284-4422

Kansas

110 East Waterman Street
Wichita, KS 67202
(316) 267-6571

Kentucky

600 Federal Plaza, Room 188
P.O. Box 3517
Louisville, KY 40201
(502) 582-5971

Louisiana

1001 Howard Avenue, 17th Floor
New Orleans, LA 70113
(504) 589-6686

500 Fannin Street, Room 5B06
Shreveport, LA 71101
(318) 226-5196

Maine

40 Western Avenue, Room 512
Augusta, ME 04330
(207) 622-6171

Maryland

8600 LaSalle Road, Room 630
Baltimore, MD 21204
(301) 962-4392

Massachusetts

60 Batterymarch Street, 10th Floor
Boston MA 02110
(617)223-3204

150 Causeway Street, 10th Floor
Boston, MA 02114
(617) 223-3224

302 High Street, 4th Floor
Holyoke, MA 01050
(413) 536-8770

Michigan

477 Michigan Avenue
Detroit, MI 48226
(313) 226-6075

West Kaye Avenue
Marquette, MI 49855
(906) 225-1108

Minnesota

12 South 6th Street
Minneapolis, MN 55402
(612) 725-2362

Missouri

911 Walnut Street, 23rd Floor
Kansas City, MO 64106
(816) 374-5288

1150 Grande Avenue, 5th Floor
Kansas City, MO 64106
(816) 374-3416

One Mercantile Center, Suite 2500
St. Louis, MO
(314) 425-4191

Mississippi

111 Fred Haise Boulevard, 2nd Floor
Biloxi, MS 39530
(601) 435-3676

100 West Capitol Street, Suite 322
Jackson, MS 39201
(601) 969-4371

Montana

301 South Park Avenue, Room 528
Drawer 10054
Helena, MT 59601
(406) 449-5381

Nebraska

19th & Farnum Streets, Fl2
Omaha, NE 68102
(402) 221-4691

Nevada

301 East Stewart
P.O. Box 7525
Downtown Station
Las Vegas, NV 89101
(702) 385-6611

50 South Virginia Street, Room 308
P.O. Box 3216
Reno, NV 89505
(702) 784-5268

New Hampshire

55 Pleasant Street, Room 211
Concord, NH 03301
(603) 224-4041

New Jersey

1800 East Davis Street
Camden, NJ 08104
(609) 757-5183

970 Broad Street, Room 1635
Newark, NJ 07102
(201) 645-2434

New Mexico

5000 Marble Avenue, N.E., Room 320
Albuquerque, NM 87110
(505) 766-3433

New York

99 Washington Avenue, Room 301
Albany, NY 12210
(518) 472-6300

111 West Huron Street, Room 1311
Buffalo, NY 14202
(716) 846-4301

180 State Street, Room 412
Elmira, NY 14901
(607) 733-4686

401 Broad Hollow Road, Suite 322
Melville, NY 11747
(516)752-1626

100 State Street, Room 601
Rochester, NY 14614
(716) 263-6700

26 Federal Plaza, Room 3100
New York, NY 10007
(212) 264-4355

North Carolina

230 South Tryon Street, Suite 700
Charlotte, NC 28202
(704) 371-6111

Ohio

550 Main Street, Room 5028
Cincinnati, OH 45202
(513) 684-2814

1240 East 9th Street, Room 371
Cleveland, OH 44199
(216) 522-4180

85 Marconi Boulevard
Columbus, OH 43215
(614) 469-6860

Oklahoma

200 Northwest 5th Street, Suite 670
Oklahoma City, OK 73102
(405) 231-4301

333 West Fourth Street, Room 3104
Tulsa, OK 74103
(918) 581-7495

Oregon

1220 Southwest Third Avenue, Room 676
Portland, OR 97204
(503) 221-2682

Pennsylvania

100 Chestnut Street, 3rd Floor
Harrisburg, PA 17101
(717) 782-3840

231 Asaphs Road, Suite 400
East Lobby
Philadelphia, PA 19004
(215) 596-5889

1000 Liberty Avenue, Room 1401
Pittsburgh, PA 15222
(412) 644-2780

20 North Pennsylvania Avenue
Wilkes-Barre, PA 18702
(717) 826-6497

Rhode Island

380 Westminster Mall
Providence, RI 02903
(401) 351-7500

South Carolina

1835 Assembly Street, 3rd Floor
Columbia, SC 29201
(803) 765-5376

South Dakota

515 9th Street, Room 246
Rapid City, SD 57701
(605) 343-5074

101 South Main Avenue, Suite 101
Sioux Falls, SD 57102
(605) 336-2980

Tennessee

502 South Gay Street, Room 307
Knoxville, TN 37902
(615) 637-9300

167 North Main Street, Room 211
Memphis, TN 38103
(901) 521-3588

404 James Robertson Parkway
Suite 1012
Nashville, TN 37219
(615) 251-5881

Texas

300 East 8th Street
Austin, TX 78701
(512) 397-5288

3105 Leopard Street
P.O. Box 9253
Corpus Christi, TX 78408
(512) 888-3333

1100 Commerce Street, Room 3C36
Dallas, TX 75242
(214) 767-0600

1720 Regal Row, Room 230
Dallas, TX 75235
(214) 767-7640

4100 Rio Bravo, Suite 300
El Paso, TX 79902
(915) 543-7580

222 East Van Buren Street
P.O. Box 2567
Harlingen, TX 78550
(512) 423-4530

1205 Texas Avenue, Room 712
Lubbock, TX 79401
(806) 762-7466

500 Dallas Street
Houston, TX 77002
(713) 226-4343

100 South Washington Street, Room G-12
Marshall, TX 75670
(214) 935-5255

Utah

125 South State Street, Room 2237
Salt Lake City, UT 84138
(314) 425-5800

Vermont

87 State Street, Room 204
P.O. Box 605
Montpelier, VT 05602
(802) 229-0538

Virginia

400 North 8th Street, Room 3015
P.O. Box 10126
Richmond, VA 23240
(804) 782-2617

Washington

710 2nd Avenue, 5th Floor
Seattle, WA 98104
(206) 442-5676

915 Second Avenue, Room 1744
Seattle, WA 98174
(206) 442-5534

West 920 Riverside Avenue, Room 651
P.O. Box 2167
Spokane, WA 99210
(509) 456-5310

Washington, DC

1030 15th Street, N.W., Suite 250
Washington, DC 20417
(202) 653-6963

West Virginia

109 North 3rd Street, Room 301
Clarksburg, WV 26301
(304) 623-5631

Charleston National Plaza
Suite 628
Charleston, WV 25301
(304) 343-6181

Wisconsin

500 South Barstow Street
Eau Claire, WI 54701
(715) 834-9012

East Washington Avenue, Room 213
Madison, WI 53703
(715) 264-5461

Wyoming

100 East B Street, Room 4001
P.O. Box 2839
Casper, WY 82602
(307) 265-5266

U.S. Territories

Pacific Daily News Building, Room 508
Martyr & O'Hara
Agana, Guam 96910
(671) 477-8420

Federal Building, Room 691
Carlos Chardon Avenue
Hato Rey, Puerto Rico 00918
(809) 753-4572

Veterans Drive, Federal Office Building, Room 283
St. Thomas, VI 00802
(809) 774-8530

Appendix D

Trade Associations

Associations are one of the largest and most powerful business and political forces in the United States today. They represent an enormous collective presence, and many offer significant benefits to their members, including

- Educational programs
- Setting professional standards
- Developing and disseminating information
- Informing the public
- Ensuring representation for private interests
- Exercising and supporting political choice
- Stimulate and organize volunteer efforts

A study of 5,500 national associations conducted by the American Society of Association Executives found the following:

- Seven out of ten Americans belong to at least one association. One out of four belongs to four or more associations.
- Associations spend $9 billion a year on educational courses.
- Ninety percent of the associations offer educational courses to their members and to the public.
- Associations spend $14.5 billion on industry standard-setting activities. More than half set and enforce product standards, and one-fourth of professional societies set professional standards.
- Associations contributed 100 million hours of member skills to community service activities.
- One-third of the associations donated money to political activities.

Most associations exist to serve their members and represent companies in an industry, professionals, or individuals who share common interests. The *Encyclopedia of Associations* is the most comprehensive source of detailed information concerning more than 22,000 American associations. To learn more about any one association listed in the encyclopedia, contact it by phone, fax, or letter. Some associations operate with small volunteer staffs and may request that written inquiries be accompanied by stamped, self-addressed envelopes. The organizations described in EA fall into several categories, which are summarized as follows:

- National nonprofit membership associations, which account for the largest number of organizations listed
- International associations, most of which are North American in scope and membership
- Local and regional organizations whose subjects or objectives are national in interest
- Nonmembership organizations, that disseminate information to the public
- For-profit organizations
- Informal organizations that do not maintain national headquarters
- Inactive and defunct associations

The *Encyclopedia of Associations* is available at the reference desk of any good library. If you would like further information, you can write or call EA's editor at the following address:

Editor
Encyclopedia of Associations
Gale Research Inc.
835 Penobscot Building
Detroit, MI 48226-9833
1-800-877-GALE

The EA's association subject of interest directory is summarized on the pages that follow. Use the index to determine if there is an association covering an area that would be of interest to you.

Academic Placement	Aerospace	Aikido
Accounting	Aerospace Medicine	Air Force
Accreditation	Afghan	Albanian
Acoustics	Afghanistan	Alcoholic Beverages
Acrobatics	Africa	Alleghenies
Actors	African	Allergy
Adhesives	African American	Alpine
Adirondacks	Agents	Alternative Education
Administration	Aging	Alternative Medicine
Administrative Services	Agnostics	Alumni
Admiralty	Agribusiness	Alzheimer's Disease
Admissions	Agricultural Development	Amateur Radio
Adoption	Agricultural Education	Ambulatory Care
Adult Education	Agricultural Equipment	Amegroid
Adventist	Agricultural Law	American
Advertising	Agricultural Science	American Legion
Advertising Auditors	Agriculture	American Revolution
Aerobics	AIDS	American West

Americans Overseas
Americas
Amish
Amusement Parks
Anarchism
Anatomy
Andean
Anesthesiology
Anglican Catholic
Anguilla
Animal Breeding
Animal Research
Animal Science
Animal Welfare
Animals
Antarctica
Anthropology
Anthroposophical
Anti-Apartheid
Anti-Communism
Antiques
Anti-Zionism
Aphasia
Apheresis
Apiculture
Appalachian
Apparel
Appliances
Appraisers
Appropriate Technology
Aquaculture
Arabic
Arbitration and Mediation
Archaeology
Archery
Architecture
Archives
Argentina
Armed Forces
Armenian
Arms
Arm Wrestling
Army
Art
Artifacts
Artificial Intelligence
Artificial Organs
Artists
Arts
Arts and Sciences
Arumanian
Asatru
Ascended Masters
Asia
Asian
Assyrian

Astrology
Astronomy
Atheist
Athletics
Atlantic
Attorneys
Auctions
Audiovisual
Australia
Australian
Austria
Austrian
Autism
Automatic Control
Automatic Identification
Automobile
Automotive
Automotive Education
Automotive Industries
Automotive Manufacturers
Automotive Services
Aviation
Awards
Badminton
Baha'i
Bakery
Baking
Ball Games
Ballooning
Baltic
Banking
Banks
Baptist
Barbados
Bartering
Baseball
Basic Education
Basketball
Basque
Baton Twirling
Batteries
Bay of Pigs
Bearings
Beatles
Beer
Behavioral Medicine
Behavioral Sciences
Behcet's Syndrome
Belgian
Belgium
Bengal
Bermuda
Beverages
Bible
Bilingualism
Billiards

Biochemistry
Bioelectrics
Bioelectromagnetics
Biofeedback
Biology
Biomedical
Biophysics
Biotechnology
Bird
Birth Defects
Blacksmiths
Blood
Boating
Bobsleigh
Bocce
Body Therapy
Bodybuilding
Bolivia
Book Clubs
Books
Boomerangs
Botany
Bottles
Bowling
Boxing
Brazil
Brazilian
Breast Diseases
Bridal Services
Bridge
British
Broadcasting
Bronchoesophagology
Brotherhood of America
Buddhist
Building Codes
Building Industries
Building Trades
Bulgaria
Burns
Bus
Business
Business Cards
Business Education
Byelorussian
Byzantine
Cadets
Californian
Cambodian
Camping
Canada
Canadian
Canals
Cancer
Canoeing
Capital Punishment

Cardiology
Career Education
Caribbean
Carousels
Cartography
Cartoons
Castles
Cat
Catholic
Cattle
Cayman Islands
Celtic
Censorship
Central America
Central American
Ceramics
Cerebral Palsy
Chambers of Commerce
Champing
Chaplains
Chariot Racing
Cheerleading
Chefs
Chemicals
Chemistry
Chess
Child Care
Child Development
Child Health
Child Welfare
Childhood Education
Children
Chile
China
Chinese
Chiropractic
Christian
Christian Reformed
Church and State
Church of God
Churches
Churches of Christ
Circumcision
Circus
Citizenship
Civics
Civil Defense
Civil Rights
Civil Service
Civil War
Classical Studies
Clinical Studies
Clowns
Clubs
Coaching
Coal

Coast Guard
Coatings
Collectibles
Collective Bargaining
Collectors
Colleges and Universities
Colombia
Colonial
Color
Coma
Combustion
Comedy
Commercial Law
Commodities
Commodity Exchanges
Communications
Communism
Community
Community Action
Community Colleges
Community Development
Community Education
Community Improvement
Community Organization
Community Service
Compensation Medicine
Composers
Computer Science
Computer Software
Computer Users
Computers
Concrete
Congregational Christian
Congress
Congressional
Conservation
Conservative
Conservative Traditionalist
Constitution
Constitutional Law
Construction
Consulting
Consumers
Containers
Contests
Continuing Education
Cooking
Cooperative Education
Cooperative Extension
Cooperative Learning
Cooperatives
Coptic
Cordage
Corporate Economics
Corporate Law
Corporate Responsibility

Correspondence
Cosmetic Surgery
Cosmetology
Cossack
Cost Estimation
Costa Rica
Costumes
Cotton
Counseling
County Government
Court Employees
Crafts
Craniofacial Abnormalities
Creative Education
Credit Unions
Crime
Criminal Justice
Criminology
Critical Care
Croatian
Croquet
Cryogenics
Cryonics
Cryptography
Cryptology
Crystallography
Cuba
Cuban
Cults
Cultural Centers
Cultural Exchange
Curriculum
Customs
Cycles
Cyprus
Cytology
Czech
Czechoslovakia
Dairies
Dairy Products
Dance
Danish
Daoist
Darts
Data Processing
Dating Services
Debt
Debt Collection
Defense
Deism
Democracy
Democratic Party
Demography
Denmark
Dentistry
Dermatology

Design
Detergent
Developmental Education
Diabetes
Disability Evaluation
Disabled
Disabled Veterans
Disarmament
Disc Sports
Discipline
Disease
Disposable Products
District Attorneys
Divine Science
Diving
Divorce
Do It Yourself Aids
Dog
Dog Racing
Dolls
Domestic Violence
Dominican Republic
Donors
Draft
Dramatics
Driver Education
Dueling
Dutch
Dyslexia
Eagles
East Timor
Eastern Orthodox
Eating Disorders
Ecology
Economic Development
Economics
Ecuador
Ecuadorean
Ecumenical
Editors
Education
Education Law
Educational Advocacy
Educational Facilities
Educational Freedom
Educational Funding
Educational Reform
Egypt
El Salvador
Elections
Electrical
Electricity
Electroencephalography
Electrolysis
Electromedicine
Electronics

Elks
Elvis Presley
Emergency Aid
Emergency Medicine
Employee Benefits
Employee Ownership
Employment
Endocrinology
Energy
Engineering
Engines
English
English Speaking
Entertainers
Entertainment
Entertainment Law
Entomology
Environment
Environmental Health
Environmental Law
Ephemera
Epidemiology
Epilepsy
Episcopal
Equal Education
Eritrea
Esperanto
Estonian
Ethics
Ethiopian
Ethnic Studies
Europe
European
Euthanasia
Evaluation
Evangelical
Evangelism
Evolution
Exhibitors
Experiential Education
Exploration
Explosives
Faculty Exchange
Fair Agencies
Falconry
Families
Family Law
Family Medicine
Family Name Societies
Family Planning
Fan Clubs
Farm Management
Farming
Federal Government
Feed
Feminism

Fencing
Ferret
Fertility
Fertilizer
Fibers
Fibrositis
Fiction
Field Hockey
Film
Film Industry
Finance
Financial Aid
Financial Planning
Finders
Finishing
Finland
Finnish
Fire Fighting
Fire Protection
Firearms
Fish
Fishing
Fishing Industries
Flag
Floor Hockey
Florists
Fluid Power
Fluoridation
Folk
Food
Food and Drugs
Food Equipment
Food Service
Footbag
Football
Footwear
Foreign Policy
Foreign Service
Foreign Students
Forensic Medicine
Forensic Sciences
Forest Industries
Forest Products
Forestry
Fortune Telling
Fragrances
France
Franchising
Frank Sinatra
Fraternities and Sororities
Free Enterprise
Free Methodist
Freedom
French
Friends
Fruits and Vegetables

Fuel
Fundraising
Furniture
Future
Futures
Gambling
Games
Gaming
Gardening
Gases
Gastroenterology
Gay/Lesbian
Genealogy
Genetic Disorders
Genetics
Geography
Geology
Georgian
Geoscience
German
Germany
Gerontology
Gifted
Glass
Golf
Good Templars
Gospel
Gothic Literature
Gourmets
Government Accountability
Government Contracts
Government Employees
Government Relations
Grain
Grandparents
Graphic Arts
Graphic Arts Products
Graphic Design
Graphics
Grass
Gravitational Strain
Great Plains
Greece
Greek
Greek Orthodox
Grounds Management
Guardians
Guatemala
Gymnastics
Haiti
Hand
Handball
Hardware
Hazing
Head Injury
Headache

Health
Health and Beauty Products
Health Care
Health Care Products
Health Law
Health Plans
Health Professionals
Health Services
Hearing Impaired
Heating and Cooling
Hematology
Hepatology
Herbalism
Herbs
Herpetology
Higher Education
Hispanic
Historic Preservation
Historical Revisionism
History
Hobby Supplies
Hockey
Holistic Medicine
Holocaust
Home Based Business
Home Care
Home Economics
Home Exchange
Home Study
Homeless
Homeopathy
Homiletics
Honduras
Hong Kong
Honor Societies
Hoo Hoo
Horse Driving
Horse Riding
Horses
Horseshoes
Horticulture
Hospice
Hospital
Hospitality Industries
Hostages
Hotel Management
Housewares
Housing
Hovercraft
Huguenot
Human Development
Human Engineering
Human Life Issues
Human Potential
Human Relations
Human Rights

Humanism
Humanistic Education
Humanities
Humor
Hungarian
Hungary
Hunger
Hunting
Hypertension
Hypnosis
Hypoglycemia
Ichthyology
Immigration
Immunology
Implements
Impotence
Independent Schools
India
Indian
Indigenous Peoples
Indonesia
Industrial Design
Industrial Development
Industrial Education
Industrial Engineering
Industrial Equipment
Industrial Security
Industrial Workers
Infants
Infectious Diseases
Information Management
Innovation
Inspectors
Instructional Media
Instrumentation
Insurance
Integration
Intellectual Property
Intelligence
Intercultural
Interdisciplinary Studies
Interior Design
Internal Medicine
International Affairs
International Cooperation
International Development
International Exchange
International Health
International Law
International Relations
International Schools
International Studies
International Trade
International Understanding
Interspecies Communication
Inventors

Investigation
Investments
Iran
Iranian
Iraq
Ireland
Irish
Islamic
Israel
Israeli
Italian
Italy
Jai Alai
Jamaica
Japan
Japanese
Jehovah's Witnesses
Jewelry
Jewish
Jewish Science
Jordan
Journalism
Jousting
Judicial Reform
Judiciary
Judo
Juggling
Juvenile
Kampuchea
Karate
Kart Racing
Kite Flying
Knights of Pythias
Knives
Korea
Korean
Korean War
Krishna Consciousness
Kurdish
Labels
Labor
Labor Reform
Labor Studies
Laboratory
Lacrosse
Laity
Lakes
Lamps
Landscaping
Language
Laotian
Laser Medicine
Lasers
Latin America
Latin American
Latter Day Saints

Latvian
Laundry
Law
Law Enforcement
Leadership
Learning Disabled
Leather
Legal
Legal Education
Legal Services
Lending
Lepidopterology
Leprosy
Liability
Libel
Liberal Arts
Liberalism
Liberia
Libertarianism
Libraries
Library Science
Lifesaving
Lighting
Linguistics
Literacy
Literature
Lithuania
Lithuanian
Livestock
Livestock Conservation
Lone Indians
Lotteries
Luge
Luggage
Lupus Erythematosus
Lutheran
Luxembourg
Lymphology
Macedonian
Magic
Mail
Maintenance
Malacology
Malaysia
Maltese
Mammalogy
Management
Manufactured Housing
Manufacturers
Representatives
Manufacturing
Manx
Marbles
Marine
Marine Corps
Marine Industries

Maritime
Maritime Law
Marketing
Marriage
Martial Arts
Marxism
Masons
Massage
Matchcover
Materials
Mathematics
Meat
Mechanics
Medical
Medical Accreditation
Medical Administration
Medical Aid
Medical Assistants
Medical Education
Medical Examiners
Medical Identification
Medical Records
Medical Research
Medical Specialties
Medical Technology
Medicine
Medieval
Meditation
Mediterranean
Meeting Places
Meeting Planners
Membrane Science
Men's Rights
Mennonite
Mental Health
Mentally Disabled
Merchant Marine
Messianic Judaism
Metabolic Disorders
Metal
Metallurgy
Meteorology
Methodist
Mexican War
Mexico
Microscopy
Microwaves
Middle East
Middle Schools
Migrant Workers
Migration
Military
Military Equipment
Military Families
Military History
Military Police

Millers
Mineralogy
Minerals
Mining
Ministry
Minority Business
Missing in Action
Missing Persons
Mission
Model Trains
Modeling
Models
Monarchy
Mongolian
Montessori
Moorish
Moose
Moravian
Morocco
Mortuary Science
Mortuary Services
Mosaism
Motor Vehicle
Motorcycle
Mouse
Mozambique
Multiple Birth
Municipal Employees
Municipal Government
Museums
Music
Mutual Aid
Mycology
Mysticism
Mythology
Namibia
Naprapathy
National Sovereignty
National Spritualist
Nationalism
Nationalities
Native American
Natural Disasters
Natural Family Planning
Natural Hygiene
Natural Resources
Natural Sciences
Naturopathy
Naval Engineering
Navigation
Navy
Nematology
Neoplasia
Nepali
Nephrology
Netherlands

Netherlands Antilles
Neurological Disorders
Neurology
Neuroscience
Neurosurgery
New Zealand
Newspapers
Nicaragua
Nicaraguan
Nigerian
Nobel Laureates
Noise Control
Nonviolence
North America
Norway
Norwegian
Notaries Public
Notions
Nuclear
Nuclear Energy
Nuclear Medicine
Nuclear War and Weapons
Nudism
Numismatic
Nurseries
Nursing
Nursing Homes
Nutrition
Nuts
Obesity
Obstetrics and Gynecology
Occupational Medicine
Occupational Safety and
Health
Oceanography
Odd Fellows
Office Equipment
Officers
Oils and Fats
Okinawa
Olympic Games
Oncology
Onomatology
Operations Research
Ophthalmology
Opticianry
Optics
Optometry
Oral and Maxillofacial
Surgery
Organization Development
Organizations
Organizations Staff
Orgonomy
Oriental Healing
Orienteering

Origami
Orioles
Ornithology
Orthomolecular Medicine
Orthopedics
Orthotics and Prosthetics
Osteology
Osteopathic Medicine
Osteopathy
Ostomy
Otorhinolaryngology
Outdoor Education
Outdoor Recreation
Owls
Pacific
Packaging
Pain
Paintball
Paints and Finishes
Pakistan
Paleontology
Palestine
Palynology
Panama
Pancreatic Disease
Paper
Papyrology
Parachuting
Paraguay
Paralegals
Parapsychology
Parasitology
Parents
Parking
Parks and Recreation
Parliaments
Parole
Particulate Science
Pathology
Patriotism
Patristics
Pattern Recognition
Peace
Peace Corps
Peat
Pedestrians
Pediatrics
Pelletization
Pennsylvania Dutch
Pensions
Pentecostal
Performing Arts
Perinatology
Personnel
Peru
Peruvian

Pest Control
Petanque
Petroleum
Pets
Pharmaceuticals
Pharmacy
Phenomena
Philanthropy
Philatelic
Philippine
Philippines
Philosophy
Phobias
Phonetics
Photogrammetry
Photography
Physical Education
Physical Fitness
Physician Assistants
Physicians
Physics
Physiology
Pigeons
Pilgrims
Pioneers
Pipe Smoking
Pipes
Pituitary
Placement
Planning
Plastics
Play
Playing Cards
Plumbing
Podiatry
Poetry
Poets
Poker
Poland
Polar Studies
Polio
Polish
Political Action
Political Federations
Political Items
Political Parties
Political Products
Political Reform
Political Science
Politics
Polls
Pollution Control
Polo
Polynesian
Popular Culture
Population

Pornography
Portugal
Portuguese
Postal Service
Postal Workers
Postcards
Poultry
Poverty
Power
Powerlifting
Presbyterian
Preschool Education
Press
Preventive Medicine
Principals
Prisoners of War
Private Schools
Probate Law
Process Serving
Proctology
Professions
Professors
Programming Languages
Property
Property Management
Property Rights
Prospectors
Protestant
Psychiatry
Psychoanalysis
Psychology
Psychopathology
Psychosomatic Medicine
Psychotherapy
Public Administration
Public Affairs
Public Finance
Public Health
Public Information
Public Interest Law
Public Lands
Public Policy
Public Relations
Public Schools
Public Speaking
Public Welfare
Public Works
Publishing
Puerto Rico
Puppets
Purchasing
Pyramidology
Pyrotechnics
Quality Assurance
Quality Control
Rabbits

Racing
Racquetball
Radiation
Radical
Radio
Radiology
Railroads
Rajneeshism
Rangeland
Rape
Reading
Real Estate
Recordings
Recreation
Recreation Vehicles
Red Men
Reform
Reformation
Refugees
Regional Government
Rehabilitation
Relief
Religion
Religious Administration
Religious Freedom
Religious Science
Religious Studies
Religious Supplies
Renaissance
Renting and Leasing
Repair
Reproductive Medicine
Reproductive Rights
Republican Party
Rescue
Research
Respiratory Diseases
Restaurant Workers
Retailing
Reticuloendothelial System
Retirees
Retirement
Reye's Syndome
Rheology
Rhetoric
Rheumatic Diseases
Right to Life
Rights of Way
River Sports
Robotics
Rodeo
Roller Coasters
Romania
Romanian
Romanian Orthodox
Romany

Rope Jumping
Rosicrucian
Rowing
Rubber
Rugby
Runaways
Rural Development
Rural Education
Rural Youth
Russian
Russian Orthodox
Sabbath
Safety
Sailboarding
Sales
Sand Castles
Sanitarians
Sanitation
Saudi Arabia
Scalp
Scandinavia
Scandinavian
Scholarship
Scholarship Alumni
School Boards
School Security
School Services
Science
Science Fiction
Scientific Products
Scientific Responsibility
Scientology
Scleroderma
Scoliosis
Scottish
Scouting
Sculpture
Seafood
Seamen
Secondary Education
Securities
Security
Security Training
Seed
Seismology
Self Defense
Self-help
Semantics
Semiotics
Serbian
Service
Service Clubs
Service Fraternities
Service Sororities
Seventh Day Adventist
Sex Addiction

Sexual Abuses
Sexual Freedom
Sexual Health
Sexually Transmitted
    Diseases
Shakers
Sheep
Sherlock Holmes
Shipping
Shooting
Shuffleboard
Sicilian
Sikh
Silesian
Singapore
Singles
Skate Sailing
Skating
Skiing
Slavic
Sleep
Slovak
Slovenian
Small Business
Smoking
Snow Sports
Snowshoe Racing
Soap Box Derby
Soccer
Social Action
Social Change
Social Clubs
Social Fraternities
Social Issues
Social Responsibility
Social Sciences
Social Security
Social Service
Social Sororities
Social Studies
Social Welfare
Social Work
Socialism
Sociology
Softball
Soil
Solar Energy
Sonography
South Africa
Southern
Southern Africa
Soviet
Spain
Spanish
Spanish American War
Spanish Civil War

Special Days
Special Education
Special Forces
Special Studies
Spectroscopy
Speech
Speech and Hearing
Speleology
Spina Bifida
Spinal Injury
Spiritual Life
Spiritual Understanding
Spiritualist
Sporting Goods
Sports
Sports Law
Sports Medicine
Sports Officials
Squash
Sri Lankan
Standards
State Government
States Rights
Stationery
Statistics
Steam Engines
Stilts
Stone
Storytelling
Stress
Stress Analysis
Stroke
Student services
Students
Substance Abuse
Subterranean Construction
Sudden Infant Death
Syndrome
Sugar
Suicide
Summer School
Support Groups
Surfing
Surgery
Surplus
Surrogate Parenthood
Surveying
Survival
Sweden
Swedish
Swimming
Swine
Swiss
Switzerland
T'ai Chi
Table Tennis

Tableware
Taiwan
Taiwanese
Tallness
Tangible Assets
Tattooing
Taxation
Taxidermy
Teachers
Technical Education
Technology
Telecommunications
Telegraphy
Telemetry
Telephones
Television
Temperance
Tennis
Testing
Textbooks
Textiles
Thai
Thailand
Thanatology
Theatre
Theology
Theosophical
Therapy
Thermal Analysis
Thermology
Thoracic Medicine
Thyroid
Tibet
Tibetian
Time
Time Equipment
Timepieces
Tires
Tissue
Tithing
Tobacco
Toxic Exposure
Toxicology
Toys
Track and Field
Tractor Pulling
Tractors
Trade
Traffic
Trails
Trainers
Trampolining

Translation
Transplantation
Transportation
Trapping
Trauma
Travel
Trees and Shrubs
Trial Advocacy
Triathlon
Trinidad and Tobago
Trivia
Tropical Medicine
Tropical Studies
Trucks
Tug of War
Turkey
Turkish
Ukrainian
Undersea Medicine
Underwater Sports
Unions
Unitarian Universalist
United Church of Christ
United Kingdom
United Nations
United States
Urban Affairs
Urban Education
Urology
Uruguay
Ushers
USSR
Utilities
Vacuum Technology
Vascular System
Vaulting
Vedanta
Vegetarianism
Vending
Venezuela
Veterans
Veterinary Education
Veterinary Medicine
Vexillology
Victims
Victorian
Vietnam
Vietnam Veterans
Vietnam War
Vietnamese
Violence
Virgin Islands

Visually Impaired
Vocational Education
Volleyball
Voluntarism
Waldensian
Walking
War of 1812
Warehousing
Waste
Water
Water Resources
Water Skiing
Weather Services
Weighing
Weightlifting
Welding
Welsh
West Indian
Western Sahara
White Supremacy
Wholesale Distribution
Widowhood
Wildlife Conservation
Wind Energy
Wine
Witchcraft
Witches
Women
Wood
Wood Trades
Woodmen
World Affairs
World Government
World Notables
World War I
World War II
World Wars
World's Fairs
Wrestling
Wristwrestling
Writers
Writing
YMCA
Yoga
Youth
Yugoslavia
YWCA
Zoological Gardens
Zoology
Zoroastrian

A Complete Business Plan

The business plan in this appendix consolidates all the subplans for Computech that we covered in the chapter material. The intent of the complete plan is to show you how all the various parts fit together. The structure of Computech's plan follows the strategic business plan outline that we presented to you in Chapter 12. The plan emphasizes cost controls, which are essential to the success and survival of any new company. This particular plan was written to attract investors and solicit a loan on behalf of the company. The parts of the plan that are included in Appendix E are summarized as follows.

EXECUTIVE SUMMARY

This section is an abstract of the company's present status and future direction. It is usually written after all the other sections of your business plan are completed because it gives readers an overview of your business and indicates how your business plan is organized. The executive summary should not exceed two pages.

COMPANY SUMMARY

The company summary covers the current condition of your organization. It's like a present-day "snapshot" of the company's current situation. It states where you want to go, what you want your company to be, and what your expectations are three to five years from now?

PRODUCT AND SERVICE ANALYSIS

This section describes the features of your products and services. How do they differ from competitive products and services? What benefits will your customers derive by using your products and services? Explain how you will satisfy customer needs and wants. Show how the products work, how the services are used, and how they have evolved over time.

MARKET ANALYSIS

This section describes the marketplace in which you will introduce your company's products and services. Describe the existing marketplace and your target or focus market in detail. Who are your customers, and how will you entice them to buy your products and services?

STRATEGIC PLAN

Identify the current and future methods you are using and will use to sell your products and services. What methods will you use to promote your products and services? Brochures, advertisements, announcements, or other promotional literature and plans are covered in this section.

MANAGEMENT

Show what the management structure is for your company and why you chose this structure. Who are the people that make up the management team, and what makes them qualified to run the company?

FINANCIAL ANALYSIS

At a minimum, the financial analysis section must include a cash flow analysis, a balance sheet, and a three- to five-year income statement with the break-even point clearly identified.

APPENDIX

The appendix section of the business plan contains all the data and information that support the statements and numbers in the main body of the plan.

Business Plan for Computech

123 Main Street
Denver, CO 80302
(303) 999-9999
May 1994

Table of Contents

1.0 Executive Summary

Computech was formed to assemble, sell, and service personal computers to take advantage of the growing personal computer business in certain sections of the country. The company's mission is to become the premier retailer of personal computers, maintenance service, and related educational seminars. We have just completed the design, development, testing, and introduction of our first personal computer, Computech 1. Now Computech is at a point where we want to take advantage of specific opportunities in our marketplace and expand our business base.

Our company has been in business for less than one year, and after the introduction of Computech 1, we reached our break-even point. Computech is currently making a profit. Revenues for next year without external funding are projected to be $400,150. We expect our product and service lines of business to continue to grow at a compound rate of 15 percent per year. Our ability to economically assemble personal computers from readily available computer components (i.e., disk drives, memory boards, etc.) and offer a complementary line of services is a capability unique to Computech.

Our strategy for dominating the market is to offer personal computers whose quality and price cannot be matched by the competition. Computech's target market includes a five-county area in Colorado known as the Denver metropolitan market region. We are rapidly moving into the market growth phase of our initial product introduction in our target market. And, our personal computers are generating a tremendous amount of interest throughout the industry.

Our service offerings cover two primary areas. First, we offer comprehensive service contracts on all Computech personal computers. Loaner computers are available to our customers while we are servicing their computers. Second, Computech's service line includes a complete series of seminars on how to use the latest and most popular software.

Responses from customers indicate that our products and services are enjoying an excellent reputation. Inquiries from prospective customers suggest that there is considerable demand for Computech retail stores in other locations. Relationships with leading businesses, retail customers, and distributors substantiate of Computech's potential for considerable growth and accomplishment in our industry.

Our objectives are to propel the company into a prominent market position. We feel that within three years, Computech will be in a suitable condition for an initial public offering or profitable acquisition. To accomplish this goal, we have developed a comprehensive plan to intensify and accelerate our marketing and sales activities by expanding our product and service lines. To implement our plans, we require an investment of $250,000 for the following purposes:

- Maximize product sales through an extensive advertising campaign.
- Add retail outlets throughout Colorado and print a directmail catalog.
- Increase our customer support services to handle the new orders.

- Augment company staff to support and sustain prolonged growth under the new marketing plan.
- Develop a new multimedia personal computer (Computech 2) to create additional sales.

In order for Computech to achieve these goals, our short-term line of credit needs to be restructured to long-term debt. This restructuring will significantly improve the cash flow of the company over the next fiscal year and will better match our objectives for long-term expansion.

2.0 COMPANY SUMMARY

The personal computer marketplace is undergoing tremendous growth. The popularity of multimedia applications is renewing interest in what was considered a mature market. For example, Colorado is currently experiencing 20 percent compound annual growth in personal computer sales. Because of the growth potential in the industry, we believe that Computech can achieve a conservative 15 percent compound annual growth rate in personal computer hardware, software, and related service sales. On the basis of Computech's 12 percent market share (Denver metro market), we estimate that our return on investment will be 9 percent. Our financial objectives over the next two years are summarized as follows:

	Last Year	This Year	Next Year
Sales			
$ volume	$325,000	$400,150	$458,156
Unit volume	335	405	450
% increase in sales	0	23%	15%
Share of market	20%	22%	25%
Gross profit	$151,000	$225,763	$266,331
Cost of goods sold	$174,000	$174,387	$191,825
Operating expenses	$147,800	$173,275	$190,542
Profit before taxes	$26,200	$52,488	$75,789
Profit % of sales	8%	23%	$28%

We believe that Computech's growth will be facilitated by the basic beliefs that are practiced by every employee in the company. Our six basic beliefs are summarized as follows:

1. Understand our customers, competition, and industry.
2. Provide the best products and services available in the markets that we choose to serve.
3. Continue to grow our business in selected fields of interest.
4. Balance our business goals with our financial objectives.
5. Make the transition from a single point of sale company to a distributed sales company.
6. Refine the company values and culture by hiring the best people.

Computech enjoys an established track record of excellent support and service to our customers. Their expressions of satisfaction and encouragement are numerous, and we intend to continue our advances in the personal computer marketplace with more unique products and services.

3.0 PRODUCT AND SERVICE ANALYSIS

Product

Computech currently offers personal computers for sale in Colorado. Development of other personal computers is in progress, and future expansion into the other states is anticipated. All Computech personal computers have standard features, such as memory, fixed disk size, and displays. We can therefore assemble any Computech personal computer from only five components, which also gives us a cost advantage over other personal computer assembly companies. Since we are able to use common parts in our personal computers, we can enjoy volume purchase discounts. Over 90 percent of our personal computers are sold through Computech's two retail stores. Our personal computers have several distinctive advantages over the competition, which are summarized as follows:

- We have a more attractive and durable external casing.
- The average price of our personal computers and maintenance service is 20 percent less than that of the competitive products and services.
- We are the only retail computer store in the Denver metropolitan market that offers a three-year unconditional warranty on our personal computers.
- All of our customers are eligible to receive a discount on any of our seminars.

Maintenance Service

Computech offers extended warranties and maintenance service on our computers. We include a three-year unconditional repair warranty on any computer we sell, which is unique within the industry. Our warranty repair return rate experience is less than 1 percent of all units sold. We also offer "after warranty" maintenance services on a contract or hourly fee basis.

Educational Seminars

Educational seminars on how to use the popular and latest software releases are conducted after retail hours in our two store locations. We believe that our seminar program is an attractive feature and an added incentive for people to buy our personal computers. We employ seminar instructors on a part-time basis and, as a result, are making money in our seminar business.

4.0 MARKET ANALYSIS

The Data Processing Management Association projects personal computer hardware, software, and service sales to be a $7,500,000 market in Colorado by the end of 1996. Conservative estimates suggest that Computech's market share, with our intensified and accelerated marketing plan, would be about 20 percent of the market by the end of 1996. The fundamental thrust of our marketing strategy is to develop personal computers that appeal to walk-in retail customers, corporate customers, and direct mail customers.

4.1 Customers

We intend to reach our customers by placing a variety of ads, mailing a full-color catalog every quarter, conducting a full-scale telemarketing campaign, and using other sales tactics. Overall, our company can be characterized as a high-profile retailer and aggressive distributor of quality personal computers. A partial list of our major commercial customers includes:

1. Sporting Stores of America

2. United Steel Corporation

3. Wal Discount Stores

Prospective major customers currently evaluating our personal computers include:

1. Colorado Tours Inc.

2. National Outdoors Inc.

3. Mart Stores

Users of personal computers are looking for quality computers that are reliable and can be maintained by a local service outlet (i.e., Computech stores). Computech's ability to assemble personal computers that are specific to the needs of our customers is what makes Computech unique. Independent market research indicates that there are only two other companies that offer competitive personal computers in the Denver metropolitan market area.

The stability of our market area is demonstrated by computer sales over the past two years. The personal computer market is growing at a rapid rate. The market for personal computers was $2,000,000 last year, representing a 22 percent increase over the previous year. According to the U.S. Department of Commerce, the area of greatest growth in the personal computer market is in multimedia units. Although most of our personal computers are sold through our two retail outlets, we intend to expand our sales and distribution through other retail outlets. Negotiations are already underway, and possible retail and wholesale outlets include:

Store Type	Total	SIC Code
Department stores	23	5311
Appliance stores	4	5251
Wholesalers	3	5199G
Discount chains	4	5063
Total	34	

Less than 20 percent of our sales are through direct channels into commercial accounts. Over the past year, we have been developing our sales strategies to penetrate commercial accounts.

4.2 Focus Group

The most typical customer for our personal computer is a professional worker who has two or more years of college. Most of our customers are already familiar with personal computers, since they use either one at work or at home. They will readily accept Computech's personal computers provided that we advertise the technical benefits and offer our computers at an attractive price. According to a recent survey that was conducted by the U.S. Department of Commerce, the personal computer market is composed of the following groups:

Young Professionals

Age:	25–35
Income:	Medium to high
Sex:	Male or female
Family:	Single or married
Geographic:	Suburban
Occupation:	White-collar
Attitude:	Innovator

Young Married Couples

Age:	20–30
Income:	Medium to high
Sex:	Male or female
Family:	Married, with or without children
Geographic:	Suburban
Occupation:	White-collar
Attitude:	Early adapters

Wealthy Rural Families

Age:	35–55
Income:	High
Sex:	Male or female
Family:	Full nest
Geographic:	Rural
Occupation:	White-collar
Attitude:	Early majority

Older Couples

Age:	55–70
Income:	High or fixed
Sex:	Male or female
Family:	Empty nest
Geographic:	Suburban
Occupation:	White-collar or none
Attitude:	Late majority

4.2 Competition

Competitive threats to Computech in the greater Denver area come primarily from two companies, Stanway Company and Bart Enterprises. In all comparisons, Computech's personal computers provide more and have better features than our competitors' products and services. The following table illustrates how Computech's products and services compare to our competitors'.

Competitive Company Roundup

	Stanway Co.	Bart Enterprises	Computech
Retail outlets	4	6	2
Estimated 1995 sales $	$733,000	$1,099,000	$458,000
Estimated share of market %	32%	48%	20%
Estimated advertising budget	$14,660	$17,890	$7,622

Competitor Ranking

Rank: 1 = Weak to 5 = Strong

	Stanway Co.	Bart Enterprises	Computech
Quality	3	4	5
Technology	4	4	4
Advertising effectiveness	2	3	3
Distribution	4	5	2
Manufacturing efficiency	3	3	5
Standing in industry	3	5	4
Future potential	3	3	5
Seriousness of competition	4	2	4
Number of employees	35	46	18
Greatest strength	Price	Sales outlets	Service
Key weakness	Quality	Price	Limited retail outlets

Personal Computer Comparison By Feature

Rank: 1 = Weak to 5 = Strong

	Stanway Co.	Bart Enterprises	Computech
Price	3	2	5
Size	4	4	4
Capacity	5	2	5
Ease of use	3	3	3
Appearance	2	3	5
Quality	1	3	5

Design	2	2	4
Useful life	3	3	5
Trade-in value	4	2	1
Technology	3	3	3
Responsiveness	5	4	3
State-of-the-art	4	4	4
24-hour availability/support	1	1	5
Technical expertise	2	2	4
Repair service	1	2	5
Guarantee/warranty	3	3	5
Upgrades	4	4	3

We have concluded from these comparisons that personal computer reliability and service are a market niche that has been overlooked by our competitors. Computech's qualifications and expertise in this area will be exploited in our advertising campaign (see advertisement and brochure layouts in the Appendix).

5.0 STRATEGIC PLAN

Computech's strategic plan is supported by a marketing strategy that has been designed to promote and support the features of our personal computers and unique service offerings. The competitive strengths of our company lie in its approach to an integrated solution, the dedication of its sales staff, and its ongoing commitment to excellence. The target market segments that Computech has chosen to focus on were identified in the Market Analysis section of our plan. Because of the special benefits of our personal computers (i.e., extended warranty and instant service), our strategic plan shows how we will address specific market and sales conditions.

5.1 Pricing and Profitability

The prices for our products and services are determined first and foremost by analyzing our costs. It is important to know that with personal computers, pricing is an important part of our market profile. Our computer prices are, on average, 20 percent below the average competitor's price. In spite of our lower price, our margin structure still allows for a 20 percent before-tax profit. This is possible because of our ability to control unit cost to the lowest level in the industry, as we have shown in the table that follows:

Personal Computer Component Part	Computech Unit Costs	Average Industry Unit Cost
Chassis	$100	$110
Power supply	$150	$200
Disk drives	$320	$385
Memory boards	$140	$200
Keyboard	$90	$75
Total costs	$800	$960

5.2 Selling Tactics

The majority of sales will be through direct sales by Computech's sales staff. We anticipate hiring additional sales representatives to cover new stores when they open. We have chosen to use a direct sales force because our products and services require considerable customer contact and post-sale support. Our pricing structure and profits justify handling our sales on an individual basis.

All regional sales are controlled out of the company's headquarters in Denver, Colorado. The primary concern of the sales force is the continued satisfaction of our clients. Sales representatives meet with store and distribution managers on a regular basis to assure account satisfaction. To assist with the ongoing contacts, Computech publishes a monthly newsletter. It contains information about our new products and services, and provides market demographic information that is important to our customers.

5.3 Distribution

One of the key elements of Computech's marketing plan is the expansion of our sales through the use of distributors. We understand the importance of selecting distribution channels that already exist and are staffed with qualified professionals. Therefore, our strategic marketing approach takes full advantage of the tremendous momentum inherent in the fact that these professionals are already involved with parallel products and services. They have the technical sales experience, and they have an existing client base.

By operating within these distribution channels, we feel that we can maintain control over our market. In addition, we can generate growth at a reasonable pace and obtain excellent sales results. Computech will use several different distribution channels. Our determining factors in choosing these channels are

- Customer profile
- Geography
- Technical competence
- Efficient use of funds
- Distributors with complementary products and services

An additional distribution channel planned for our personal computers is direct mail through catalog advertisements.

An important advantage of these alternative channels is flexibility. By using more than one method, Computech will have more control and options with which to respond to the special needs of our customers.

Coverage

Regional target areas for our personal computers include major market areas outside our current Denver metropolitan market area. Reports indicate the highest level of consumer computer interest is in the cities of Fort Collins, Colorado Springs, and Grand Junction. Because our distribution network is partially set up in these cities, we can enjoy a quick start-up operation in these areas (see table that follows).

Selected Manufacturers' Representative

Name	Territory Covered	Type of Operation
ABC Sales Systems	Fort Collins	Retail Stores
Distribution, Inc.	Colorado Springs	Wholesale Distributor
GHI Stores	Grand Junction	Department Stores

Customer service

Our customers have emphasized that maintenance service and education support are among their major concerns when they purchase a personal computer. They are impressed with Computech's customer service. A service hot line is currently available to all customers. We intend to provide maintenance service at our customers' location in the near future, which will be an attractive feature to our commercial customers. The purpose of our extended service options is to assure customer satisfaction and to allow us to increase sales, as well as maintain a high profile within our service area.

Educational support is provided to our customers at our retail locations. We offer training on how to use all of the popular and new software products. As an added incentive for customers to buy Computech's personal computers, we often include a free seminar as part of a personal computer purchase.

Returns policy

If for some reason our personal computer is not right for a customer, he or she may return it for a full refund within thirty days of the product receipt date. Refunds are made only on the price and do not include shipping costs. Credit card refunds are credited to customer accounts.

5.4 Advertising and Promotion

Computech recognizes that the key to the success of our sales program is extensive advertising and promotion. To accomplish our sales goals, we will need the services of an advertising agency and a public relations firm. Once we receive funding, an agency selection shall be made. With the agency's assistance, a comprehensive advertising and promotion plan will be drafted. Advertising will be done both independently and cooperatively with distributors, retailers, and companies with whom Computech has joint marketing and sales relationships. The objectives of our advertising and promotional campaign are summarized as follows:

- Position Computech as the market leader in personal computers.
- Increase company awareness and brand name recognition among retailers, distributors, and customers.
- Use market research to develop our long-term marketing plans.
- Coordinate sales literature, demonstration materials, and direct response promotions to increase sales.

To get the most out of our promotional budget, our media coverage will be focused on the business audience. We will develop an advertising campaign built around innovative personal computer ideas, beginning with a "who we are" position supported by ads that reinforce our image and message. Our ad campaigns will have a consistent reach and frequency throughout the year. Computech's media strategy is summarized as follows:

- Increase awareness of the company's leadership in personal computers.
- Establish Computech's image as a professional and highly reliable company.
- Select primary business publications with high specific market penetration.
- Schedule ads frequently to impact the market with product and service messages.
- Select specific media to reach dual markets.
- Employ special high-interest issues of major publications whenever possible.
- Maximize ad life with weekly and monthly publications.

Advertising campaign

The best way to reach our potential customers is to develop an intense advertising campaign promoting our basic premise: "In today's economy, paddling isn't enough. You need a Computech personal computer to help you get to where you want to go." To establish our computer image and create excitement in our messages, ads will convey the look and feel of a "we know where we are going" company. Consumers will actively seek out our advice, products, and services as a result of our advertising program. Because our combined products and services are so innovative, it is important that we develop a promotional campaign that is consistent. Accordingly, Computech has created a system of easy-to-understand ads to ensure the maximum benefit from our advertising dollars.

Preliminary Media Schedule

	Circulation	Monthly Budget
Radio	50,000	$1,500
Newspapers	350,000	$2,400
Magazines	100,000	$3,722
Total	500,000	$4,400

Anticipated response expected = 0.001 percent, or 1 customer per 1,000 reached by advertising

$$\text{Advertising cost per customer} = \frac{\$4,400}{0.001 \times 500,000} = \$8.80 \text{ per customer}$$

We expect to reach 500,000 prospective customers per month and plan to maintain that contact rate. Compared to industry averages, Computech is investing more in all advertising areas to assure the successful promotion of our personal computers, as is demonstrated in the following table.

Computech's Advertising Spending vs. Industry Average
($ per $100 net sales)

	Industry	Computech
Advertising	$1.25	$1.35
Sales promotion	$0.55	$0.75
Trade	$0.35	$0.38
Consumer mail	$0.24	$0.45

5.5 Public Relations

Our public relations objective is to position Computech at the leading edge in providing personal computers. We intend to increase the public's awareness of our brand name. To accomplish this objective, we intend to communicate on a regular basis with three target groups:

1. Business and editorial staffs of major local publications

2. Key management personnel in Denver metropolitan area companies

3. Local professional groups and associations

We will develop a sustained public relations effort with ongoing contact with key editors of the major news media. A regular and consistent product update program is already in place to keep key editors abreast of our personal computer enhancements. At a minimum, four technical articles per year will be written by our employees for the major trade journals.

We intend to establish relationships with editorial staffs for the purpose of being included in product comparisons with competing products and services. This exposure will build credibility and market acceptance. We will publish a document covering Computech's background that will be used as a primary public relations tool for target media contacts, press kits, dealer kits, and sales packages.

Trade shows

We plan to attend COMDEX, the annual computer trade show, and will share a booth at the show to reduce costs. These shows will be attended both independently and with companies with which Computech has joint marketing and sales agreements. Our staff will write technical reports and papers that will be presented at computer conferences throughout the year.

We plan to use trade shows as another method for maintaining a high profile with the editors of key target media. Whenever possible, Computech's major product announcements will be made at trade shows to increase publicity and media coverage.

Newsletters

A four-page newsletter will be prepared to serve as an informational piece for internal personnel and for our customers. It will cover Computech activities (sales, marketing, manufacturing, R&D) and include a message from the president. The newsletter will also include highlights of major developments in the computer industry, key sales stories, significant marketing events, and product development news.

Joint marketing agreements

Joint marketing agreements with established computer supply companies will help us to increase revenues and market presence. Computech is pursuing joint marketing agreements with several organizations to further promote Computech's products and services. Our plans include having computer supply companies market our personal computers as a part of their existing product line.

Joint development efforts

Computech has joint computer development efforts underway with several multimedia disk drive companies. Financial and technical ideas are being shared, and several joint development projects are in process, but have not yet begun.

5.6 Manufacturing and Service Cost

All of Computech's personal computers are assembled at the main store, which is located in Denver. The assembly area is located directly behind the retail storefront and includes 800 square feet of assembly space. Each of the four assembly stations occupies 100 square feet of space, for a total of 400 square feet. The remaining 200 square feet have been set aside for packaging and shipping. People who visit our operation are impressed with our utilization of space. Every square foot is fully utilized to minimize our overhead cost. Complete sets of personal computer components are packaged into kits (one kit per computer), which are delivered to the work stations to increase the efficiency of our assembly process. We can assemble and package a complete personal computer in 1.5 worker-hours. Our manufacturing assembly costs are among the lowest in the industry, which are shown in the table that follows

Average Costs to Assemble One Personal Computer

	Industry	Computech
Floor space	$3.25	$2.35
Utilities and overhead	$0.55	$0.75
Direct labor	$62.95	$41.00
Indirect labor	$7.25	$6.45
Total	$74.00	$50.55

Cost for expansion

We will need to expand Computech's personal computer manufacturing area in the near future. The cost of the expansion should not present any financial problems, since we are currently using more expensive retail space to assemble personal computers. If we were to relocate the assembly operation into one of the many available and remote industrial parks, we could reduce our cost per square foot by 40 percent.

Transportation cost and access

Products and supplies are moved between Computech's two retail stores using a company-owned van. This mode of transportation has proven to be highly efficient, since our employees are always traveling between the two stores. Our vehicle liability insurance covers all company employees. Personal computers that are ordered by our commercial accounts are shipped and delivered by UPS carriers.

Available suppliers

As we indicated earlier, only five component parts are used to build a Computech personal computer. Each component is supplied to Computech by one primary supplier. Hence, we have five primary suppliers, which allows us to take advantage of volume purchase discounts for all of the components that we order. However, we have identified and qualified two backup suppliers for each primary supplier in the event that we encounter problems such as quality control with a primary supplier.

Labor pool availability

Qualified labor is readily available in the Denver area. There are a number of large computer assembly companies to draw labor from, including IBM and StorageTec. To attract the best candidates from the larger companies, Computech offers a competitive salary and fringe benefit package, plus a company equity ownership benefit designed to retain the best employees. As a result, our voluntary employee turnover rate has been less than 5 percent a year.

Service program and costs

All of our manufacturing personnel are qualified to service any of Computech's personal computers. Therefore, we do not need to maintain a separate service department. In the event that a customer delivers a faulty computer to one of our retail outlets, it is immediately dispatched to our Boulder manufacturing facility. We interrupt the least busy assembly station with what we call an "ASAP order" to repair the customer's personal computer. Overtime is authorized if a repair order seriously disrupts the production cycle of new personal computers. Our hourly computer maintenance charges are the same as our assembly hourly rate ($50.55 ÷ 1.5 hours, or $33.70 per hour) plus a 20 percent profit add-on (20% of $33.70, or $6.75) to assure that we cover all associated overhead costs and company profit objectives.

Seminar program and costs

Elsewhere in this business plan, we have talked about the benefits and various features of Computech's seminar program. To control the cost of this program, all of the personnel that present our seminars are hired on a contract basis at $25 per hour. Our average fee for a seven-hour seminar is $70 per person. Seminars are held after retail hours in Computech's two retail stores and are promoted through our monthly newsletter. On average, we conduct ten seminars per month and have consistently made money on the program, as shown in the following table.

Costs and Income for Average Computech Seminar

Instructor salary	$175	(7 hours @ $25 per hour)
Utilities and overhead	$20	(floor space, utilities, an insurance)
Advertising	$175	(Cost of newsletter and postage)
Total costs	$370	
Total income	$700	(10 students at $70 each)
Profit	$330	($700 - $370 = $330)

6.0 MANAGEMENT

The legal form of Computech is a general partnership. Each partner owns a percentage of the company. Computech's founders and key managers have combined experience in the computer industry exceeding 100 years. The strength of Computech's management team stems from its combined expertise in both management and technical areas. The leadership characteristics of the company's management team have resulted in broad and flexible goal-setting capabilities to meet the ever-changing demands of the quickly moving marketplace requiring our products and services. This is evident when the team responds to situations requiring new and innovative capabilities.

Key Managers and Responsibilities

- John Doe, President
  Chief executive officer also responsible for market planning, advertising, public relations, sales promotion, ad layouts, and sales support services. Identify new markets and corporate market research activities.
- Susan Jones, Vice President of Sales
  Manage field sales organization, territories, and quotas. Manage sales office activities, including customer support services.
- David Crosby, Vice President of Finance
  Manage working capital, including receivables, inventory, cash, and marketable securities. Perform financial forecasting, including capital budget, cash budget, pro forma financial statements, and external financing requirements.
- Ed Rye, Vice President of Product Development
  Oversee product development, including quality control, physical distribution, packaging design, new product development, and improvements on existing products and services.
- Cheri Dengel, Vice President of Operations
  Perform service, manufacturing, raw materials management, and cost allocation functions. Evaluate supplier alternatives to assure that quality and cost performance objectives are being met.

7.0 FINANCIAL ANALYSIS

Computech has developed a line of personal computer products and services that are superior to the competitive products and services in the market today. In order to support our target markets, a significant capital infusion into the company is required. The financial statements and projections that are included in this section will show that Computech is in a strong financial position and has adopted a responsible attitude toward the management of the company's assets and funds.

7.1 Five-Year Sales Forecast

The sales forecast shows revenue and expense projections over a five-year period. It provides the foundation for our other financial statements and projections (see Figure E-1).

Figure E-1
Computech's Five-Year Sales Forecast

Sales	Year 1	Year 2	Year 3	Year 4	Year 5
Product A	$140,052	$160,354	$186,005	$220,751	$254,160
Percent of total sales	35%	35%	35%	35%	35%
Product B	$100,037	$114,539	$132,861	$157,679	$181,542
Percent of total sales	25%	25%	25%	25%	25%
Product C	$88,033	$100,794	$116,917	$138,758	$159,757
Percent of total sales	22%	22%	22%	22%	22%
Service A	$72,027	$82,648	$95,660	$113,529	$130,719
Percent of total sales	18%	18%	18%	18%	18%
Total sales	$400,150	$458,156	$531,445	$630,717	$726,171
Total cost of goods sold	$174,387	$191,825	$220,159	$263,188	$302,073
Gross profit	$225,763	$266,331	$311,286	$367,529	$424,098
Gross profit percent	56%	58%	59%	58%	58%
Total operating expenses	$173,275	$190,542	$215,009	$251,214	$287,306
Percent of total sales	43%	42%	40%	40%	40%
Income from operations	$52,488	$75,789	$96,277	$116,315	$136,792
Percent of total sales	13%	17%	18%	18%	19%
Total expenses	$347,662	$382,367	$435,168	$514,402	$589,379
Percent of total sales	87%	83%	82%	82%	81%
Net profit before taxes	$52,488	$75,789	$96,277	$116,315	$136,792
Percent of total sales	13%	17%	18%	18%	19%

7.2 One-Year Cash Flow Statement

The cash flow statement shown in Figure E-2 projects Computech's cash receipts, cash disbursements, and financing activity on a quarterly basis over a one-year period. Computech's sales forecast was used to support this schedule.

Figure E-2
Computech's One-Year Cash Flow Requirements Budget

Cash Flow Item	1st Quarter	2nd Quarter	3rd Quarter	4th Quarter
Beginning cash balances	$2,500	$12,456	$29,515	$51,598
Net sales	$90,170	$96,758	$103,785	$111,296
Other income	$550	$675	$900	$875
Total available cash	$93,220	$109,889	$134,200	$163,769
Cash disbursements				
Payroll	$12,115	$12,056	$12,390	$12,862
Advertising	$2,062	$2,045	$1,765	$1,750
Sales commissions	$5,038	$6,019	$8,230	$10,500
Cost of goods sold	$22,180	$23,094	$24,275	$21,437
Interest expense	$4,038	$4,019	$4,130	$4,287
Taxes	$8,076	$8,037	$8,260	$9,970
Equipment leases	$8,884	$8,841	$9,086	$9,432
Building rent	$15,345	$15,271	$15,694	$15,517
Total cash disbursements	$77,738	$79,378	$83,830	$85,746
Cash after disbursements	$15,482	$30,511	$50,370	$78,023

7.3 Five-Year Income Projection

The income statement that is shown in Figure E-3 forecasts the earnings of the company over a five-year period. The sales forecast in Figure E-1 is included in the income statement projections.

Figure E-3
Computech's Five-Year Income Projection

Income Account	Year 1	Year 2	Year 3	Year 4	Year 5
Sales					
Wholesale	$220,083	$251,986	$292,295	$346,894	$399,394
Retail	$180,068	$206,170	$239,150	$283,823	$326,777
Total sales	$400,150	$458,156	$531,445	$630,717	$726,171
Cost of Goods Sold					
Cost of materials	$95,913	$105,504	$121,087	$144,753	$166,140
Direct labor	$78,474	$86,321	$99,072	$118,435	$135,933
Total cost of goods sold	$174,387	$191,825	$220,159	$263,188	$302,073
Gross profit	$225,763	$266,331	$331,286	$367,529	$424,098
Operating expenses					
Utilities	$15,991	$18,581	$22,251	$27,682	$31,745
Salaries	$44,655	$48,108	$53,002	$60,243	$65,661
Payroll taxes and benefits	$10,397	$11,433	$12,901	$15,073	$16,698
Advertising	$6,931	$7,622	$8,600	$10,048	$11,132
Office supplies	$3,466	$3,811	$4,300	$5,024	$5,566
Rent	$60,646	$66,690	$75,253	$87,925	$97,407
Depreciation	$5,198	$5,716	$6,450	$7,536	$8,349
Interest expense	$25,991	$28,581	$32,251	$37,682	$41,746
Total operating expenses	$173,275	$190,542	$215,009	$251,214	$287,306
Net profit before taxes	$52,488	$75,789	$96,277	$116,315	$136,792
Profit percent of sales	13%	17%	18%	18%	19%

7.4 Three-Year Balance Sheet Projection

The balance sheet in Figure E-4 shows the financial position of the company at year-end over a three-year time period.

Figure E-4
Computech's Three-Year Balance Sheet Projection

Balance Sheet Account	Year 1	Year 2	Year 3
Current Assets			
Cash	$82,024	$137,680	$200,923
Accounts receivable	$22,000	$24,000	$27,000
Inventory	$13,000	$12,000	$19,000
Total current assets	$117,024	$173,680	$246,923
Plant and equipment			
Buildings and land	0	0	0
Equipment	$3,000	$3,000	$3,000
Less: Depreciation	$600	$1,200	$1,800
Total plant and equipment	$2,400	$1,800	$1,200
Total assets	$119,424	$175,480	$248,123
Liabilities			
Accounts payable	$2,000	$2,000	$2,000
Short-term debt	$1,000	$1,000	$1,000
Long-term debt	$22,000	$22,000	$22,000
Total liabilities	$25,000	$25,000	$25,000
Owners' equity	$94,424	$150,480	$223,123
Total liabilities and equity	$119,424	$175,480	$248,123

7.5 Sources and Uses of Funds

The sources and uses of funds schedule in Figure E-5 summarizes the sources of funds (i.e., financing) and the uses of funds (i.e., investing activities of the company). Changes in our working capital over a three-year period are also covered.

Figure E-5
Computech's Sources and Uses of Funds

Account Description	Year 1	Year 2	Year 3
Sources of Funds			
Net profit	$41,924	$56,055	$72,643
Depreciation	$600	$600	$600
Private investors	$50,000	0	0
Increased long-term debt	$25,000	0	0
Total sources of funds	$117,524	$56,655	$73,243
Uses of Funds			
Building	$29,381	$14,164	$18,311
Purchased equipment	$23,505	$11,331	$14,649
Loan repayment	$32,907	$15,863	$20,508
Research and development	$31,731	$15,297	$19,776
Total uses of funds	$117,524	$56,655	$73,243
Changes in Working Capital			
Cash	$88,143	$42,291	$54,932
Accounts receivable	$11,752	$5,666	$7,324
Short-term debt	$5,876	$2,833	$3,662
Investments	$4,701	$2,266	$42,930
Accrued liabilities	$7,051	$3,399	$4,395
Increased working capital	$117,524	$56,655	$73,243

7.6 Five-Year Break-even Analysis

The break-even analysis in Figure E-6 shows the effect of changes in costs and sales levels on Computech's profitability over a five-year period.

Figure E-6
Computech's Five-Year Break-even Analysis

Account Description	Year 1	Year 2	Year 3	Year 4	Year 5
Sales					
Total sales dollars	$400,150	$458,156	$531,445	$630,717	$726,171
Total sales units	40,500	39,900	40,900	40,690	40,500
Average price per unit	$9.88	$11.48	$12.99	$15.50	$17.93
Fixed Costs					
Sales and marketing	$41,719	$45,884	$52,220	$61,728	$69,645
Research and development	$52,149	$57,355	$65,275	$77,160	$87,056
General and administrative	$27,813	$30,589	$34,813	$41,152	$46,430
Total fixed costs	$121,682	$133,828	$152,309	$180,041	$203,133
Variable Costs					
Cost of goods sold	$139,065	$152,947	$174,067	$205,761	$232,152
Other variable costs	$86,916	$95,592	$108,792	$128,601	$145,095
Total variable costs	$225,980	$248,539	$282,859	$334,361	$377,246
Total costs	$347,662	$382,367	$435,168	$514,402	$589,379
Break-even unit volume	35,188	33,300	33,491	33,186	32,871
Units over/(under) break-even	5,312	6,600	7,409	7,504	7,629
Profit per unit	$1.30	$1.90	$2.35	$2.86	$3.38

APPENDIX

Resumes of key people

Data supporting sales projections:

    Actual orders

    Personally known prospective key accounts

    Potential customers

Product and service price schedules

Market survey data

Equipment in inventory

Drawings and drafts

Agreements

Articles and publicity

Patents, trademarks, and copyrights

Financial projections

Five-year market projection

Eighteen-month disbursement schedule

Advertising and promotion disbursement schedule

Staff and equipment disbursement schedule

Personal computers and development disbursement schedule

Increased expenses disbursement schedule

Summary of all disbursement spreadsheets

Five-year projected income statement

Sales forecasts for year 1995

OEM and maintenance revenue forecast

New sales revenue forecast

Other revenue forecast

Summary of all revenue forecast

Index

definition of, 38
process, 48-49
in a sample business plan, 266-270
market examination, 30
market fit, 172
market information, definition of, in
market research, 38
market research
correlating primary and secondary
information, 49
data, 50-53
definition of, 38
firms, 45-46
sampling procedures, 46-47
survey sample size, 47
tabulating survey results, 48-49
market segmentation, 169
market share
forecasts, 74-76
formula for calculating, 75
market specialty periodicals, 41
market strategy, 51-53
marketing
definition of, 37
functions, definition of, 65-66
information, evaluating, 39-43
plan, developing a, 12, 49-53
organizations, 42-43
role in strategic plan, 173
Marketing News, 92
maturity, of loan, extending, 122
mean, role of, 48
media
advantages and disadvantages,
87-90
alternatives for advertising, 79-87
median, role of, 48
MEWA (Multiple Employer Welfare
Arrangements) health insurance,
193
mission statement, for a business,
190-191
mistakes, avoiding, in business,
183-184
mode
median and mean calculation, 48
role of, 48
Money, 41, 192
money purchase plan, as employee
retirement option, 194-195
monitor, computer, 161
morale, employee, 189-190
Robert Morris Associates, 78

N
name, of company, selecting a, 136
National Association of Small
Business Investment Companies,
120
negotiation close, in sales, 72
net losses, calculation of, 99
net profit, calculation of, 99
net worth, calculation of, 113
networks, computer, 162
new business, high failure rate of, 30
newspaper advertising, 87
nondisclosure
agreement, 147-149
example of, 148
form, 147-149
numbers test, to measure health of
business, 182-183

O
office
equipment, 13, 155-165
furniture, 159-160
supplies, 165
tax deductions, 165-166
on-demand faxes, 158
open-ended leases, for business
equipment, 123 (*see also* operating
leases)
operating
expenses, 99
leases, for business equipment, 123
systems, computer software, 163
oral contracts, 144
organization chart, function of an,
133-134
owner's equity, definition of, 96 (*see
also* retained earnings)

P
paper stock, for business forms, 142
partner
general, 129
limited, 129
partnership
advantages and disadvantages, 128
business, 13
agreement, 127
general, 127-128
limited, 128-129
mistakes, contract, 183-184
payments
balloon loan, 123

About the Author

David E. Rye brings over a decade of experience to The Adams Business Advisor series. His books include *Two for the Money* and *The Corporate Game*. As a small business owner, he offers a series of seminars on entrepreneurship and a wide variety of other business and human development subjects.